THE THAMES PATH

titles so far published in this series

Offa's Dyke Path South
Offa's Dyke Path North
Cleveland Way
The Ridgeway
Pennine Way South
Pennine Way North
Pembrokeshire Coast Path
South Downs Way
North Downs Way
Yorkshire Wolds Way
Peddars Way and
Norfolk Coast Path
The Thames Path
Hadrian's Wall Path
Glyndŵr's Way
Pennine Bridleway:
Derbyshire to the South
Pennines
The Cotswold Way

South West Coast Path
Minehead to Padstow
Padstow to Falmouth
Falmouth to Exmouth
Exmouth to Poole

The Thames Path

David Sharp

Photographs by Rob Fraser

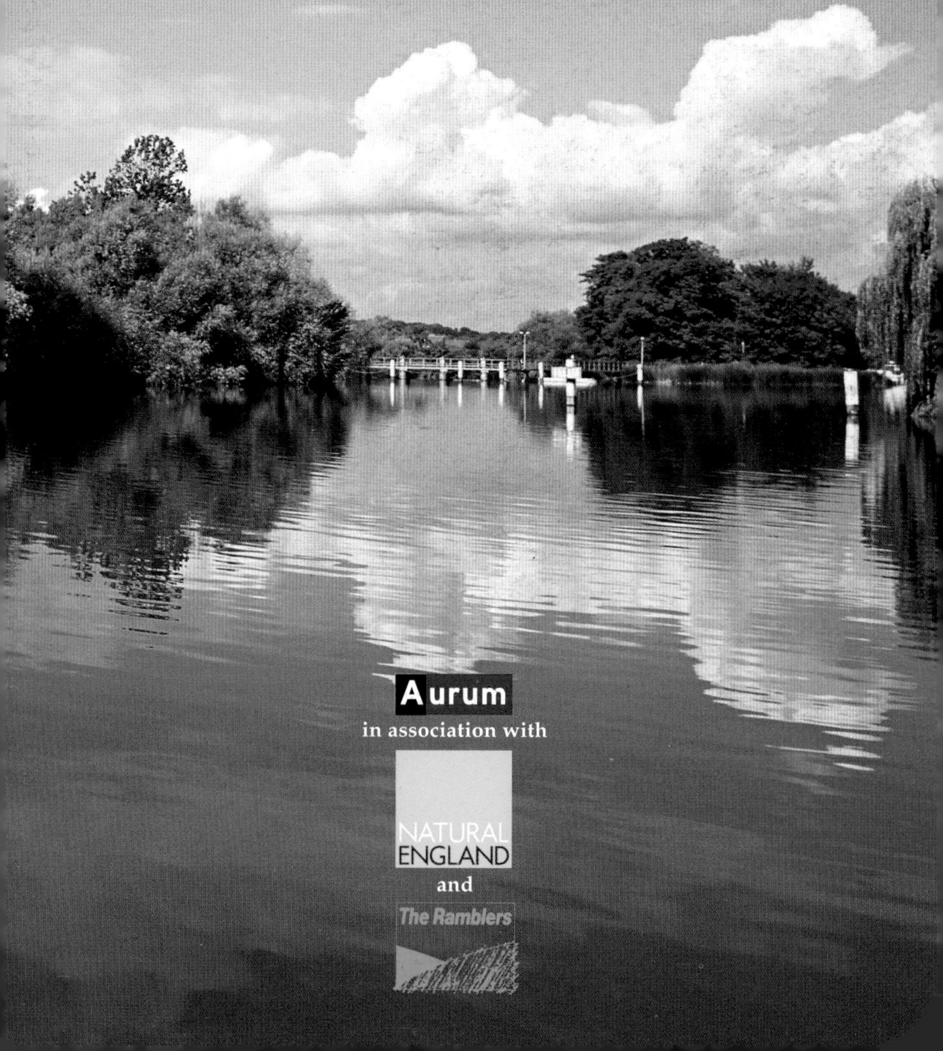

Aurum

in association with

NATURAL ENGLAND

and

The Ramblers

Acknowledgements

On behalf of all who enjoy the Thames Path, now or in the future, I would like to record my thanks to those who made it possible. To Leigh Hatts for proving that it was feasible; to Jenny Blair for drawing it all together in a massive report; and to Jane Bowden, Simon Fisher, Maggie Grenham and Karin Groeneveld for all their efforts in turning it into reality. My personal thanks also go to Andrew McCloy for his help in compiling the information sections of this guide, and to Dr David Varcoe for his guidance on the sources of the Thames.

David Sharp is a Vice President of the Ramblers' Association. Having masterminded the Ramblers' first survey of a potential route along the Thames, he then led the campaign to gain its recognition, especially as author of the bestselling Ramblers' guide to the walk. He has written on many other aspects of walking, but always returns to his first love – the Thames. With his wife Margaret, he has explored the river for over 30 years, watching the Thames Path gradually take shape.

The photographs on the cover and pages 13, 27, 43, 66, 80, 114, 116, 118, 147 and 182 are by David Sharp and that on page 38 by Lisa Hooper. All other photographs by Rob Fraser, © 1996 by Natural England.

This revised edition first published 2007 by Aurum Press Ltd
in association with Natural England and The Ramblers' Association

A catalogue record for this book is available from the British Library.

ISBN-10 184513 266 1
ISBN-13 978 184513 266 8

Book design by Robert Updegraff

Cover photograph: *Wittenham Clumps seen from the riverbank*
Title page photograph: *The Thames approaches Sonning Lock and Weir*

Printed and bound in Italy by Printer Trento Srl

The Ramblers' Association aims to help everyone enjoy walking in the countryside, to foster care and understanding of the countryside, to protect rights of way, to secure public access on foot to open country, and to defend the natural beauty of the countryside. See under Useful Information for address.

CONTENTS

How to use this guide

The chapters which follow give precise guidance for following the Thames Path, with maps placed alongside the text to which they relate. Each chapter starts by quoting the total distance covered along the Thames Path itself, but also suggests how you can break this into shorter walks by using public transport at convenient points. This sometimes involves leaving the path and following a link route to the station, and you should always allow for this extra distance when judging the length of your walk. Instructions for reaching stations or bus stops given in the text are set in italic type.

By convention, the banks of a river are usually referred to as 'left' and 'right' when travelling downstream, but as the text frequently uses these directions in other contexts, we avoid confusion by referring to 'north bank' and 'south bank' where necessary. Where short distances have been quoted in yards, this can be taken as meaning long paces, and metric equivalents are therefore not deemed necessary.

Maps

These have been prepared for this guide by the Ordnance Survey®, using their 1:25 000 scale Explorer™ maps as a base.

Special features of interest are numbered, both in the text and on the maps. Letters have been used in the same way, to identify key points along the route. Public houses have been identified in rural stretches, but not in towns and large villages, or in London, where you will easily find refreshments. *Arrows (➞) at the edge of the maps indicate the start point.*

Along the rural Thames Path from the source to Teddington Lock, the maps are reproduced at the 1:25 000 scale and the route is shown as a continuous yellow line, or dotted yellow line where the route is only temporary. These temporary sections will soon be improved, and you should look around for signs and waymarks that may be guiding you onto a better route. Usually the yellow line will be identifying an existing footpath, track or road used by the Thames Path, but paths have been newly created or diverted for it in places and this may not be recorded on the map yet, so do not be surprised if occasionally the yellow line shows a new route: you can confidently follow it. Station links as described in the text are shown on the maps as a dotted line.

Along the London Thames Path from Teddington Lock to the Thames Barrier, the same map base has been enlarged to a 1:16 666 (6 centimetres to 1 kilometre, or 3 ¾ inches to 1 mile) scale to allow more detail to be recorded. The text on each spread covers routes on both banks of the river, and the text for the north bank is printed on a blue background and that for the south bank on a pink background. Points of interest and key points on the two banks are indicated on the maps by numbered or lettered spots of the corresponding colours. Features of interest are numbered as in the rural chapters, but as route-finding in London often depends on knowing which road you are in, the key letters are used to identify street names as mentioned in the text. Station links are also shown as in the rural chapters, but only to selected stations as mentioned in the text.

Through much of London and Docklands, the riverside access is constantly changing and improving as redeveloped sites open up, providing us with new walkways by the Thames. This guide describes the best riverside route currently available, but do not be surprised if you meet even further improvements. Every year we gain a little more of the London Thames to enjoy.

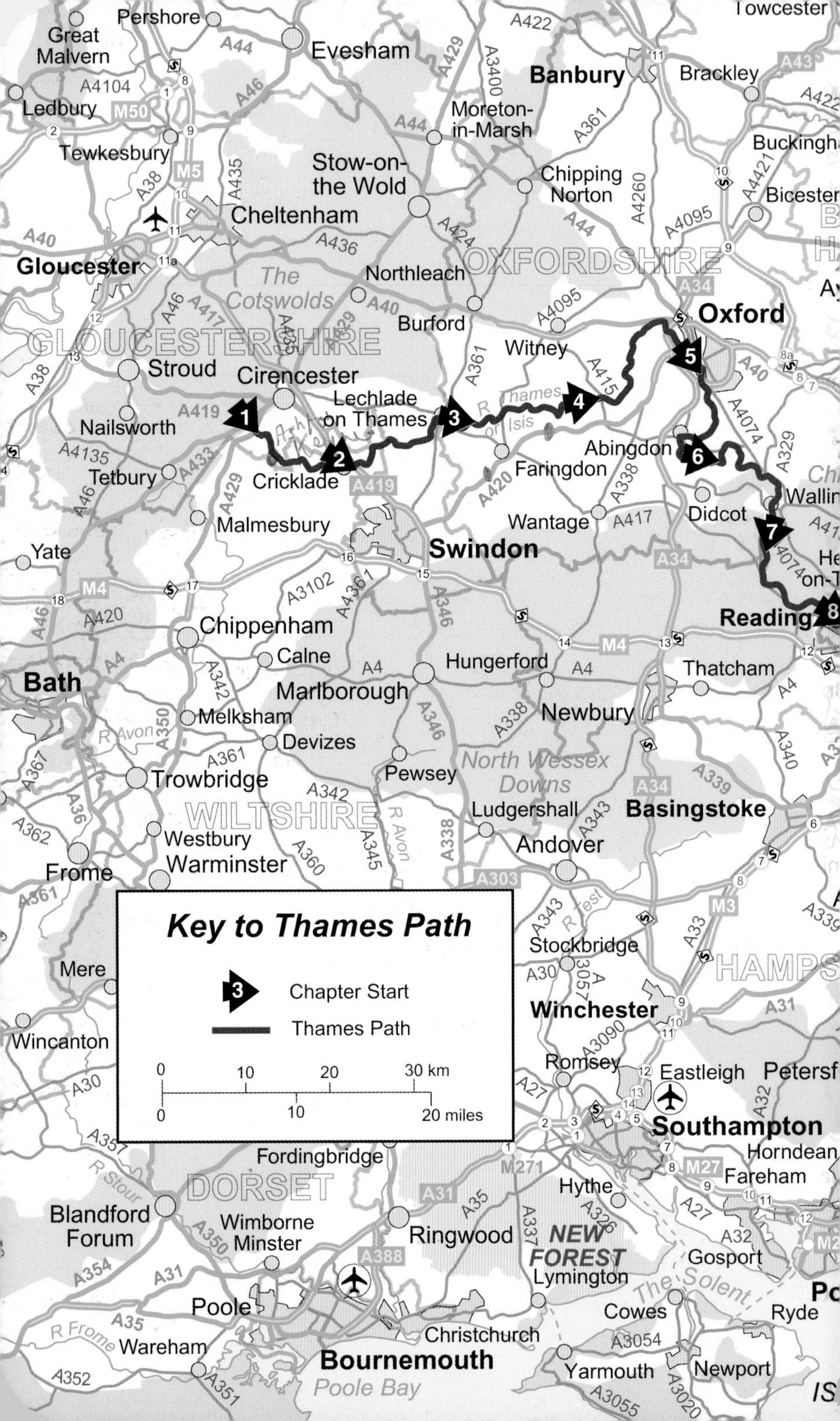

Key to Thames Path
Chapter Start
Thames Path
0 10 20 30 km
0 10 20 miles
Pershore
Great Malvern
Evesham
Banbury
Brackley
Ledbury
Moreton-in-Marsh
Tewkesbury
Stow-on-the Wold
Chipping Norton
Bicester
Cheltenham
OXFORDSHIRE
Gloucester
The Cotswolds
Northleach
Oxford
Burford
Witney
GLOUCESTERSHIRE
Stroud
Cirencester
Lechlade on Thames
R Thames or Isis
Nailsworth
Abingdon
Faringdon
Tetbury
Cricklade
Wallingford
Didcot
Malmesbury
Wantage
Swindon
Yate
Reading
Chippenham
Calne
Hungerford
Thatcham
Bath
Marlborough
Melksham
Newbury
Devizes
Pewsey
North Wessex Downs
Trowbridge
Ludgershall
Basingstoke
WILTSHIRE
Westbury
Andover
Warminster
Frome
Stockbridge
Mere
HAMPSHIRE
Winchester
Wincanton
Romsey
Eastleigh
Southampton
Fordingbridge
Horndean
Fareham
Hythe
DORSET
Blandford Forum
Wimborne Minster
Ringwood
NEW FOREST
Gosport
Lymington
The Solent
Poole
Cowes
Ryde
Christchurch
Wareham
Bournemouth
Yarmouth
Newport
Poole Bay

Bedford
Biggleswade
Haverhill
Saffron Walden
Royston
Milton Keynes
Letchworth
Baldock
Buntingford
ESSEX
Luton
Stevenage
Bishop's Stortford
Braintree
Luton Airport
Stansted Airport
Great Dunmow
Dunstable
Hertford
HERTFORDSHIRE
Hemel Hempstead
St Albans
Harlow
Chelmsford
Hatfield
Epping
Chipping Ongar
Amersham
High Wycombe
Billericay
Brentwood
Watford
LONDON
Beaconsfield
Ilford
Dagenham
Basildon
Slough
Maidenhead
Windsor
Dartford
Tilbury
Richmond
Staines
Gravesend
Orpington
Bracknell
Sutton
Chatham
Croydon
Esher
Woking
Leatherhead
Surrey
Maidstone
Farnborough
SURREY
Aldershot
Dorking
Redhill
Sevenoaks
Hills
Tonbridge
Guildford
Reigate
KENT
Godalming
Royal Tunbridge Wells
Gatwick
Bordon
Crawley
East Grinstead
R Medway
Haslemere
High Weald
Crowborough
R Arun
Horsham
Haywards Heath
Billingshurst
R Rother
Heathfield
Midhurst
Burgess Hill
Pulborough
EAST SUSSEX
Sussex Downs
WEST SUSSEX
Lewes
Hailsham
Havant
Worthing
Arundel
Chichester
Bexhill
Littlehampton
Brighton
Newhaven
Bognor Regis
Eastbourne
Beachy Head
Selsey Bill
OF WIGHT

Distance Checklist

location	*approx distance from previous location*			
	miles		*km*	
The Source	–		–	
Ashton Keynes	7.0		11.3	
Cricklade	5.3		8.5	
Castle Eaton	4.2		6.8	
Lechlade	6.7		10.8	
Radcot	6.4		10.3	
Newbridge	10.0		16.0	
Swinford	7.8		12.6	
Oxford	6.2		10.0	
Abingdon	9.9		16.0	
Culham	2.2		3.5	
Wallingford	11.3		18.2	
Cholsey	3.2		5.2	
Goring	3.9		6.3	
Pangbourne	4.2		6.8	
Tilehurst	3.5		5.6	
Reading	3.4		5.5	
Shiplake	6.7		10.8	
Henley	2.2		3.5	
Marlow	8.7		14.0	
Maidenhead	7.6		12.2	
Windsor	6.7		10.8	
Staines	8.2		13.	
Shepperton	5.5		8.8	
Hampton Court	6.1		9.8	
Teddington	4.8		7.7	
	N bank	*S bank*	*N bank*	*S bank*
Richmond	3.9	3.4	6.3	5.5
Putney	10.2	8.2	16.4	13.2
Westminster	7.0	8.0	11.3	12.9
Tower Bridge	3.3	2.5	5.3	4.0
Greenwich	5.5	5.8	8.8	9.3
Thames Barrier	–	4.2	–	6.8

Preface

The 184-mile (294-km) Thames Path is the only National Trail to follow a river for the whole of its length. Beginning at the source of the River Thames in the Cotswolds, the Trail meanders with the river through peaceful water meadows, historic towns and cities and many unspoilt villages, before cutting through the heart of London to the Thames Barrier at Greenwich just a few miles from the sea.

Lots of visitors are drawn to the Thames Path National Trail for a day trip or to enjoy it over a series of weekends, often inventing circuits between bridges and locks to suit. But there are still many, enchanted by the river, who manage to find a couple of weeks to indulge themselves by walking the whole length from the source to the sea. Being level, this Trail is accessible to walkers of most ages and abilities.

The Thames Path National Trail is exceptionally well served by public transport, making it possible to plan trips using trains, buses or boats and to explore without the need for a car.

National Trails are managed, promoted and funded by Natural England and local authorities, with the latter also being responsible for maintenance. In addition, the Thames Path greatly benefits from the work of a group of enthusiastic local volunteers who carry out much of the maintenance.

I hope you will enjoy this book during many hours of delightful walking alongside one of Britain's greatest rivers in some of our loveliest countryside.

Sir Martin Doughty
Chair
Natural England

INTRODUCTION

River of contrasts

It may not always be where you expect it, but at one spring or another in the gentle folds of Cotswold meadow around Ewen you will meet the first trickles of moving water, and know that you have found the birthplace of Thames. At the other end of your 184-mile (294-km) journey, you will see that same water surging through the great barrier into an estuary broadening to greet the sea. Between the two, you will experience a living river, from gentle birth, through the artless freedom of youth, to the proud symbols of maturity – the castles and colleges, churches and royal palaces that line its banks. All rivers can be rewarding to explore, but the Thames is something special, one of the world's great rivers, flowing serenely through the pages of our history.

For many years, such a journey was more dream than reality, but the launch of the Thames Path in 1996 opened it up to join our other National Trails. As a walking experience it is distinctly different from the other National Trails. Firstly, because it is a very easy walk, as accessible to the stroller as to the die-hard long-distance walker. It offers no rugged hill climbs or vast moorland expanses by way of challenge; indeed the Thames never seems to be going anywhere in a hurry, and the mood is catching. The good public transport facilities along the Thames valley help, as they make it temptingly easy to plan short walks. Many people explore the Thames in this way, taking it in easy stages – covering a single section on one day and then returning a few weeks later to carry on where they left off. Thus you can walk the Thames Path in two weeks, two years, or a lifetime. Old Thames seems to encourage this leisurely approach, always there to welcome you back and see you off on the next stage.

The second difference is in the remarkable variety it offers, a progression of experience from the lonely, open watermeadows of its headwaters to the vistas of a great city and its regenerated docklands. Even a single day's walk can offer this variety as the Thames Path takes you from the busy waterside of a little township, Henley perhaps, around a bend or two into river scenes of total tranquillity, where a heron will flap away in surprise that anyone has intruded into its solitude.

Your walk may be by a modest field path, just visible in the grass of the riverbank, or along a broad and popular promenade, or, in London, via a handsome walkway opened as part of a new riverside development. But at almost every point the Thames Path provides easy going, with no call for specialist gear, except perhaps after prolonged rain in the upper reaches,

The cottages of Strand on the Green look over their walkway to the Thames – one of several village-like communities along the London Thames Path.

when wellies are advisable on a short walk along a soggy towpath. Generally the clay and gravel of the Thames valley will compact underfoot when dry, to make a pleasant walking surface through most seasons, and the work of volunteer teams keeps the riverside path clear of summer foliage.

Of course, the Thames Path can be walked in either direction. In this book we have chosen to describe it in the downstream direction, in part because many people find it easier to read maps from left to right and most of the time your back will be to the prevailing wind, but also because of the gradually growing sense of climax as you follow the river down to London.

As on the other National Trails, you can expect to find the route well signed with 'Thames Path', and the familiar National Trail acorns. Many fingerposts also indicate the distance to the next main access point along the walk, and there are Thames Path information points at nineteen locks that not only remind you of the route but give extra information about nearby features. The signs in London will vary in style and colour in order to conform with local requirements, and may even be incorporated into other signing, but the words 'Thames Path' and the acorn are constant elements to look out for.

Along the rural Thames many new riverside paths have been created, but this work is ongoing and there are still a few points where you have to follow a temporary route away from the river. The maps identify these temporary stretches, and when you come to the start of one it is advisable to look around for new 'Thames Path' signs that will guide you to a recently created section. Along the London Thames new stretches of riverside access are becoming available month by month, and it would be confusing to try to distinguish temporary from permanent sections of path. But the signing will always guide you along the best route currently available, so keep alert for possible changes.

The old Thames towpath was used by men and horses to tow barges, but despite this tradition it should be noted that its legal status is only that of a public footpath. Short stretches of the Thames Path are bridleways, easily identifiable on the maps; but most of the route is along footpaths. In urban London the legal status varies – some sections are public rights-of-way, others are subject to walkway agreements which may restrict public access to daylight hours. The path even crosses several parks where gates will be locked at sunset. So it must be stressed that, although there are a few bridleway sections and stretches with either formal or informal cycleway status, in general the Thames Path is a National Trail for walkers.

Remember, too, that throughout the rural Thames your walk is through farming land, so keep to the riverside path, resist the urge to take short-cuts across the meadows, and be sure to leave gates as you find them. You will often meet anglers, and at times their gear tends to spread across the towpath, so be tolerant and step quietly and carefully around them. Boating parties frequently stop and picnic, placing their mooring lines where they might trip you up – another case for cheerful tolerance. In truth, Old Father Thames seems to pass on his genial good nature to all his followers. The boating family will give you a wave as they pass, the lock-keeper will usually have time for a chat as you pause to admire his flowerbeds. If there is one piece of essential advice for the Thames Path walker, it must surely be – don't hurry!

Dream into reality

The creation of a long walk by the Thames is no new idea. Even in the early 1930s, local authorities along the river were getting together to discuss how the old Thames towing path could be put to new use. It was no longer needed for its original purpose, yet it was there, following the river from Putney, deep in London, up to Lechlade on the edge of the Cotswolds. The Thames Commissioners were responsible for establishing the towpath back in the late 18th century, at a time when the river was beginning to play an essential role in the burgeoning canal system. It proved a difficult task as the Thames is no canal but a living river, and every so often the towpath met obstacles, natural or man-made, and got around them by changing to the opposite bank. At these problem points, a navigation ferry had to be provided, to carry the towing teams across. A mile above Lechlade, the towpath left the Thames entirely to follow a new navigation, the Thames and Severn Canal.

Visionary though they were, those 1930s debates could do little to create a long-distance walk, and it was not until 1949 that Parliament provided the means of doing this, on a national scale. Not surprisingly, the embryonic idea of re-using the Thames towpath came top of the list of routes for consideration. But, ironically, this proved to be the worst possible time for considering a walk along the river. The navigation ferries, so vital to the continuity of the towpath, were no longer economical and were closing down. Other routes were clearly easier to create, and the Thames idea was put to one side, all too likely to be forgotten.

Two bodies were determined that this should not happen – the River Thames Society and the Ramblers' Association. They worked together, and in 1977 the Ramblers published a new concept for a walk that would require no ferries. Moreover, it enlarged on the original idea of a towpath walk by carrying it on via little-used paths to discover the source itself, in that faraway Gloucestershire meadow.

It revived interest to a point where, in 1984, the Countryside Commission (now part of Natural England) published the results of a study that declared the concept to be feasible, the likely costs reasonable and the recreational value high. The route was officially declared a National Trail in 1987, and since then a vast amount of work has gone into improving its line and raising it to the highest standards. Three new footbridges provide much-needed river crossings, miles of new riverside footpaths have been patiently negotiated with landowners, and stiles replaced by gates to make the Thames Path more easily accessible.

Through London and Docklands in particular, the Thames Path sees exciting developments almost month by month. Once it seemed that the walk must end where the towpath ends, at Putney Bridge, but now you can keep on along either bank, often on lively new walkways created as features of new riverside developments. Of course there are still a few points where you have, briefly, to leave the river. Perhaps a stubborn warehouse blocks the way, a site where the cranes and the hard hats are still working away, or even a fragment of surviving riverside industry. But today's Thames Path is complete enough to give you a breathtaking new view of a great city – the view from the river. And even the few rough passages have something to say about the fabric of London, interludes before the next vast river scene opens up. And there could be no more powerful image with which to end the walk than the mighty engineering triumph of the Thames Barrier.

Hambleden Mill, residential now, but still one of the best of the surviving Thames watermills, reached via the spectacular right-of-way over Hambleden Weir.

Infant Thames

All the Cotswold rivers, Churn, Coln, Leach, Windrush, Evenlode and lesser names, flow down to add their waters to the Thames. There have been disputes as to the true source of the Thames, but the river we follow from Trewsbury Mead through the Keynes villages has for centuries been called Thames, and locals have never known it by any other name. This must be because it has always unquestionably been the main stream, and indeed barges once traded up to wharves at Waterhay Bridge.

So in the meadows above the hamlet of Ewen, the source springs of Thames are all around you, though only rarely, in very wet seasons, will you see water at the highest spring marked by the stone where our Thames Path begins. Just above it ran the summit level of the Thames and Severn Canal, now dry, and through the years when a steam pump was raising water to it, this was naturally blamed for the absence of water

In a tree-shaded hollow on Trewsbury Mead, a circle of pebbles lies beneath an elderly ash tree, and a simple inscribed stone marks the source.

in the valley springs. Now it is evident that the water table is lower. A Victorian visitor records walking hereabouts and producing fountains of water just by thrusting his stick into the grassy hillocks. It wouldn't happen today. But the water is down there still, and it would be fair to say that the true source of the Thames is beneath your feet. The lush valley slopes down to Ewen at a considerable angle, as do the water-bearing strata below, and from one spring or another water will burst to the surface. Walking down the valley, you will pass several springs, the first in the bowl of meadow just beyond the Foss Way, which can be transformed into a lake after a rainy spell – and probably has the best claim to be the source. In another half mile you walk above Lyd Well, reputedly a Roman well and often flowing vigorously in its boggy enclosure. In Ewen itself, across the lane behind The Wild Duck Inn, you can look over the fence to a pool in a deep tree-circled hollow – Monks' Pond, another spring which reliably feeds the Thames. Ewen comes from the Saxon Æwylme meaning source of a river – and that says it all.

Lonely Thames

As it flows through Cricklade to Lechlade the Thames grows from modest stream to lovely young river, broad and confident enough to carry the big white cruisers that gather at the head of navigation. Then from St John's Lock down to Oxford it takes on a quality of loneliness, meandering through its wide, flat flood plain of Oxford clay. Beware those loops; they can make your walk far longer than it appears from a glance at the map. No villages, no farmsteads come near the river, the only human habitation is the occasional lock cottage or isolated inn. With no sound of road or rattle of railway, to some this is a stretch of blissful escape. A string of communities, like the market town of Bampton, and villages such as Aston, Longworth, Buckland, Appleton and Northmoor, would consider themselves to be 'by the Thames', but they keep to the gravel terraces a mile or two back from the river.

The routes to the river crossings have always been important here, leading first to fords, then trackways down to the early bridges. Thus the town of Faringdon once had a castle standing guard over the ancient packhorse crossing at Radcot. At times of unrest, the crossings were fought over. Radcot Bridge saw the Earl of Oxford's defeat by Henry Bolingbroke's forces in 1387, then became a Royalist outpost in the Civil War, when its final capture by Fairfax forced King Charles to abandon Oxford. Newbridge, too, saw bitter Civil War encounters, but it is difficult today to associate these peaceful spots with the clash of arms. This is a Thames of far-stretching watermeadows under a vast, open arc of sky, bringing an odd 'top of the world' feeling as you walk for miles with just a herd or two of inquisitive young cattle for company. Past travellers made constant reference to the elms, and their stately presence must have added a grander dimension to the landscape. The elms were lost in the 1970s, but still it is the trees that define and punctuate these river scenes, taking the Thames Path through ever-changing compositions that are the very essence of English countryside.

Early Thames

From Oxford on, you are meeting the earliest valley settlements. Access was good and, especially as trade began to move along the river and along the downland line of the Icknield Way, prehistoric man made his home on the dry gravel by the Thames. For sure, New Stone Age people brought agriculture, evidenced by many finds around Abingdon, and the later Beaker Folk left numerous traces between Abingdon and Stanton Harcourt, including a fine collection of bronze weapons found in the Thames near Sandford Lock. But though we can learn much from finds and crop-marks, it is not until you reach the hill fort on the Sinodun Hills, and the great earthworks of the Dyke Hills below, that the work of prehistoric man becomes obvious. The major settlements seem either to have been based on defensive needs or on fords. Oxford itself grew as an island stronghold between Thames and Cherwell, while Iron Age, Roman and Saxon Dorchester all sheltered between Thames and Thame in the same way.

As trade increased, the ford settlements like Wallingford grew in importance – in Saxon times the town even had a Royal mint. Abingdon rose to prosperity with the foundation of its abbey, which soon become one of the richest in the land. Indeed, the old town still clearly stands around the abbey gates. For long it out-shone its rival, Wallingford, but its fords were long and treacherous, and Wallingford had not only a

At Rushey Lock, the Thames Path crosses an early form of Thames weir, and here the lock-keeper's house of 1896 is framed by weir paddles.

ford but also a bridge by the time William the Conqueror came seeking a crossing for his army. The Cotswold merchants preferred to take their precious woolpacks over Wallingford Bridge rather than risk a ford, so the Abingdon merchants had to raise money to build both Abingdon and Culham bridges and a long causeway between them. Thus, in 1422, they won their trade back. The bridges and the causeway still stand, and Wallingford has both Saxon ramparts and the battered traces of a castle demolished after falling to the Roundheads – visual reminders of how the early pages of our history unfolded along this stretch of the Thames.

Victorian Thames

Below Reading you are walking into the Thames of Victorian high summer, and at Henley you cannot escape reminders of its famous Royal Regatta, the spectacle the Victorians elevated to the very top of their social calendar. In the late 19th century everyone, from Cockney to society belle, flocked here, and in 1888 the peak day of the regatta brought 6,768 people along the little branch line to Henley. They saw the course lined by over 80 houseboats decked with colourful awnings, floral garlands and bunting. Fashionable crowds, the men in white flannels, striped blazers and straw hats, the ladies in their latest finery, spread across the river in punts, rowing boats and gondolas. Musicians entertained, picnic parties strolled the banks, and by evening light the lanterns and coloured globes of a Venetian carnival turned the river into fairyland. The rowing, of course, took second place!

Every Thames-side town from Oxford to Richmond had its regatta; indeed when Henley ended, the crowds would teem down to Marlow Regatta, which started the following day. And it was not just the regattas; the Victorians took passionately to boating along the river, either camping or putting up in riverside taverns. Some wrote philosophically of their experiences, and Jerome K. Jerome, author of the classic *Three Men in a Boat*, was only one of many who followed the vogue. The Thames brought literary inspiration in other ways, too. When Charles Dodgson, a lecturer at Christ Church, Oxford, rowed three little girls to picnics at Godstow, he told them the fanciful stories that were published in 1865 as *Alice's Adventures in Wonderland*. Kenneth Grahame lived much of his life at Cookham and used his beloved stretch of river up to Pangbourne as a setting for the tales of Toad, Mole and Ratty told first to his young son, then later published as *The Wind in the Willows*. The Victorians, with their hampers and parasols, have departed but their spirit still haunts the middle Thames.

Royal Thames

As the Thames Path passes beneath Windsor Castle, you are forcefully reminded that you are following a Royal river. As you travel downstream from here you will pass the sites of a succession of palaces that have stood by the water's edge, vying for royal favour from reign to reign. From the formalities of court and the foul air of London, our sovereigns escaped to their country estates, travelling by river with far more comfort and pageantry than by road. The gilded royal barge would be accompanied by musicians, courtiers and household in procession. The last state barge was retired after centuries of use to the Royal Maritime Museum, Greenwich, but the Queen's Bargemaster and Royal Watermen still attend state occasions in their finery.

Most monarchs since Henry II have favoured Windsor Castle, especially for its vast hunting forest, and today the Queen's standard often flies from the Round Tower. Victoria spent over £1 million on modernising her castle, and broke with tradition by travelling here by Royal Train. Cardinal Wolsey gave his vastly ostentatious palace of Hampton Court to Henry VIII in a vain bid to regain favour. Henry accepted it, and spent so much of his extravagant life there that two of his unfortunate wives still haunt it. The great Palace of Shene was more magnificent even than Hampton Court, but when Richard II's queen died there of the plague, he ordered it to be 'thrown down'. The Tudors rebuilt it and renamed it Richmond, and in her old age Elizabeth I came to love it as her 'warm winter box'. At Kew, the smallest of all the royal palaces was built in 1631 by a Dutch merchant and acquired by George III to house his growing family – he had fifteen children.

Few traces remain of the palaces by London's riverside. Westminster survives only in the squat Jewel Tower and the Great Hall deep within the Parliament building; and of nearby Whitehall Palace only the Banqueting House survives. Baynard's Castle, by Blackfriars, has vanished.

Along the riverside at Henley, hireboats line up to await custom, and the towers of

Brakspear's brewery peep over the roofline of mellow Georgian houses.

Downstream of the City, the great royal palace of Placentia stood by the Greenwich riverside, ideally placed for hunting and for receiving state visitors. Henry VIII was born there, and Elizabeth made it her favourite summer court. James I settled Placentia on his queen and commissioned Inigo Jones to add the little Queen's House, which must have sat oddly beside the rambling Tudor palace. With the palace in ruins, the elegant buildings you see today were built in its place as a hospital for seamen, with the Queen's House preserved within it. Thus has Royal Thames served our monarchs through the centuries.

Matchless Thames

When the poet James Thomson penned the line 'Slow let us trace the matchless Vale of Thames' he was enjoying the 18th-century view from Richmond Hill. Today, that view is little changed; indeed it was protected by Act of Parliament in 1902, and still provides a panorama of palaces, parks and villas that is quite unique – a fact now recognised by the application of a visionary Landscape Strategy for its restoration and future. This stretch of Thames from Hampton to Kew served as an out-of-town retreat for royalty and for the leaders of society and the arts, and as their ambitions extended to creating gardens, always with the Thames as a central feature, so the river took on an Elysian quality. As you pass by riverside Hampton with glimpses of Garrick's villa and temple, you are entering a stretch of the Thames which still displays the garden concepts of famous creators, Alexander Pope, Charles Bridgeman and William Kent in classical mode, and 'Capability' Brown with his more naturalistic eye. Hampton Court Palace stands within an elaborate garden scheme of patios and vistas, its Privy Garden recently restored to the William and Mary plan, thanks to discovery of its earlier layout beneath overgrown shrubbery. Around Ham House, a remarkable network of lime avenues and vistas can still be traced, and the garden has been restored to its 17th-century plan. Across the river stands the little villa of Marble Hill, perfectly sited in relationship to the Thames. The great parks, Bushy, Hampton Court and Richmond Park, hardly impinge on the river scene, but walking along the Syon Reach you are at the meeting point of two landscaped gardens. Across the river is the 'Capability' Brown setting for Syon House, while on the towpath bank the gardens of two royal estates have been re-landscaped into the botanic gardens.

London and Dockland Thames

Through central London the Thames Path reveals the very heart of a great city, with cathedral and abbey, palace and castle all contributing to the grand panorama. As you pass Lambeth Bridge, you join the Jubilee Walkway. You will see its waymark discs beneath your feet, and this 14-mile (23-km) walk could take you exploring through much of London's colourful history.

Shakespeare's Globe, a faithful reconstruction of the Elizabethan theatre where many of the great plays were performed, has brought visitors flocking to Bankside.

It was relaunched to celebrate Queen Elizabeth II's Golden Jubilee, and a guide leaflet is available from tourist offices or from www.tfl.gov.uk/walking. But this is the London shared with visitors from around the world, there are many guides, and it is not until you enter Docklands that the river again has an environment that is uniquely its own.

Below Tower Bridge you are walking into the area of Docklands where, even in the 1960s, you would have been intruding into busy scenes, with merchant ships lining every quay, cranes hoisting cargo, dockers and lightermen swarming everywhere. Then, over 60 million tons of goods went through London's docks every year, but all this activity was to vanish with startling suddenness.

It began back in the 1790s when London merchants realised that mooring piers along the river itself could no longer cope with the trade flowing in. They persuaded Parliament to approve the building of enclosed docks, which would not only take more ships but would also reduce the pilfering that was traditional along the open river. The West India merchants were first with their new docks on the Isle of Dogs, and others followed within a few years. The Surrey Docks were created piecemeal by combining several older docks in Rotherhithe. St Katharine Dock was opened quite late, in 1828, carved ruthlessly from slums where 11,000 people lost their miserable homes. Thus by the end of the 19th century, London's trade was being handled by the world's biggest enclosed dock system. Work conditions were appalling as an army of cheap casual labour gathered daily for the 'call on' at dock gates, hoping for a day's tough work. In 1889 strikers demanded a wage of sixpence an hour.

World War II brought violent disaster to the docks. On 'Black Saturday', 7 September 1940, bombs set vast areas ablaze, and Londoners could all see the pall of smoke as their docks burnt. But when war ended, the ruins were rebuilt and Docklands flourished for another 20 years. The end came abruptly. Bigger ships needed deeper water, and the old docks could not handle containers or the new roll-on, roll-off technology. So they died, and in 1981 a new body, the London Docklands Development Corporation, set about restoring life to a derelict area. From the Thames Path you will see the results, and how the docks have found new uses. Where the West India Company first built, the towers of Canary Wharf now rise. But the noisy, hectic bustle of a working port can only be re-created in your own imagination.

The Thames Path

1 The Source to Cricklade

12¼ miles (19.7 km)

Transport Options

After the ease of reaching Kemble by train, you are dependent on occasional buses. A 7-mile (11.3-km) walk from the source brings you to Ashton Keynes, where there is a reasonable bus service to Swindon, Monday to Saturday, while Cricklade has a similar but rather more frequent service.

Although the source of the Thames lies, seemingly, in a remote Gloucestershire meadow, it is in truth only a short walk from Kemble station **A**. So your walk of discovery will very likely begin at the station forecourt on the London-bound side, taking the approach road to join another road. Turn left here, and, in just 75 yards, a signed path on the right crosses a stile to follow a stream that sometimes flows into the infant Thames but which can, like the Thames itself, be just a dry dip in the meadow in summer. Just to assert that it is sometimes a vigorous little tributary, a footbridge crosses just before it enters the main stream. Turn left over this bridge **B** and follow the bank of the Thames for a while up a broad valley, the course of the river quite apparent, even when dry. Soon, the right-of-way climbs to the left-hand side of the field through a gate. At this point, just below you, a grove of trees and the low retaining wall of a pond mark the location of Lyd Well **2**, an ancient spring where, often, the very first Thames water will be gushing up from a little, grassy dell.

When you see, opposite, a big house of Cotswold stone, take the path bearing right across the meadow. In the dip, you can easily trace the line where an infant Thames occasionally flows, and even the tumble of stones that was once a footbridge. Ahead, you can see the traffic on the Roman Foss Way; from here aim for a flight of stone steps leading up to a stile. Cross the road cautiously – the traffic is fast here – then continue down a farm approach opposite, over a stile on the right, and carry on along a track with a fence to your left. The track goes through a gate in the long stone wall ahead, so use the green squeeze stile beside it, and keep on by a faint track marked by a straggly line of trees; ahead, the tower of Coates Church acts as a useful guide. One more stile and you are there – the pebbles of the head spring beneath an elderly ash tree, and the simple stone placed by the

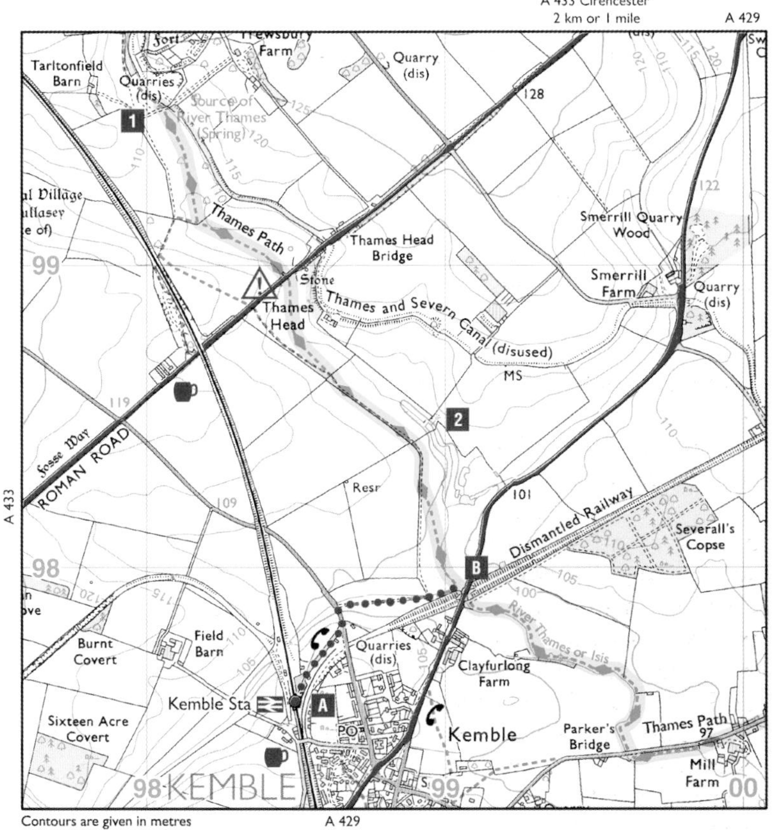

Thames Conservators to confirm that your walk truly starts here **1**. For sixteen years up to 1974, *Old Father Thames* himself resided here to greet you, but, today, he reclines in greater security at St John's Lock, where you will pass him later.

So, suitably inspired, and in the certain knowledge that it must all be downhill from here on, you set out back along the track towards Kemble, along the line of trees, via the squeeze stile and the clear way back across the Foss Way. After a wet season, the bowl of grass to your left can be a lake of Thames water, fed by the first springs. The right-of-way climbs to the right-hand field boundary for a while, but, towards the end of the field, you should branch left again to find the Thames channel, already quite broad, and the stile beside the two-arch bridge that takes it under the road into Kemble village. Just to the right, across the road, go through a gate and carry on along a rough path by the riverbank, the Thames now to your right, with the spire of Kemble Church visible over the fields beyond. Coming up to Parker's Bridge, bear left across the road and take the little path that wends its way along the green strip between river and road. When it gives up, keep on along the road into the farms and cottages of Ewen. Ahead, through the village, is the picturesque Wild Duck Inn.

But your route turns right at the first road junction in Ewen. Immediately after crossing the Thames, turn through a gate **C**. Now the path keeps along the riverbank, leading into open meadows and on to Upper Mill Farm. So modest is the flow of water here, it is difficult to believe that it worked watermills, yet your path passes by the one-time millrace, turning left in another 25 yards to take a footbridge over the mill stream **D**. Once over, turn right to follow the field boundary, now with the Thames to your right. Cross a plank footbridge, with Somerford Keynes in view over the fields, turn right again and continue by the river past Old Mill Farm. In the next big field, the serene grouping of church and manor house of Somerford Keynes **3** is visible just a field or two to your left. Footpaths lead that way, should you want to explore, or sample The Baker's Arms in the village. But the Thames Path keeps by the field edge until a long, wooden footbridge **E** takes it into Neigh

An infant Thames runs shyly through its meadows, near Waterhay Bridge.

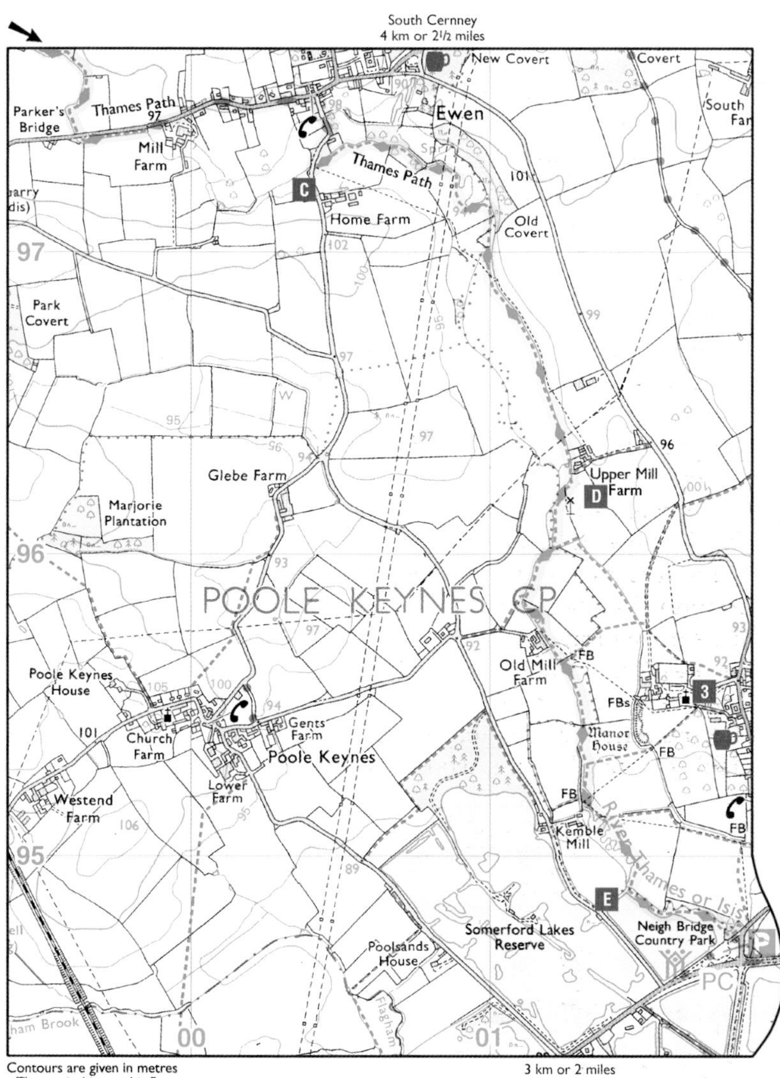

Bridge Country Park. Here, even if your walk so far has been by a stubbornly dry Thames, you will find a lake full of water. Turn left after crossing the bridge and continue on the path by the riverside until you finally come up to the lane by Neigh Bridge itself. Just to the right, across the head of the lake, the Country Park has toilets, open during the summer.

Cross the lane and turn right to walk on the grass verge, then left along the broad Spine Road of Cotswold Water Park. You will

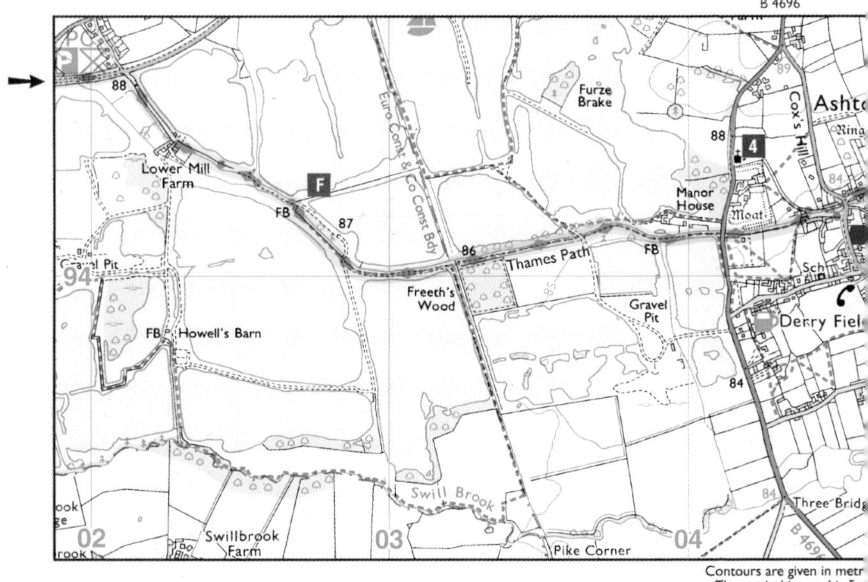

go over the Thames again in another 150 yards, then cross the road to take the gravel path beside the lane opposite. The water park lakes are flooded gravel workings put to new uses. Very soon you are looking over Mill Lake to your left as the Thames appears beside you again, to your right. Beyond the Lower Mill Estate housing, keep on by the broad track where you will now see even more water to the right – Lower Mill Nature Reserve.

When the track comes to the gate into Farmhouse Lake, take the footbridge over the Thames **F**, turn left and continue, with the river now on your left, towards Ashton Keynes. After the vast, watery expanses, the sylvan path through Flood Hatches Copse comes as a complete contrast. The Thames follows several courses through and around Ashton Keynes, and you will cross one channel flowing away to the right before the path crosses a road, then squeezes between cottages into a charming village scene. A mini-Thames flows in its stone-edged channel across the grass and under an equally diminutive bridge – the glow of Cotswold stone all around. Walking ahead to the road you will pass one of the four preaching crosses in Ashton Keynes – headless but ancient. Why the village had so many is a mystery, but the church, reached by a path leading away behind you, is appropriately called Holy Cross **4**.

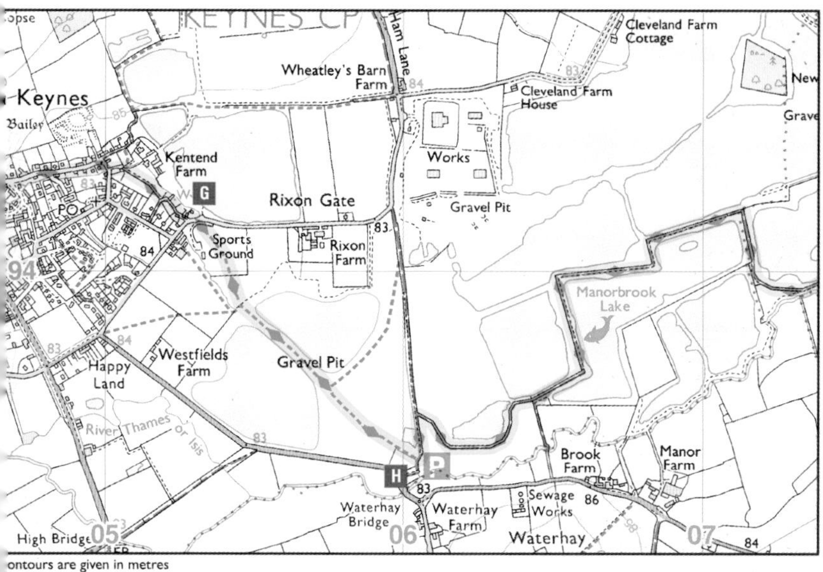

ontours are given in metres
The vertical interval is 5m

The nearest village pub is now The White Hart, reached by turning right in the road, past the cross. But the Thames Path turns left in the road, then right down Back Street. This quiet lane turns right to cross a little watercourse, and you go immediately left into the Kentend Farm drive. At the farm gates, go right through a kissing-gate and along the field edge with the water channel to the right. Through another kissing-gate, bear left with the path until you come to a drive that passes several houses and leads up to a road.

For the next half-mile (800 metres) to Waterhay, the Thames Path crosses an area transformed by recent gravel workings. Across the road to your left, go through a gate **G** into a sports field, cross their drive to a kissing-gate, then continue straight ahead with the pavilion to your right. A further gate leads out of the sports field and across Ashton Keynes Millennium Green to take a causeway between two new lakes. Once, this path followed a minor channel of the Thames, but you would not realize this today – the quarrying has ruthlessly swallowed it up. At Waterhay you join a more firmly established crossing way **H**, where you turn first left, then right. This bridleway winds its way through the Cleveland Lakes, more of the Cotswold Water Park. The first great water expanse on the right is Manorbrook Lake,

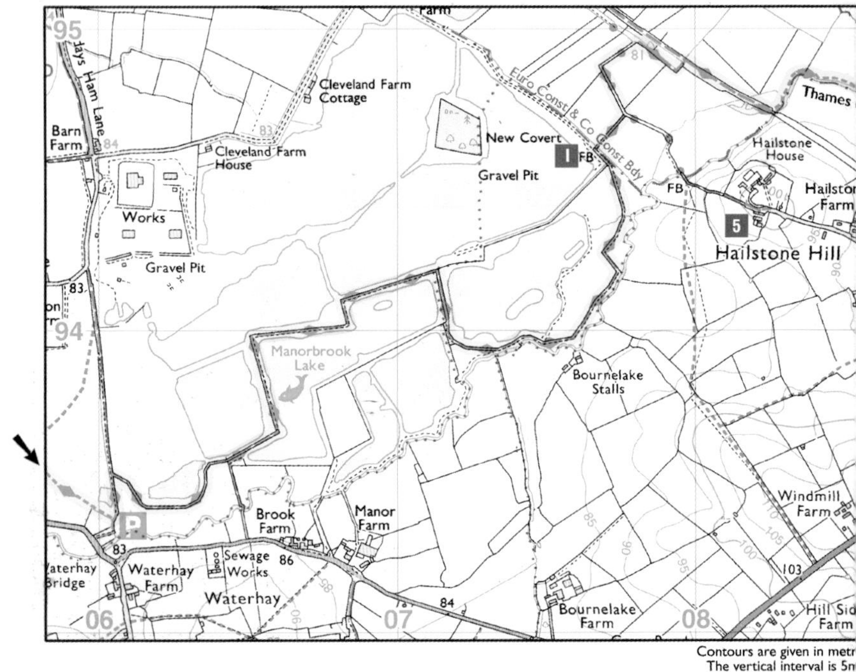

part of which is devoted to fishing. Your way turns left to follow its bank, the waterscape around you becoming quite attractive as nature softens the rawness of former gravel workings. Several turns later, you finally leave Manorbrook through a gate. Carry on for a few yards, then turn right to skirt one more lake, Cleveland Lake. Away to the left is Hailstone Hill **5**, a point to aim for. Turning towards the hill, you will be pleasantly surprised to discover that you have joined the Thames again, flowing now just to your right under old Bournelake Farm bridge. But this is only a brief encounter before the bridleway swings away to the left, coming to a gate labelled 'private road' where your journey continues to the right **I** over a bridge leading down to a broader crossing track, where you turn left.

At the next junction, turn right on a track that turns up onto the converted bed of the railway that once served Cricklade. After a gate, with a bridge clearly visible up ahead, turn left over a stile and follow a track down to the riverside. Follow the Thames now, first on the track, then on a meadow path until you reach another bridge on the line of the North Wiltshire Canal, which crossed the Thames here by a low

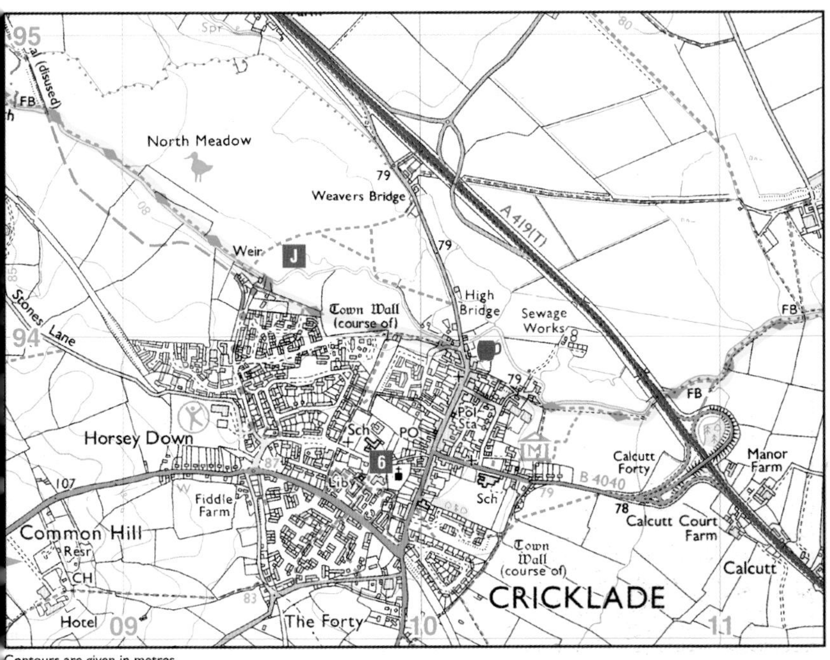

Contours are given in metres
The vertical interval is 5m

aqueduct. By the bridge, a stile and steps lead down into the vast, open vista of North Meadow. The nature reserve established here in 1973 protects one of the finest remaining examples of ancient meadowland, still opened to common grazing on the old Lammas Land principle. Among rarities to be seen here, towards the end of April each year is the best display anywhere of snake's-head fritillary.

Follow the riverbank now past several stiles and gates, with the magnificent tower of St Sampson's Church **6** ahead, the focal point of several river compositions. After you have passed a gauging station, go through a gate and cross the river over a farm bridge **J**. Walk up the track and around a bend, keeping to the left-hand gated path, then left over a plank footbridge and on by a fenced path. Keep ahead over an open field to a kissing-gate and the first houses of Cricklade, where immediately you turn left along an estate path. Where the path, Bailiff's Piece, turns right, keep on through a gap in the hedge and head straight across an open and obviously popular meadow. Several paths aim for the far end, where a gate leads into a road, North Wall, and thus to the foot of Cricklade High Street.

2 Cricklade to Lechlade

10¾ miles (17.3 km)

Transport Options

Castle Eaton after 4¼ miles (6.8 km) and Upper Inglesham 4¼ miles (6.8 km) further on are the only staging points on this walk. One bus a day runs from Castle Eaton to Swindon, but Upper Inglesham is reasonably served by buses between Lechlade and Swindon, Mondays to Saturdays.

Cricklade is the first township on the Thames, and, like many on the route, seems to have begun as a favoured crossing point. The Roman Ermine Street crosses nearby, and, ironically, Cricklade's much-needed bypass has restored the Roman line. From the Town Bridge over the Thames **7**, the High Street climbs steadily with that marvellous English country town mix of styles and periods, all living harmoniously together. St Sampson's Church **6** stands back behind the houses, and while its massive Tudor tower with its four great corner pinnacles dominates the meadows for miles around, it can hardly be seen from the High Street. Very visible, however, is the smaller, much-restored Norman church of St Mary, which has – in an unusual move – been rededicated as Cricklade's Catholic church. In its churchyard is a fine 14th-century preaching cross with figures in a four-sided lantern head.

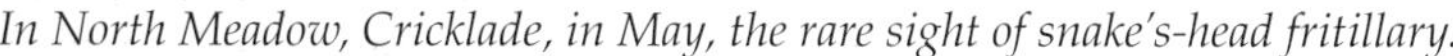

In North Meadow, Cricklade, in May, the rare sight of snake's-head fritillary.

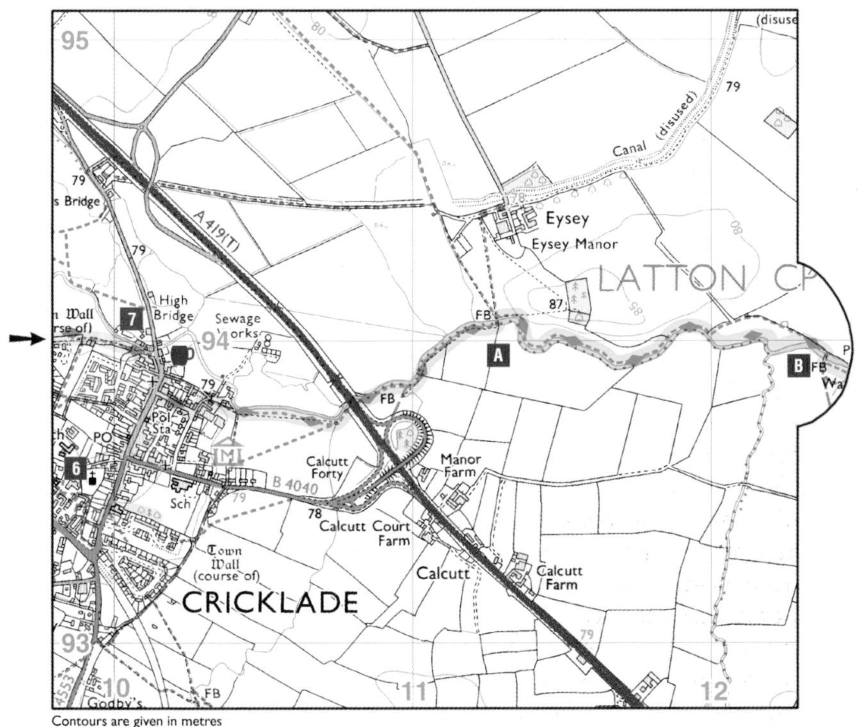

Contours are given in metres
The vertical interval is 5m

Almost opposite St Mary's, the Thames Path leaves the High Street via Abingdon Court Lane. Where the lane turns right, leave it and turn left into a drive. Coming to a point where the ways divide in several directions, cross a stile in the hedge on the right where there are steps going over a large stone slab. Turn left and follow the fence to a hedge gap leading into open meadows, once more by the Thames, now swollen by the waters of the Churn, and soon by two other tributaries, Key and Ray. Cross the first of these by means of a concrete farm bridge, then follow the Thames bank under the bypass and on to Eysey Footbridge **A**. At this pretty spot, you cross the Thames itself, and take to paths along its north bank. Walk on through the riverside meadows, now beneath the gentle slope of tree-clad Eysey Hill, until a stile and a length of path through dense foliage leads out to the lonely Water Eaton Footbridge **B**.

Once over the footbridge, turn left to follow the river bank with the barns of Water Eaton Farm up to your right. The river-

The church of St Mary, Castle Eaton, stands by the bank of a reed-filled Thames, where even the smallest boats seldom try to navigate.

side path from here into Castle Eaton was created specially for Thames Path walkers. It crosses a succession of double-gated footbridges over water channels, one of them with a venerable willow of awe-inspiring size nearby, still displaying a defiant flourish of greenery. After running through open meadows, the path comes to a crossing track and has to skirt briefly leftwards in order to pass a plantation of young trees that comes down to the river. Then, after following the meanders of the Thames through several vast meadows, the path brings you to within sight of the cottages of Castle Eaton up ahead. As you approach the village a faint track leads off to the right, away from the river, to a footbridge and gate leading into the foot of Mill Lane.

Walk on up the lane, soon with houses on either side, and keep ahead in The Street **C**. Follow it past mellow stone cottages to the large Georgian inn, The Red Lion. Just before the inn, a quick diversion down the Kempsford turning will give you a glimpse of the Thames, but the route from here on is not by the river, so keep on, turning right by the big barns of Manor Farm. On the left here, a stone-roofed lych-gate leads to the church **8** poised on the bank of the Thames. An 1860s restoration added a little bell turret with spire on the nave roof, a distinctive feature presumably intended to hold a Sanctus bell.

The village road passes Long Row, a terrace of cottages on your right, then returns to the main road. Turn left, go round a bend and turn left again into the farm lane leading to Blackford Farm.

Follow the lane around several bends, then, as you pass barns on your left, carry on until you pass the little farmhouse itself on your right. Walk on over grass, then left **D** to follow the field boundary down to another brief meeting with the Thames. The river here is a reedy channel with farms and the tall, graceful tower of Kempsford Church **9** just over the meadows beyond. Your path follows the Thames bank, then a side channel, over several stiles and into a lane opposite cottages at Hannington Bridge.

Turn right now, and continue until, where the lane turns right at a junction of ways, you turn left onto a track that leads to a house. Just before reaching this, fork right **E** onto the start of a fine old bridlepath to Inglesham. For 1½ miles (2.4 km) this rolls along with, for the most part, a ditch and hedge to the left, and open fields to the right. The Thames is just a field or two away, but out of sight. Eventually, following a temporary route, a bridleway gate leads to a ford over a tributary stream with a footbridge just to the right. Cross and walk forward 50 yards into the corner of a field **F**; here turn right and walk, with the boundary hedge on your right, up to the cottages of Upper Inglesham. On this field, you can easily see the lines of mediaeval ridge-and-furrow cultivation, first parallel to your route, then running across it. Coming into the lane, turn left up to the A361 road, and then left again. You now have over a mile of busy road and speeding traffic, so it is best to cross to the east side, where there are wider verges that are regularly cut for you.

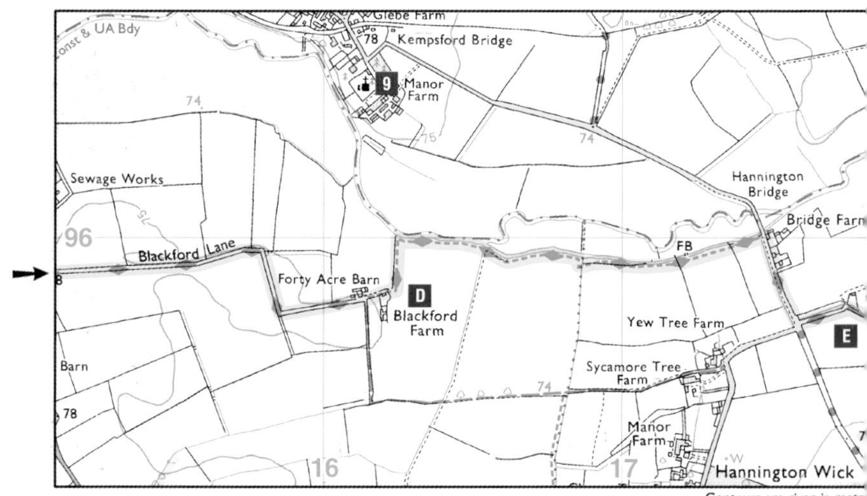

The river winds gracefully across the flood plain at St John's Lock, Lechlade.

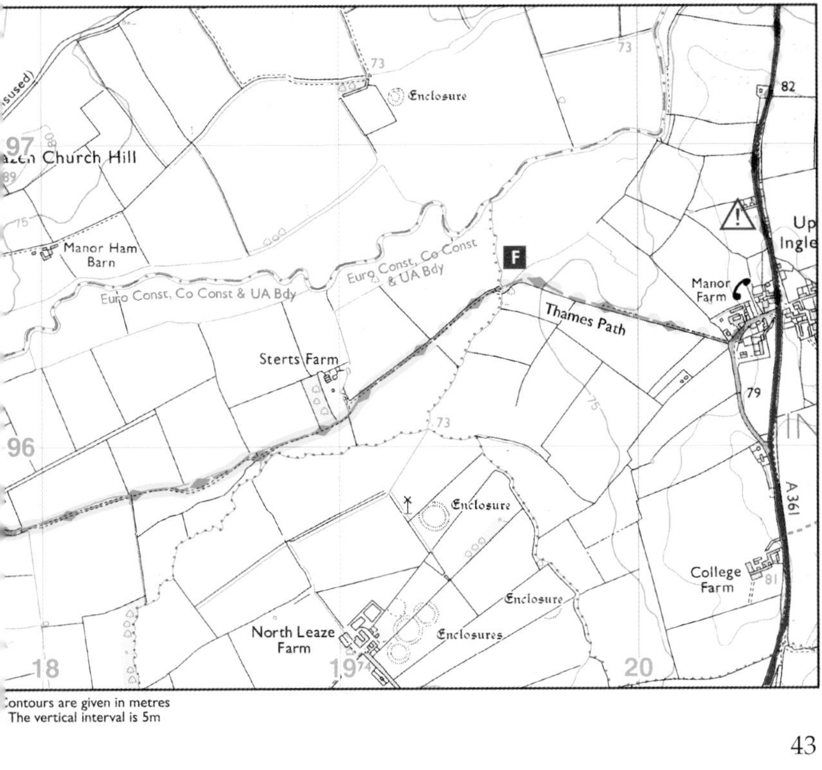

Enclosure
97
Church Hill
Manor Ham Barn
Euro Const, Co Const & UA Bdy
Euro Const, Co Const & UA Bdy
F
Thames Path
Sterts Farm
Manor Farm
Up
Ingle
82
79
96
A 361
Enclosure
Enclosure
Enclosures
North Leaze Farm
College Farm
18
19
20

Contours are given in metres
The vertical interval is 5m

At the end of this tramp, you can turn, with relief, down the lane signposted to Inglesham Church **10**. Your reward is a marvellous little building: St John the Baptist, which served an almost vanished village, and which restoration in Victorian times returned to its earlier character – rather than the Victorian Gothic inflicted on so many of its fellows – a miracle brought about by William Morris. So, here, you have a kind of time capsule – a parish church of a bygone era with venerable 13th-century stonework, wall paintings and texts from the 13th century onwards, a Jacobean pulpit and box pews, including private pews for squire and vicar. It is tended by the Churches Conservation Trust, and, except at certain times of year when altar furnishings are in place, you should find it open.

Retrace your steps a little until, just beyond the first house along the lane leading to the church, a stile **G** takes you into the meadows towards Lechlade. From the stile, walk diagonally left across the field to a footbridge by the Thames. Follow its bank now around the first bend, where you find yourself looking across to a stonebuilt farmhouse and, behind it, an odd roundhouse – Roundhouse Farm **11**. Here, the Thames and Severn Canal left the Thames to carry its trade, via the Sapperton Tunnel and the Golden Valley, down to Stroud. One of the most

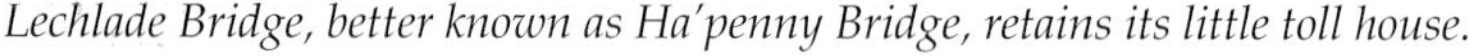

Lechlade Bridge, better known as Ha'penny Bridge, retains its little toll house.

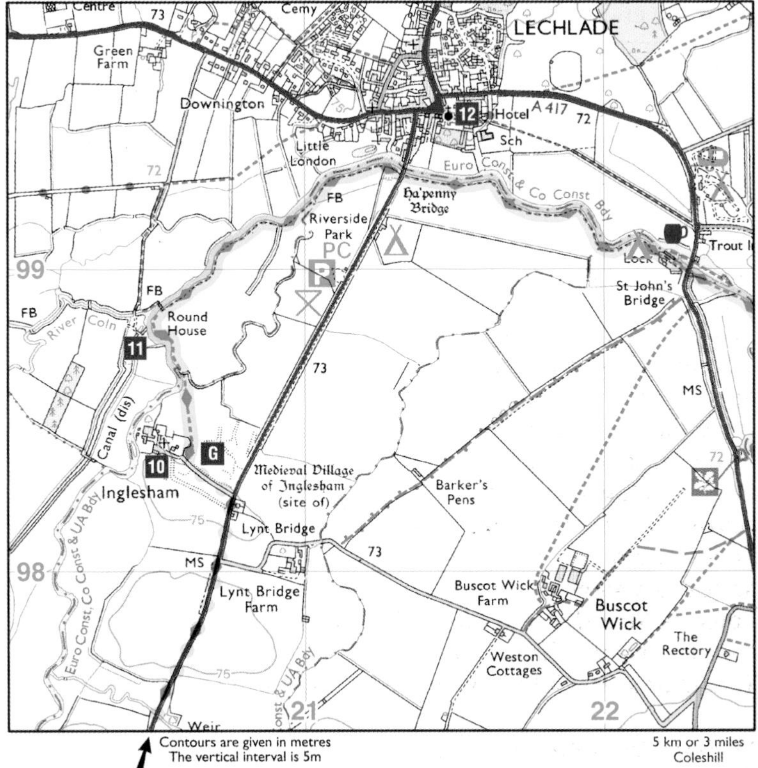

ambitious of canal concepts, the waterway was never really successful; water leaked from its summit level constantly, and the last boats to travel between the Severn and the Thames did so in 1927. The roundhouses were the unusual quarters for lock-keepers, and several survive, though much of the canal is now dry. Across the Thames, you can see the willow-hung entry of the River Coln, but can only guess where the canal began.

You have now reached an important landmark on your walk. On the bank opposite the farmhouse is a modest block of stone, the abutment of a bridge that brought the canal towpath over the Thames to your feet, from where it followed the river down to Putney. From here on, it will provide many days of easy walking by the Thames. So, set off with new assurance through Lechlade's riverside park to the 18th-century Town Bridge, usually called Ha'penny Bridge, from the toll once charged. An archway with gates will take you on to St John's Lock, but you may wish to cross the bridge and explore Lechlade.

3 Lechlade to Newbridge

16¼ miles (26.1 km)

Transport Options

This is remotest Thames, and the staging points, Radcot Bridge, after 6¼ miles (10 km), and Tadpole Bridge, after another 4 miles (6.4 km), have no transport. Buses serve villages north and south of the Thames, and from Newbridge to Abingdon and Witney, but otherwise this is B & B country.

Lechlade has all the feel of a small, prosperous town. From the marketplace, with its several coaching inns, the streets radiate out, their golden Cotswold stone mingling with the greys of Oxfordshire. The spire of St Lawrence **12**, truly one of the great 'wool churches', draws the whole composition together. Indeed, Lechlade owes its location and its prosperity to having long been the highest point on the Thames that laden barges could reach. The riverside is still busy, but where once Cotswold stone and Gloucestershire cheeses were loaded up for London, it is now the gleaming, white pleasure cruisers that congregate at the head of navigation.

Under Ha'penny Bridge, a towpath arch with two gates will take you from the riverside park, around bends of the river, to St John's Lock. Here, in front of the lock house, you can pay your respects to Old Father Thames **13**, reclining with symbols of commerce around him. He was first commissioned in 1854 for the grounds of Crystal Palace, then bought by one of the Thames Conservators and set beside the Thames Head spring to gaze at occasional visitors from a cage of railings. Doubtless he is happier here, watching the boats. St John's Bridge, beyond the lock, is Victorian, but earlier versions were administered by St John's Priory, established here in 1250. Nothing remains of the priory, but probably some of its stones were reused in the nearby Trout Inn. For anyone who wants to avoid the steps built into the new Bloomers Hole footbridge ahead, an alternative route crosses St John's Bridge to turn right beyond The Trout, then right again in 350 yards on a track back to the Thames. But the Thames Path itself keeps to the old towpath, squeezing beneath the bridge arch, then through a gate into the meadows beyond. A footbridge crosses a broad sidestream, then the footbridge at Bloomers Hole **A** takes you over the Thames itself. Turn downstream again to follow the serpentine loops of the Thames – here firmly fenced off and no short-cuts allowed.

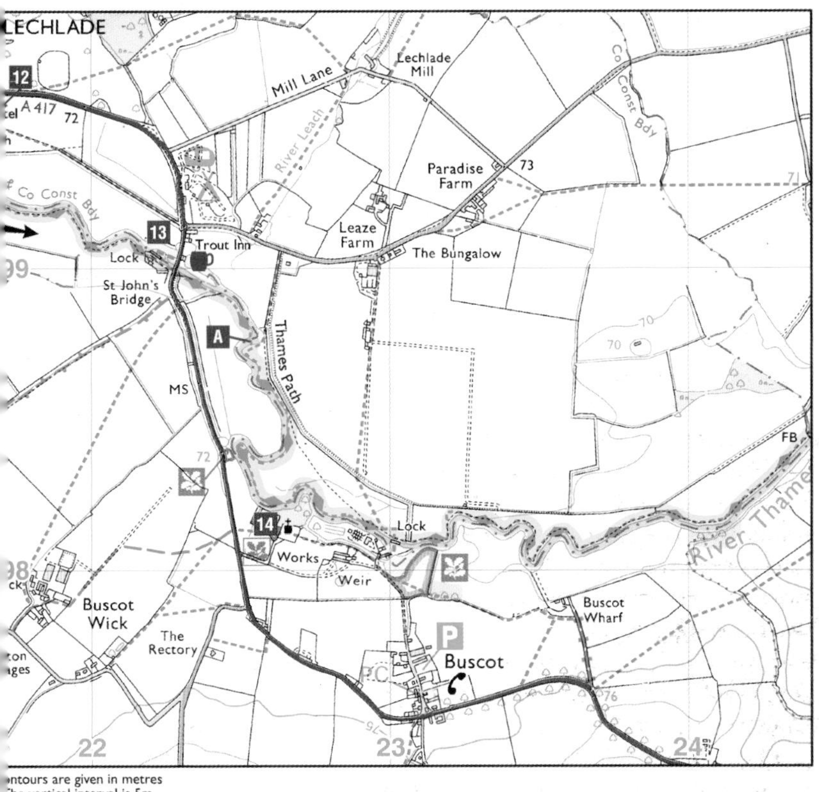

ntours are given in metres
'he vertical interval is 5m

Here, in the open meadows, you are very aware of the concrete pillboxes of World War II vintage, some so eroded as to look like tiny medieval castles. In this tranquil setting it is difficult to believe that, in 1940, the natural defence line of our river was Stopline Red, a last desperate bid to keep invaders from the Midlands. Across the Thames, you can see Buscot Church **14**, and beside it the fine Old Parsonage of the Queen Anne period, part of the National Trust's Buscot estate. Then, coming to Buscot Lock, go through the gate to walk ahead (not the stile on the left) and over the weir bridge to the lock. To visit Buscot village, cross the upper lock gates and the old weir on a path that passes the stone weir-keeper's cottage and the weir pool.

The Thames Path, however, continues on the grass along the lock edge, through a gate and along the water's edge before crossing a big concrete bridge over the main weir stream, and thus back to the riverside again. Around more meanders, in a

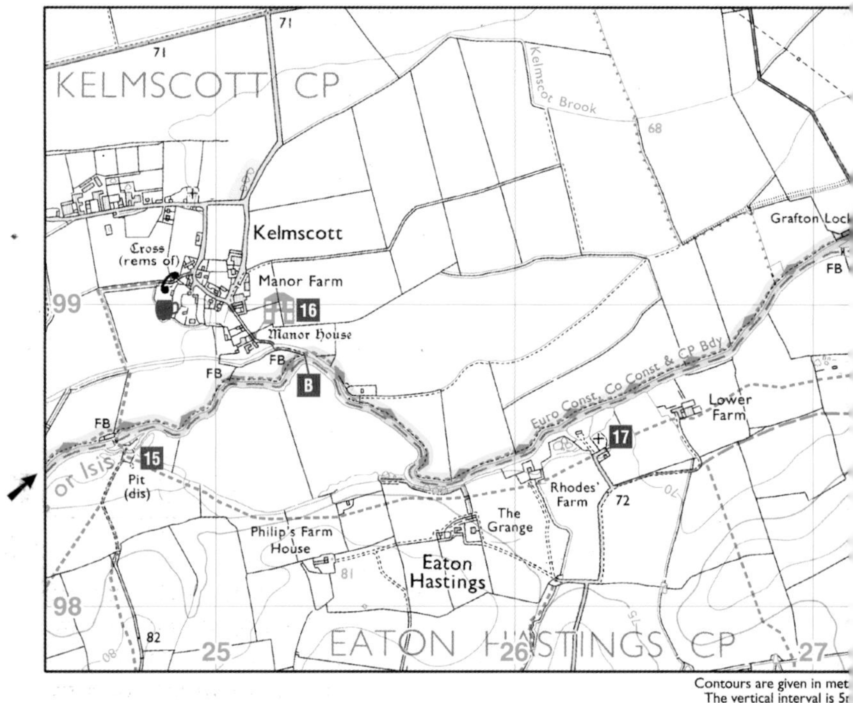

Contours are given in met
The vertical interval is 5r

grove of trees ahead, you come to Eaton Weir **15**, a pretty spot with a rustic bridge and a tiny cottage; but no weir – this was one of the last of the primitive flash-weirs on the Thames, and was taken up in 1936. A touch of sadness lingers here: the inn that stood on the far bank was destroyed by fire some years ago in tragic circumstances, and no trace remains. Stay on the same bank, squeeze past the footbridge and carry on, with the river still to your right. Soon, a footbridge and gate **B** lead you into a broad track.

Your route lies onward, but, to the left, this track will take you, in just a couple of minutes, to Kelmscott Manor **16**, the serene Elizabethan house that William Morris fell in love with and made his country home for 25 years. The grey, stone gables and mullioned windows peep at you from over high walls, but if you are shrewd enough to visit on a Wednesday in summer, the house will be open. Many days further on, your journey will take you past Kelmscott House on Hammersmith Mall, London, William Morris's town address. Legend has it that, on occasions, he rowed family and guests the 130 miles (209 km) from house to manor.

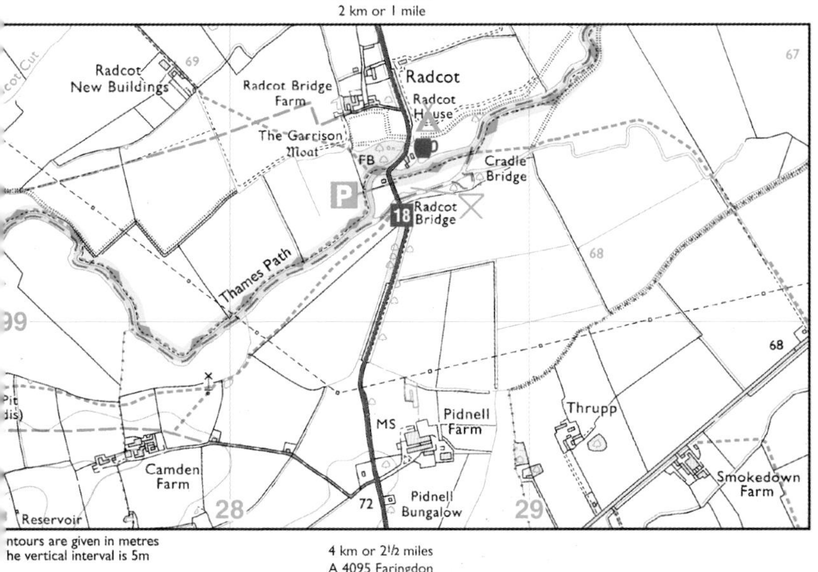

Further up the lane is Kelmscott village, where, in the churchyard of the little church of St George, Morris was buried under a simple, decorated, stone slab, the work of his friend Philip Webb.

But all that is a diversion. Keep on along the broad track by the Thames, then through a kissing-gate into open meadows again. Soon, across the river, a lawn, a house or two and a glimpse of a simple church among the trees tell you that you are passing Eaton Hastings **17**. In the next grove of trees is Grafton Lock, where you walk through the gate, along the lawn, between the flowerbeds and straight on towards Radcot. Here, the river divides, and while you follow the left-hand branch up to the road beside the narrow, much-scraped navigation bridge, you can see that the other branch flows under a far older bridge **18**. Indeed, parts of old Radcot Bridge date to the 12th century, a time when only the religious houses had building skills like this. The three Gothic arches are ribbed beneath like a cathedral roof, and one parapet still carries the niche that once held a statue of the Virgin Mary. Radcot is simply the oldest bridge on the Thames, preserved because the river traffic was diverted along the other channel.

Coming to the road, you cross the newer bridge, then turn down the steps and go through a gate into the picnic meadow, at the further end of which a bridge takes you over the old channel and straight on.

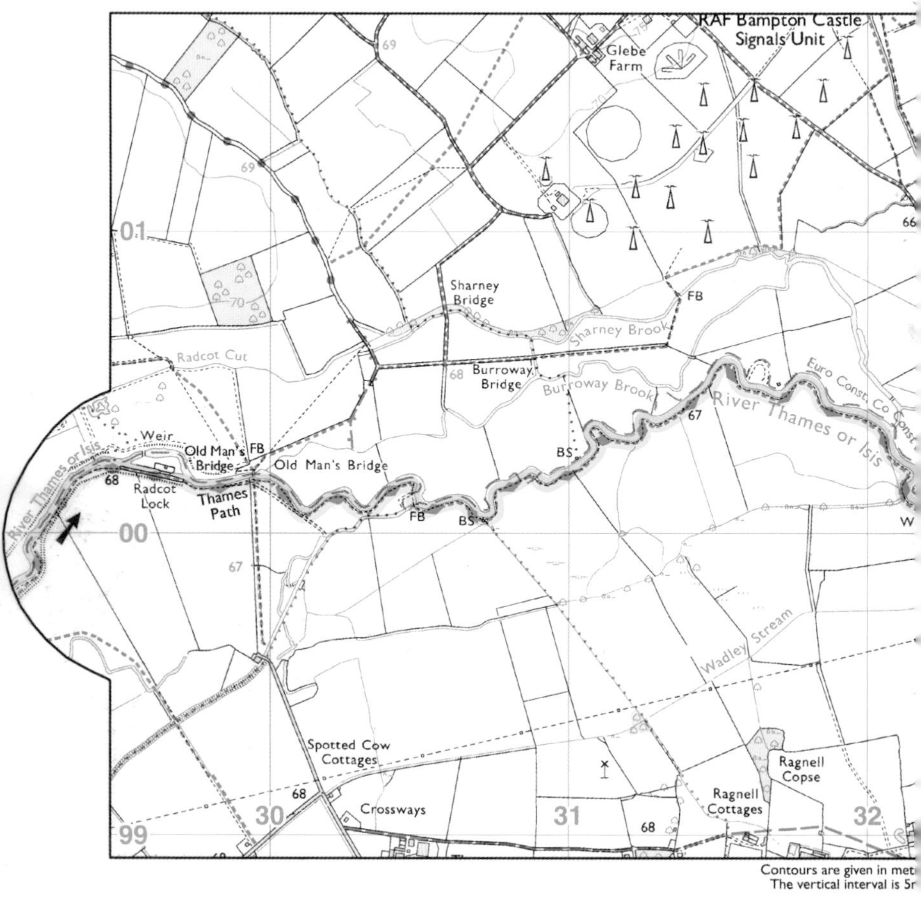

At Radcot Lock, take the grassy path past the lock itself, then walk briefly along the access drive before leaving it to return to the riverbank. Past Old Man's Bridge, lonely in the fields, there are more meanders in the river; in fact, you can try guessing where the Thames will wander to next. At Rushey Lock **19**, your way crosses the weir, then takes a gravel path across the garden past the charming, stone lock cottage, and over the lower lock gates to the road. While crossing, you may sense that Rushey Weir is something unusual: an increasingly rare example of an old Thames paddle-and-rymer weir. There are paddles stacked by the path, and you can see how they are dropped into place between the heavier posts with handles, the rymers, to hold the water back. Before the arrival of pound locks, a weir like this

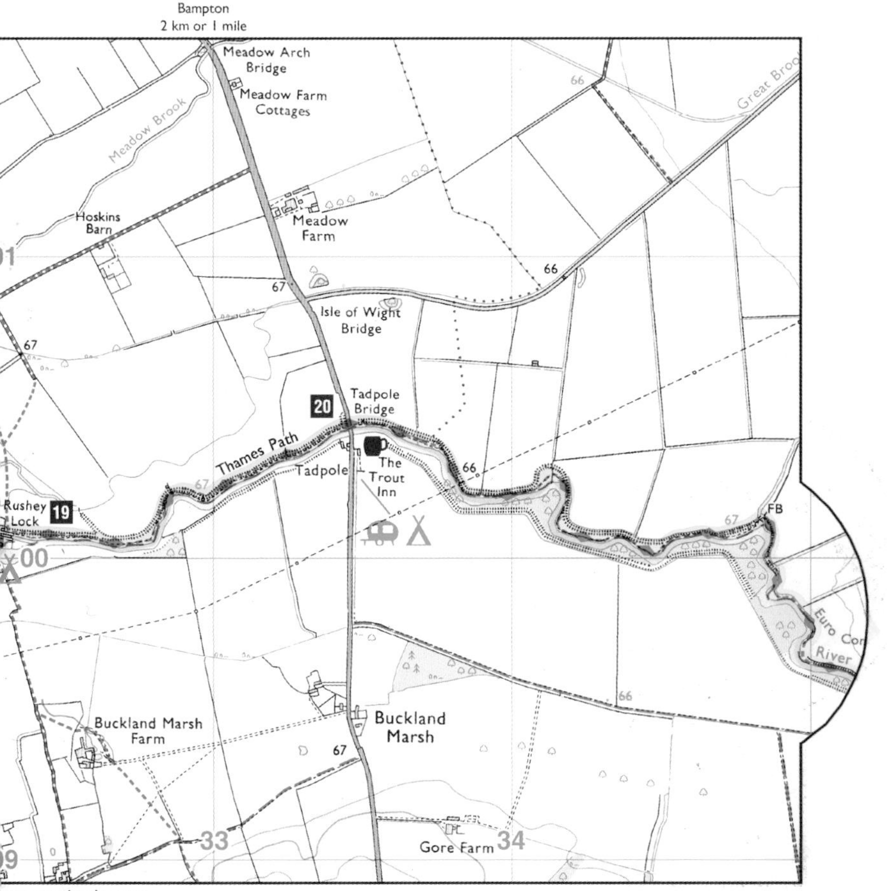

had to be opened by drawing out some of the paddles and rymers – the river traffic going through the gap as soon as the resulting 'flash' of water had subsided.

The lock access road follows the river now to Tadpole Bridge **20**. This remote bridge, with its delightful name and solitary inn for company, was built to carry the turnpike road to Bampton. The steps on the right take you up to the road, where you cross straight over and drop down to the towpath again. The path takes you through open meadows, at the end of which is a gate a little way up from the river. Here, avenues of slender trees provide a useful guide to where the Thames runs, as you wend your way via a gate into Chimney Meadow Nature Reserve, one of the largest areas of unimproved meadowland in

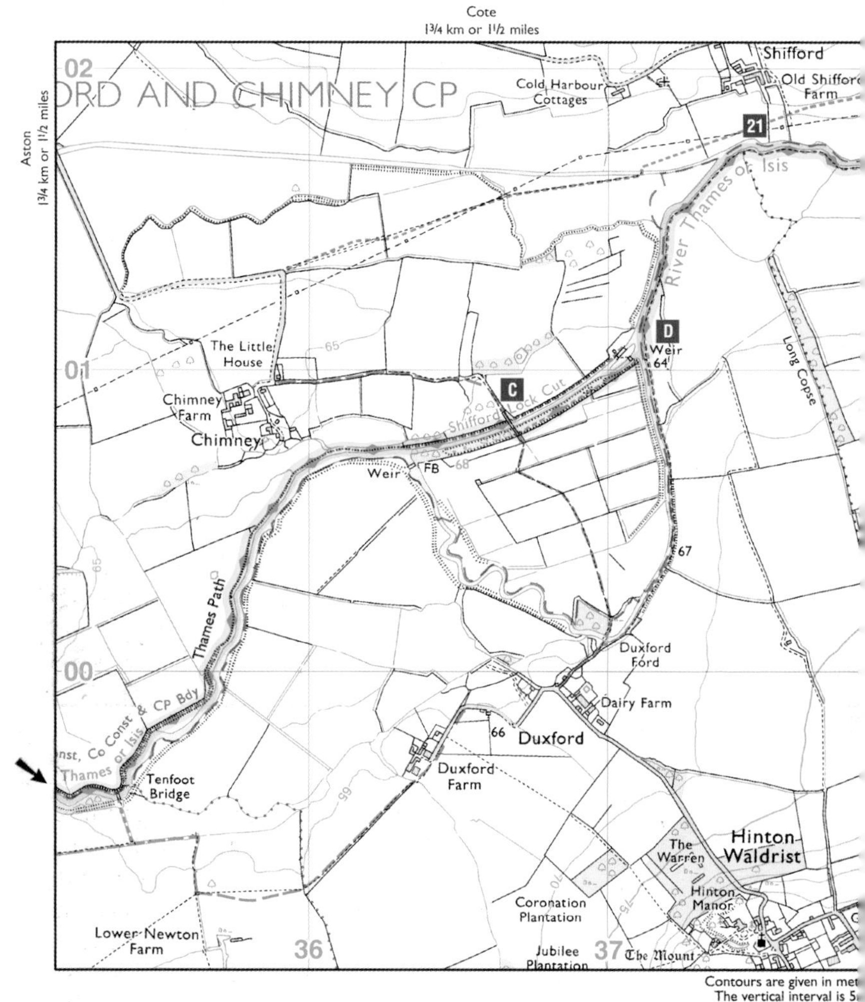

England, rich in hay meadow plants. Your path keeps to the bank beside the river, taking you to Tenfoot Bridge. Like several other lonely footbridges on the upper Thames, Tenfoot is on the site of a flash-weir, taken up in 1870. Although the weir has gone, the right-of-way claimed by locals crossing over it has been preserved by a footbridge like this. The 'tenfoot' probably referred to the opening in the weir that let barges through.

Do not cross here, but keep on along the river bank. Soon you will see the distant buildings of Chimney Farm to your left, then across the river a weir that takes the old Thames channel looping

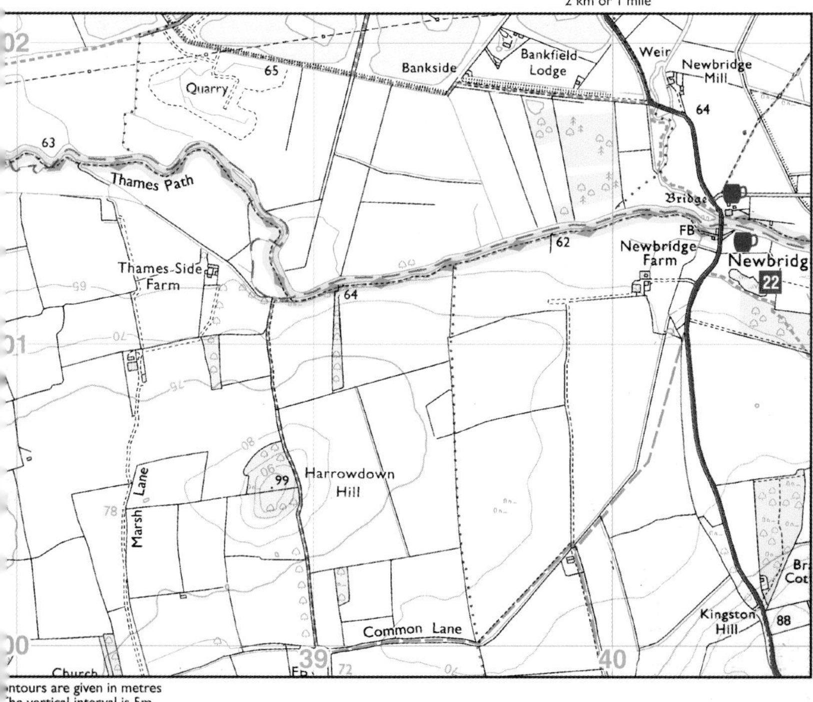

away towards Duxford, still, as the name suggests, a genuine Thames ford. Now you are following an artificial cut, soon crossed by a wooden bridleway bridge **C**. Climb the steps and cross the bridge, turning left in a few yards through a gate onto a path along an open green strip. Now the lock cut is to your left, and, walking on beneath a fine, tall stand of poplar, you can hear the water surging over Shifford Weir. Just beyond it, bear right over a footbridge **D**, and turn leftwards along the riverbank, round the edge of a vast field. Just a meadow away, across the Thames, you can see a farm, a scattering of cottages and a tiny 19th-century chapel. This is Shifford **21** and, unbelievably, there must have been a major town here a thousand years ago. King Alfred held a meeting of the English Parliament at Shifford with 'many bishops, learned men, proud earls and awful knights'. They would not recognise it now. After one more bend of the river, and a wooded stretch beneath Harrowdown Hill, you are on a straight run to Newbridge **22**. Go through one last gate and walk alongside the garden of the Maybush pub, up to the road.

4 Newbridge to Oxford

14 miles (22.5 km)

Transport Options

From Newbridge, a 7¾-mile (12.5-km) walk brings you to Swinford Bridge, and, from nearby Eynsham and Farmoor, there are good bus links every day into Oxford.

Newbridge **22** is a spot to be savoured in the tranquillity of early morning before the traffic has begun to rumble through. Then the glowing stone of the bridge is reflected in the still waters, the incredibly ancient arches caught in perfect mirror image. Newbridge is 13th-century work, little altered and probably 'newer' than the bridge you passed at Radcot by 50 years or less. Its stone surely came from the Taynton quarries near Burford, rafted down the Windrush that enters here. Indeed, this must once have been a busy wharf – the point where Taynton stone began its journey down the Thames to help build the Oxford colleges and even St Paul's Cathedral. Today, there is just the bridge and, on either bank, the hostelries with their dreamily poetic names – Maybush and Rose Revived.

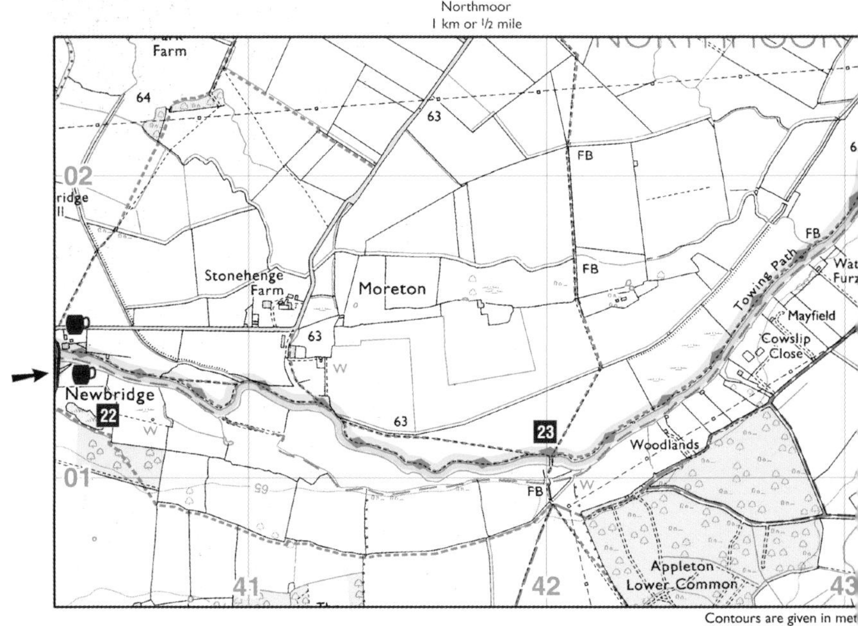

The Rose Revived Inn stands by the warm Cotswold stone of medieval Newbridge, providing a useful overnight stop for walkers between Oxford and Lechlade.

Your walk starts out along the riverside terrace of The Rose Revived, which is reached by a white garden gate. Following the water's edge over the lawn, you will find the towpath again, ready to take you round more amiable meanders of the Thames. Soon, you come to another lonely bridge, Hart's Weir Footbridge **23**, which links one remote meadow with another in puzzling fashion. Like others you have passed, this crossing preserves the right-of-way over an early Thames weir, long since taken up.

Now the river is beginning its great loop around the high ground of Cumnor and Wytham Hill. On the right day, this stretch can be sheer joy. Forget about route-finding and just stride out over the springy turf while the Thames unfolds an endless variety of compositions worthy of the brushes of a Constable.

At Northmoor Lock, go through the gate and over the grass to pass by the lockside. Here too you will see that the weir retains its paddle-and-rymer construction, and the lock-keeper tells of a 20-year campaign to keep it that way. It survives, and you would never suspect that the paddles are now fibreglass! After another mile or so, the gleam of white river craft and the hint of caravans through the trees ahead tell you that you are approaching Bablock Hythe **24**, the best known of all the Thames crossings. The Romans forded here, then a ferry crossed for perhaps a thousand years. In World War II, a chain-hauled vehicle ferry was kept busy, but today, even with an inn called The Ferryman nearby, you are only likely to get across if you book well in advance. Standing by the ferry point, you can't help recalling Matthew Arnold's Scholar-Gipsy who 'oft was met crossing the stripling Thames at Bab-lock-hythe'. In his search for solitude, the Scholar-Gipsy would not have approved the chalet estate that mars this spot now.

Here, you leave the river for a while. From the ferry point, turn up the approach lane, with the chalet estate to your right, keeping straight ahead at a junction along the Stanton Harcourt road. After another 300 yards by a passing place, go through a gate on the right onto a bridleway **A**. Through several more gates, the bridleway follows the left-hand field boundary, with views opening out onto the high ground of Wytham Great Wood over to the right. The metalled track you finally enter comes down from Stanton Harcourt, a village well deserving a visit, if you have the time. Thatched cottages, church, manor house and 17th-century parsonage make an impressive group; the church is outstanding for its Harcourt chapel, and the manor house equally so for the medieval great kitchen and nearby Pope's Tower.

The Thames Path turns right along the track, back towards the river. When it ends, at a gate **B**, go through the kissing-gate alongside and turn left to walk near to the field boundary on your left. Through a gate into the next field, your way bears right along a faint track over the grass towards an exit point, visible in the far corner. Go right through a gate over a concrete bridge, then through a further gate and into another meadow. Using the distant hill as the point to aim for, cross through the centre of the meadow until you again meet the Thames at the bottom. Two paths come to the riverbank at this spot **C**, where, until the 1930s, a footbridge crossed at the site of another ancient weir,

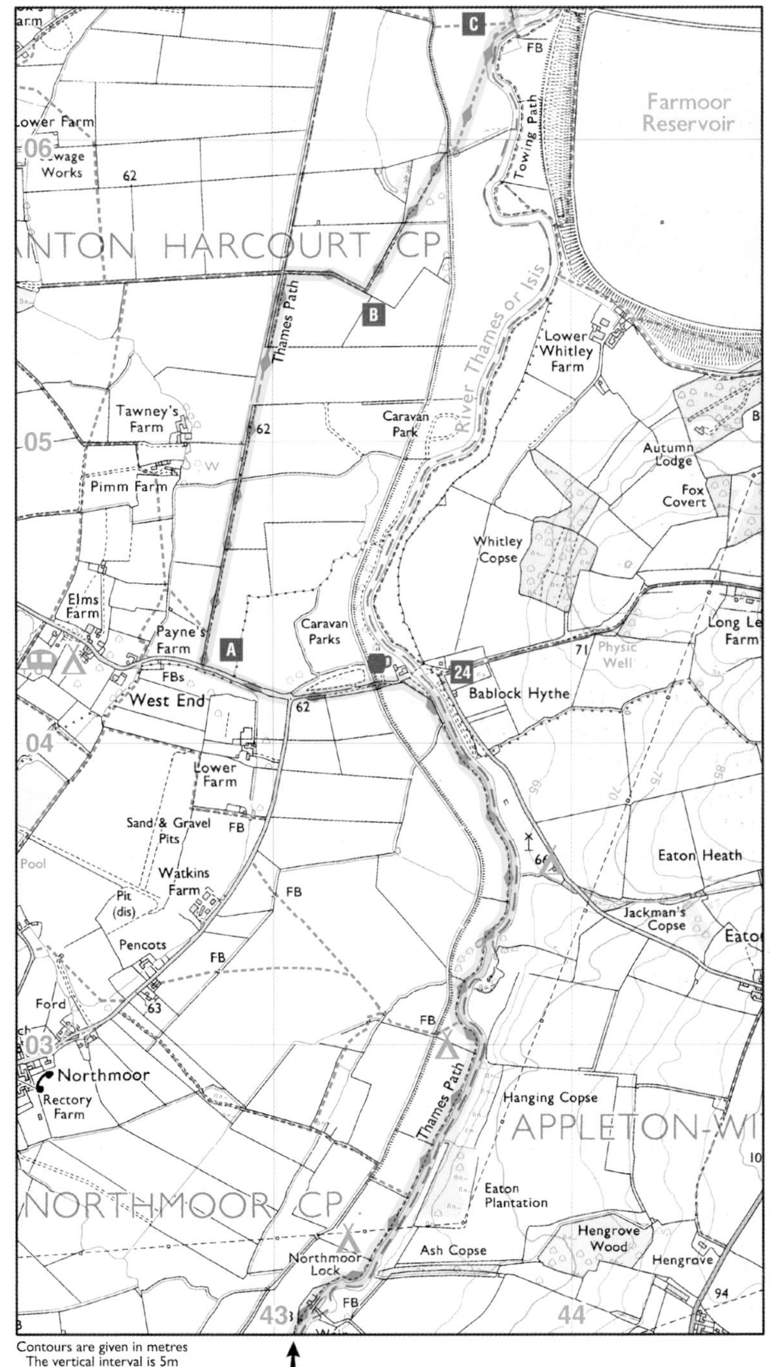

Contours are given in metres
The vertical interval is 5m

Skinner's Weir. No trace remains today, so bear left and follow the bank through a gate, leaving it briefly to skirt around a marvellously verdant backwater. Through a kissing-gate, you can see your path cutting off a river loop and heading directly across the grass to Pinkhill Weir **25**. Cross the weir bridge, then take a path over the grass of the lock island to cross over the upper gates of the lock. Go through a gate on the right, then turn left over the gravel outside the lock enclosure, to reach the towpath again.

At the next bend, beyond a footbridge, the old towpath has been eroded away and lost, so a short diversion away from the river is necessary. Take the path up to the road, turn left and, after 250 yards, turn left again down the drive to Oxford Cruisers **D**. Just through the gate into the riverside area, bear right to a gate onto the towpath again. More twists and loops lead on to the elegant arches of Swinford Bridge **26**, first of the two remaining privately owned toll bridges on the Thames, which was built for the Earl of Abingdon around 1770. Your path goes under one of the arches and on, *but for Eynsham, The Talbot Inn and buses to Oxford, take the steps up to the road and cross Swinford Bridge.* The bridge is free to pedestrians, but it is a hectic job collecting the 5p tolls from every passing car on this busy road.

On Port Meadow, horses and cattle still graze on ancient common land.

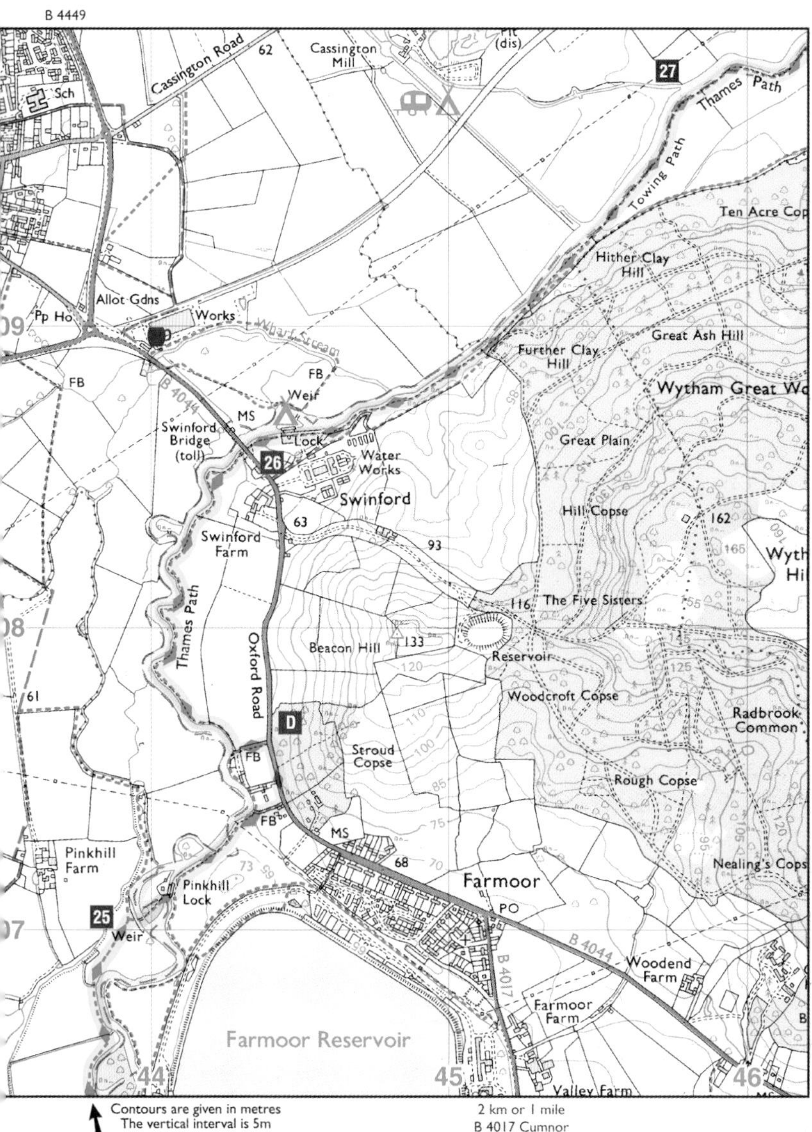

Beyond Swinford Bridge and Eynsham Lock, a modest path leads on to the point where Wytham Great Wood comes steeply down its hill to the water's edge. This fine 600-acre (243-hectare) wood, a wildlife haven, was bequeathed to Oxford University. Back in open pasture again, the Cotswold stream with the delectable name of Evenlode slips modestly into the Thames **27**. Then

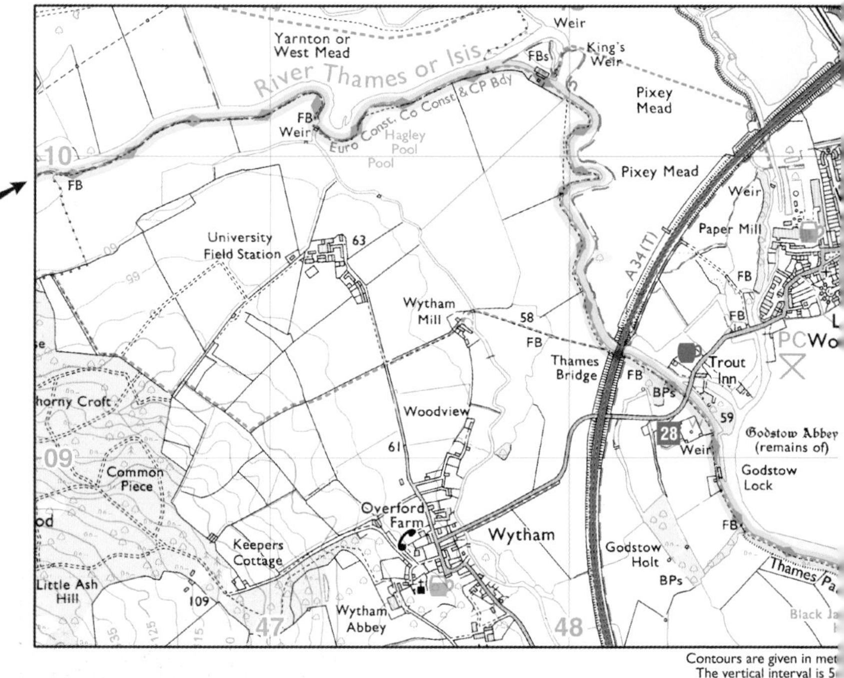

comes King's Lock; once beyond this, continue onwards by the river, and go under the Oxford bypass bridge. You pass an iron boundary marker of 1886 with the ox of Oxford on top, and then arrive at Godstow.

To the left, you can see the old channel flowing under the ancient two-arch bridge, which has, like Radcot Bridge, been preserved by diverting the navigation to a new channel. Your path goes up to the road and straight across into the meadow, where you pass by all that remains of Godstow Abbey **28** – just a walled enclosure with, in one corner, the shell of a 16th-century chapel. Romantic associations here are with Rosamund de Clifford, mistress of Henry II. The abbey was founded in 1139, and became a kind of finishing school for daughters of the nobility. Rosamund was a favoured pupil, and after a mysterious death was brought back for burial here. Ironically, the best-surviving fragment of her abbey is the lovely old Trout Inn over the bridge, first built in 1138 as its hospice.

The track past the abbey leads to Godstow Lock, then continues with the vast, open grazing of Port Meadow across the river – unchanged since William the Conqueror presented it to the burgesses of Oxford as free common. As the river curves, the famous skyline of Oxford opens up across the meadow. On your bank, a footpath soon leads off to the thatched Perch pub at Binsey, but the little line of cottages stays hidden until you near the end of their open green. Look back for a moment here, to Binsey, tucked beneath the backdrop of Wytham Woods. Then carry on past Bossom's Boatyard to cross Medley footbridge **E** and proceed along the other bank.

Soon, another footbridge to your left crosses into Port Meadow, but your path continues over the bridge ahead, which follows a causeway bank now, the Thames to the right, the tall grasses of a wetlands strip to the left – a surprisingly lush and rural entry into Oxford. Finally, cross by footbridge over a feeder waterway signposted to the Oxford Canal, and walk by the backs of cottage gardens up to the road at Osney Bridge **29**. *Oxford station is just along the road to your left now.*

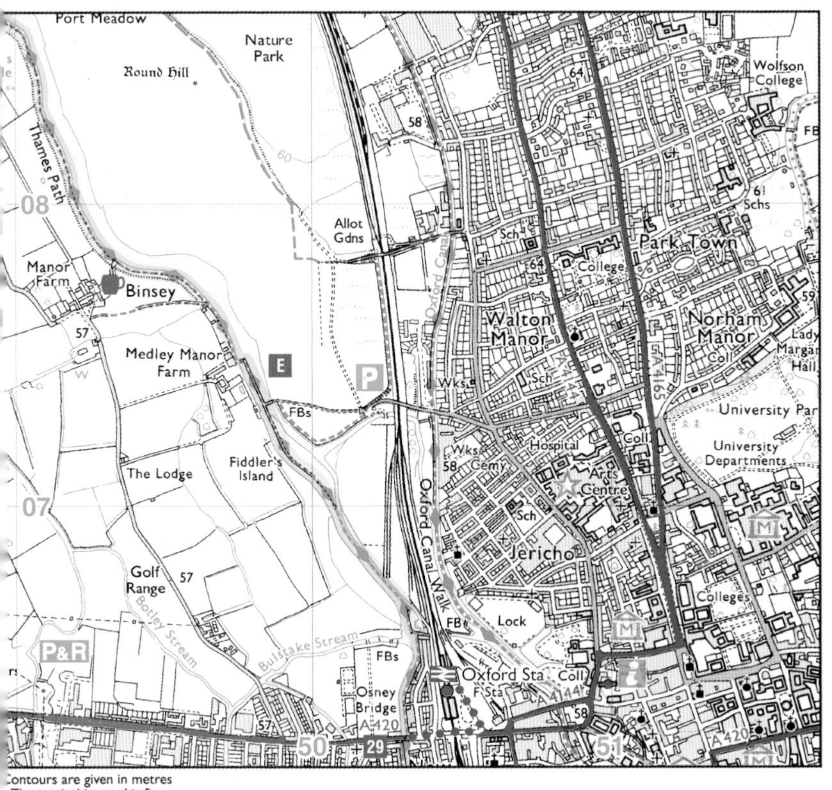

Contours are given in metres
The vertical interval is 5m

5 Oxford to Culham

12 miles (19.3 km)

Transport Options

From Osney Bridge, a 6-mile (9.7-km) walk brings you to Lower Radley, where there is a nearby rail connection; another 3¾ miles (6 km) further on, Abingdon has a frequent bus service from the High Street back to Oxford, St Aldate's, or to Didcot railway station Mondays to Saturdays. Culham has a railway station, but services are infrequent and it is some way from the river.

You will see little of dreaming spires from the Thames Path as it skirts around Oxford's edge. Indeed, unless you succumb to the urge to break off and explore, your encounter with the city will be pleasantly green and surprisingly brief. From Osney Bridge **29**, you set off on the south bank via a girder bridge over a tributary stream, then along the grass in front of a charming terrace of riverside cottages.

Beyond The Waterman's Arms, the path leaves the road to cross the weir streams of Osney Lock, then passes the lock itself, with the gaunt shell of a mill looming beyond. This reminds us that, by repute, the earlier main channel of the Thames ran under Hythe Bridge nearer the city centre until the monks of now-vanished Osney Abbey directed it this way to work their mill.

Beyond the lock, the path is mercifully screened from nearby industry by foliage. On the far side of the railway bridge, the path continues along the riverside, but here you may be tempted to sample the unexpected views from Grandpont Nature Reserve on your right. It was created on the site of Oxford Gasworks. By the river you pass a handsome new college residence, then, beyond Jubilee Terrace, your path curves with the Thames and climbs up to the road on Folly Bridge **30**. Grandpont was the earlier name, but the better-known label comes from a building that once stood over the north end of the earlier bridge. Known as Friar Bacon's Study, it was named after the 13th-century friar, Roger Bacon, who used it as an observatory. The Victorian house by today's bridge, with its castellated skyline and assortment of statues in niches, keeps the 'folly' theme intact.

To explore Oxford, it is best to turn left across Folly Bridge and walk up St Aldate's. Otherwise, cross the road via the pedestrian lights and drop down to the Thames again. Once across, you have the traditional home of Salter Bros. steamers on your left,

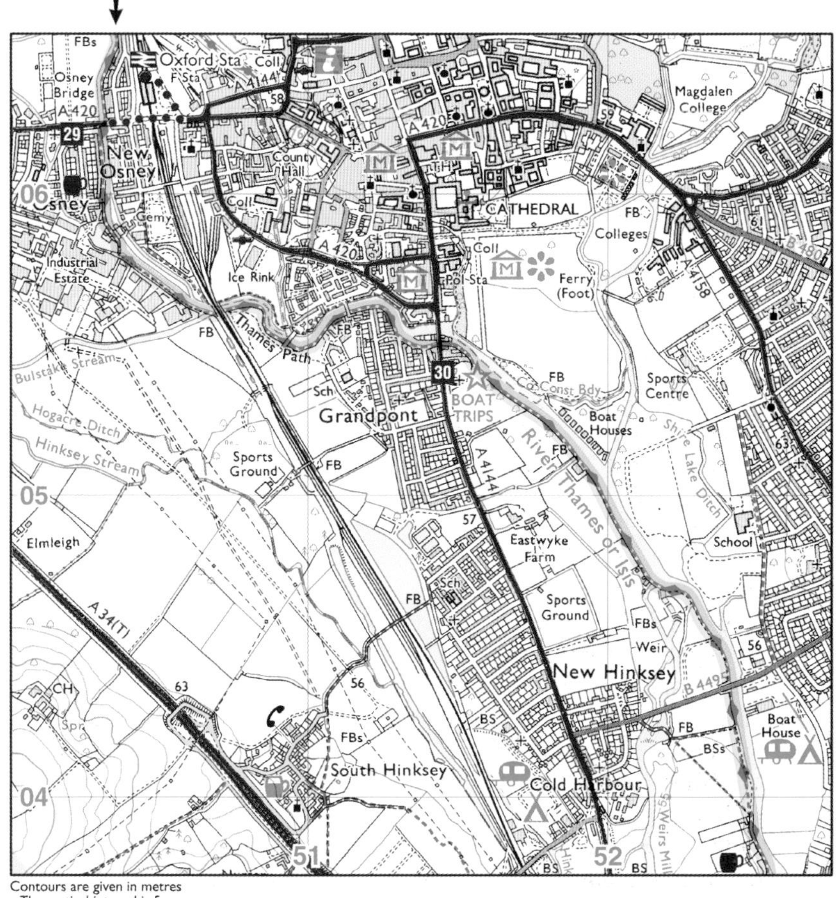

Contours are given in metres
The vertical interval is 5m

then the tree-lined banks of Christ Church Meadow across the river. This is a rowing reach, and once the bank would have been lined with ornate college barges serving the double duty of club-houses and grandstands. Alas, they have gone, either rotted away or converted to humbler uses. But through the trees, you can glimpse a little of the Oxford skyline: a part of Merton College, the dome of the Radcliffe Camera – even a spire or two.

Now you are walking through open fields with Oxford left behind; indeed, beyond the next road bridge you come to Iffley Meadows, 82 acres (33 hectares) of ancient watermeadow, where regular winter flooding enriches the clay soil with silt. The drooping purple heads of the rare snake's-head fritillary can be seen here in late April. Surrounded by meadow land, The Isis

Iffley Lock, with its odd, bridged-over weir crossing, is the site of one of the first pound locks on the Thames, built here in the 1630s.

Tavern here depends largely on river trade – the bars are full of oars, skiffs and photos of stiffly posed rowing crews. Then comes Iffley Lock, and over the trees, on the far bank, can be seen the sturdy tower of the superb Norman church of Iffley **31**. St Mary's is 12th century, richly decorated in Romanesque style with fantastic beasts and zig-zag stonework inside and out. You can reach it by the path over the rustic footbridge, then by the lock and weirs, and finally by climbing the little lane up from the river and turning right. On the way, you may notice a plaque on the site of the first pound lock on the Thames, and then a millstone – all that remains of Iffley Mill.

Beyond Iffley, a substantial footbridge takes you over the Hinksey Stream, then open meadows owned by Oxford Preservation Society lead on to Sandford. A steel footbridge crosses the weir stream, almost as broad as the Thames itself, and soon you hear turbulent water to your right. The lock up ahead has the greatest fall of water on the Thames, and the water thunders over the impressive weir known as the Sandford Lasher. Impressive and sometimes lethal, for the Lasher has claimed several lives; a memorial column stands on the weir as a reminder.

The Victorian mill that once stood by the lock has been replaced by housing, but The Kings Arms and its colourful little group of cottages across the lock are still attractive **32**. Thirsty walkers will be relieved to know that they can reach it by crossing the lower lock gates and the former millstream. There was a ferry here as early as the 13th century, and, just beyond the lock, a stone mounting block is preserved from it. Continue past the lock over a bridge and turn left along a narrow strip of car park where you will find the towpath continuing at the end **A**.

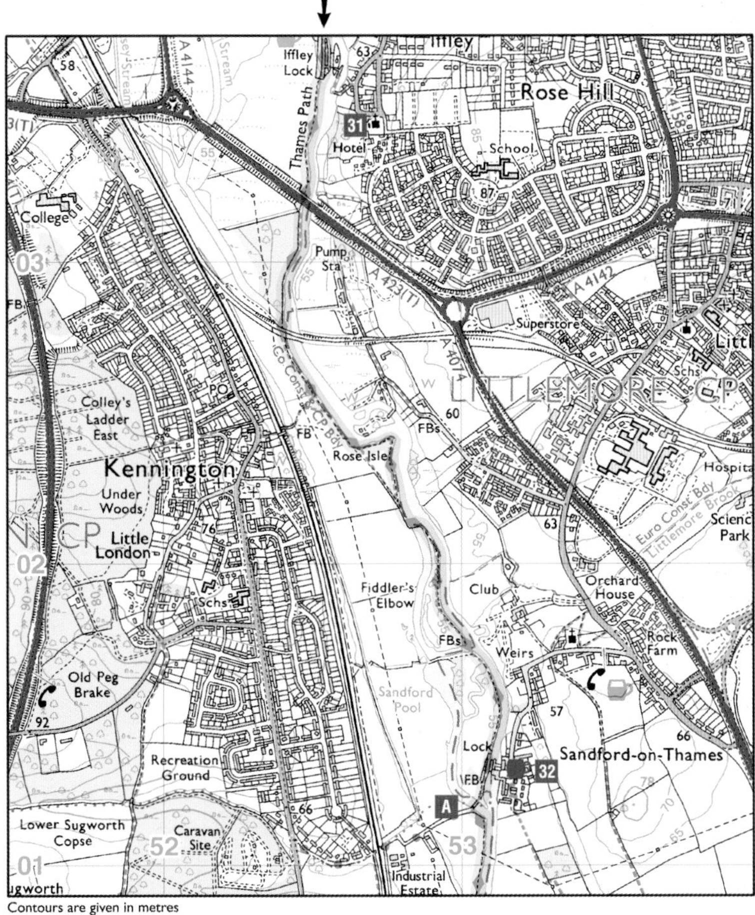

Contours are given in metres
The vertical interval is 5m

A lush, wild stretch follows, with low hills rising across the river, and good farmland on your side. Eventually you come to the boathouses of Radley College, a public school with a strong rowing tradition **33**. Cross the slipway to the boathouse by footbridge, and keep on by the Thames. *For Radley station, take the tree-lined lane on the right just beyond the college buildings, and turn right at a T-junction.*

Beyond the boathouses, the mansion on the rise across the river is Nuneham House **34**. The original house of 1756 has been altered and added to several times, but the landscaping potential of the site seems to have been the big attraction; Lord Harcourt even had a village *moved* to give the famous Capability Brown full scope to beautify it. Little of the landscaping survived World War II, but as you walk past you will see, prominent on its hill, the Jacobean Carfax Conduit, once a feature of Oxford's water supply, now serving simply as a garden ornament.

Your path keeps by the Thames, crossing the well-kept lawns of a riverside house. Then, beyond the railway bridge comes a wild area of high grasses and scrubland left over from gravel workings, with paths heading off in several directions. Resist

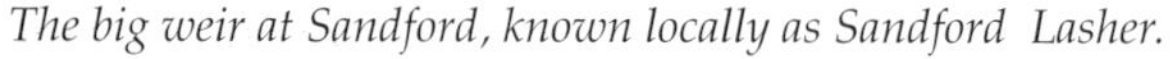

The big weir at Sandford, known locally as Sandford Lasher.

temptation, and follow the river past recently planted community woodland. As you pass the second of two picnic sites you will see a weir across the Thames – one of the overgrown entries into the Swift Ditch **35** (named Back Water on the map), a morsel of Thames history that you will meet again soon.

Beyond the woodland planting, your path skirts around a verdant inlet **B**, a wildlife haven with several viewing points for enjoying a watery scene of reeds and bulrushes. Back with the Thames again, cross a footbridge and take the path with just a ditch between you and the riverbank. At a crossing path **C**, turn left and go over another lush channel, the Abbey Stream, then turn left by its bank on the path to Abingdon Weir. Cross the weir, take the fenced path and cross the lower lock gates, then go right through a gate onto the towpath again; ahead are Abingdon and the spire of St Helen's **36** – a classic Thames view.

As you walk through the arch of Abingdon Bridge, take a look back: you will see that it is far longer than you imagined – truly a causeway with many arches. The original, built by the Fraternity of the Holy Cross in 1422, had 14 arches, and although largely rebuilt last century, the bridge has kept its medieval feel. To explore Abingdon, go up the steps on either side of the bridge, and walk up Bridge Street to the market place. Here, at the heart of Abingdon, stands the magnificent county hall with all the major features around you, St Nicholas and the Abbey Gateway to one side, St Helen's Street leading to St Helen's Church on the other.

Your walk continues through riverside gardens, with a fine view of St Helen's spire and some of the surrounding almshouses – the earliest dating from 1446. Across open meadows now, you cross a footbridge **D** over the same Swift Ditch that left the Thames a long mile back. This ancient channel was once probably the main navigation, until Abingdon Lock opened on a channel dug by the monks of Abingdon Abbey centuries ago. So, from the footbridge, look left for an unchanged vision of medieval times: Old Culham Bridge, which was built when Abingdon Bridge was built, but now, unused and unrestored, peacefully sleeps more centuries away.

Now the Thames-side path skirts the vast, open field that virtually surrounds the hamlet of Culham. At a sharp bend in your path, the old Thames channel can be seen leaving to meander via Sutton Courtenay, leaving you to follow the lock cut. Approaching Culham, the first thing you see is the gabled dove-

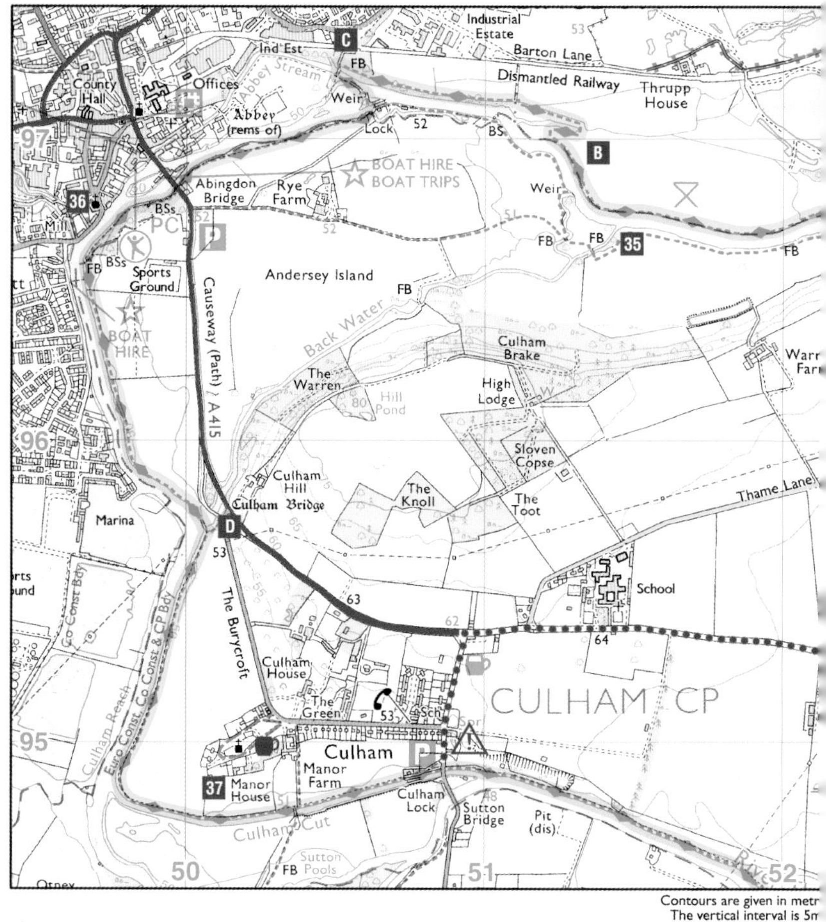

cote, which is big enough for 4,000 nesting places. Then comes Culham Manor House **37**, partly rebuilt in the 17th century on the base of what was originally a 15th-century grange of Abingdon Abbey. The whole ensemble of manor house, church, pub and cottages around a little green makes a perfect entity, charming to behold across the fields.

A footbridge over the cut carries a path that leads over the weirs of Sutton Pools to Sutton Courtenay village with its long, attractive green. Another path on the left leads to Culham, but the Thames Path keeps resolutely on along the cut, past Culham Lock and up to the road. *From this point, Culham station is reached by walking left up the road, then right along the A415 for over a mile.*

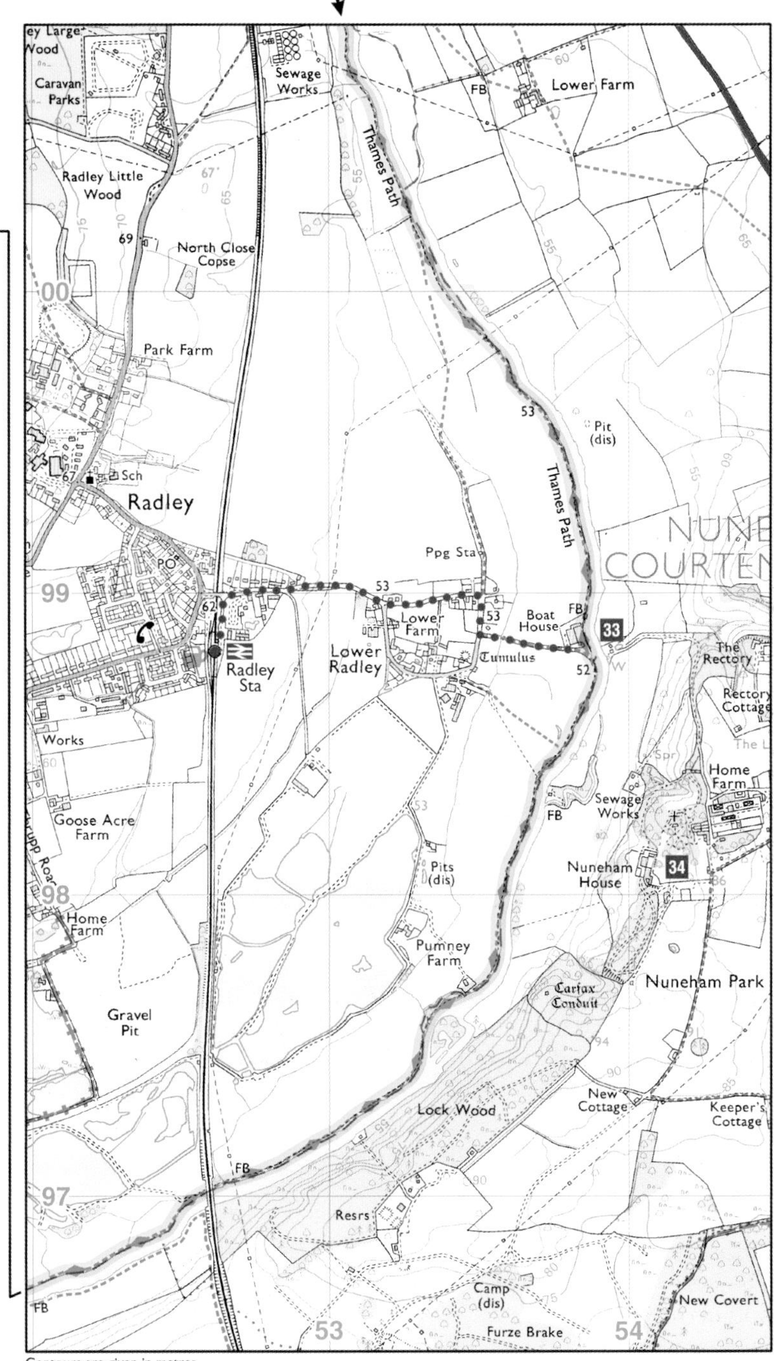

Contours are given in metres
The vertical interval is 5m

6 Culham to Cholsey

14½ miles (25 km)

Transport Options

From Culham Lock, a 5¾-mile (9.3-km) walk brings you to Day's Lock near Dorchester; then it is a further 5½ miles (8.8 km) to Wallingford. Dorchester has bus connections to Wallingford, then on to Cholsey or Goring.

From Culham Lock access track **A**, your path forks right by the waterside to cross the road alongside the narrow lock cut bridge and over the stile directly opposite. This is another bridge with one-way light control, so watch out for the traffic flow. You will now be looking along an unusually straight, tree-hung reach, and very soon, back over your shoulder you can see the old loop of the Thames rejoining the cut, under the three-arched Sutton Bridge. Until the early 1800s, when both bridges and the lock cut were built, the barges had to follow this loop up to Sutton Courtenay village, then literally under a very obstructive Sutton Mill. Everyone must have seen the new cut as a big improvement except the miller, who thus lost his tolls.

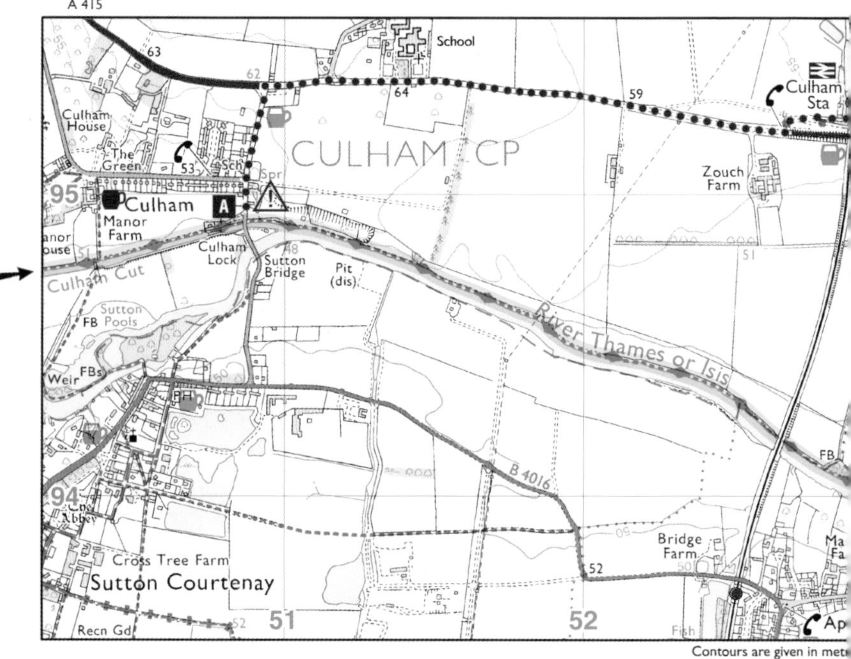

Follow the riverside path until it becomes a rough, narrow way by the edge of fields, with the towers of Didcot Power Station looming distantly over the river. Beyond a railway bridge, barns, cottages and the unusual, fat spire of Appleford Church **38** are just a field away over the Thames. Then, a pattern is repeated as a weir on the right takes an old loop up to Long Wittenham, and again you are following a lock cut.

Past Clifton Lock, the whole scene is transformed and opens out as though some artistic hand had composed the landscape. A red-brick, Gothic bridge spans the river, a little church spire rising beyond it, while rustic cottages peep through a tasteful arrangement of trees. This is Clifton Hampden, and if a name had to be given to that artistic hand, it would be that of Sir George Gilbert Scott. He designed the bridge that replaced the ferry in 1864, and restored the little church on its viewpoint bluff **39**, which can be reached by a long flight of steps.

Walk on towards the bridge where your path goes left up to the road; but note that another path goes under the bridge and across the meadow beyond – should you want to visit the church. To the left now are the renowned cottages of Clifton

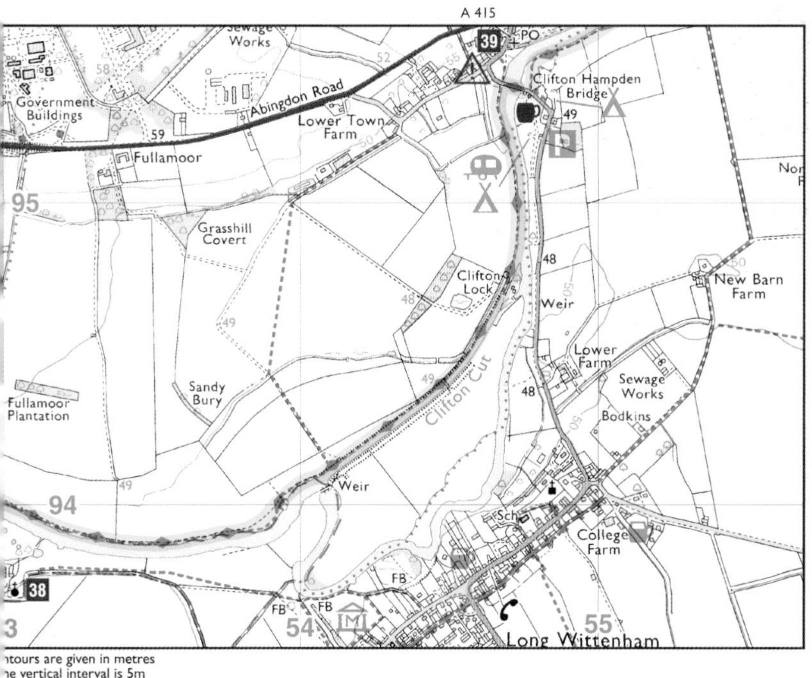

ntours are given in metres
he vertical interval is 5m

Hampden with their steeply pitched, thatched roofs, while across the bridge, just around a bend, is The Barley Mow, the best-known of all Thames pubs, its low thatch and ancient 'cruck construction' timber frame facing you as you approach. As Jerome K. Jerome pointed out in *Three Men in a Boat*, the doors are low, too. 'Duck or grouse', as the sign says over the entrance.

Your route now crosses the bridge, where, once more, you need to watch the one-way traffic flow; then, on the other side, a path on the left goes down rough steps to the riverbank again. Now, a vast curve of the Thames swings round to Little Wittenham, and you can measure it by noting the lie of the Sinodun Hills way over to the right with the Thames flowing at their feet. Pass the elegant lawns and villas of Burcot, then, as you come nearer to the hills, the tower of the abbey church of Dorchester is seen rising above the trees to your left.

Under the tumbling branches of elderly willows, your path comes up to Day's Lock, first crossing the weir **B**, then the upper lock gates to the Dorchester bank. From the weir bridge, you can see past the lock to Wittenham Clumps **40**, with Little Wittenham Bridge tucked beneath, giving scale to the delectable scene.

Walking along the grass by the lockside to the footbridge now, you have almost too many options as regards taking a detour. Over the bridge and up the lane past Little Wittenham Church, a clear path up Church Meadow takes you to the summit beech-clump of the nearer hill, Round Hill, which offers superb views all around. This whole area is a 250-acre (101-hectare) nature reserve owned by the Northmoor Trust, and you are welcome to explore. Alternatively, a path from the footbridge leads, in a left diagonal, back across the meadow towards Dorchester, taking you first through a bridleway gate and then by an enclosed path running alongside the impressive ramparts of the Dyke Hills.

From this spot, you really can see the three ages of Dorchester: across the Thames, the second of the Sinodun Hills, Castle Hill, is ringed by the massive banks of an early Iron Age hill fort, the first settlement; by your side, the Dyke Hills were the landward defences of a pre-Roman town, protected on the other three sides by the Thames and the Thame; and, across the fields, today's Dorchester, built over a Romano-British town which grew by the Roman road from Silchester.

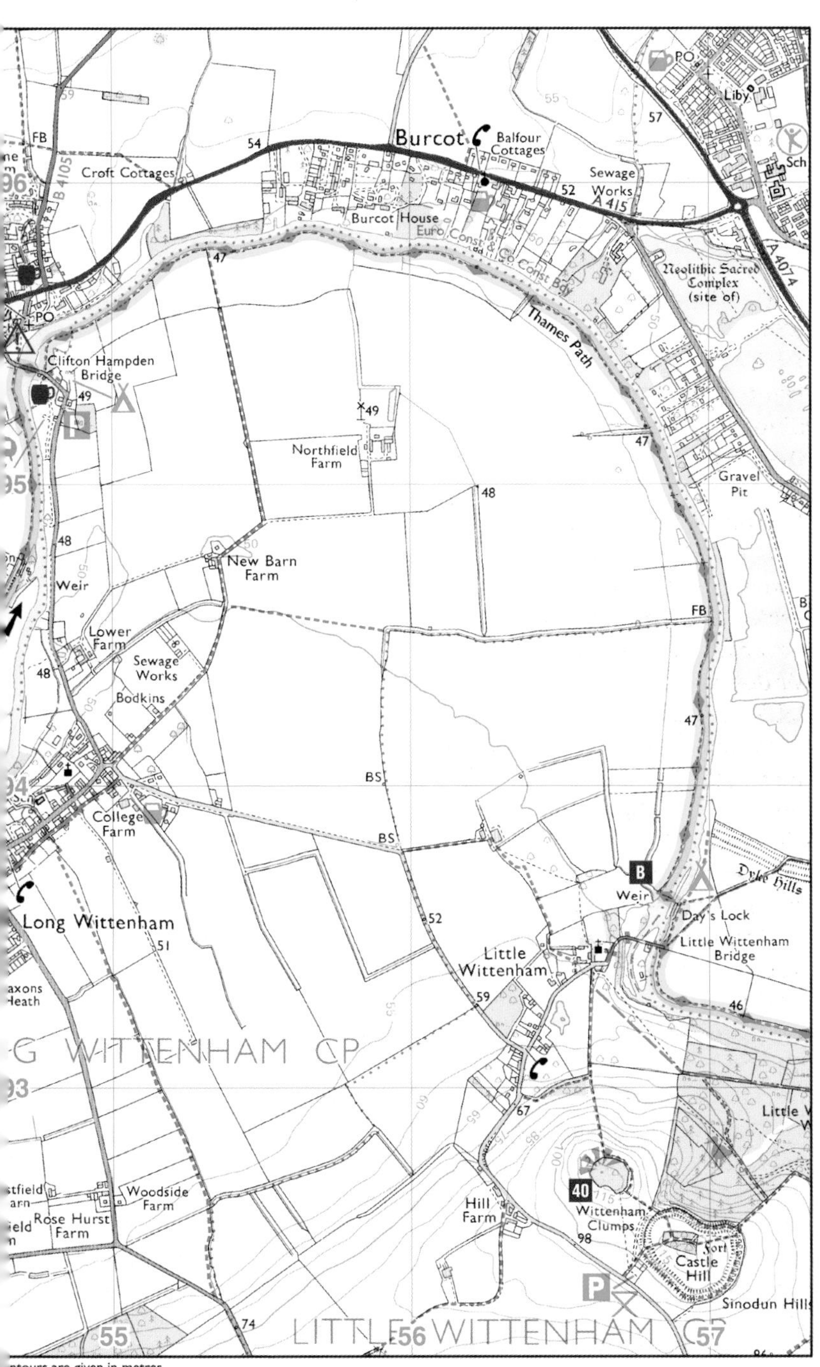

Contours are given in metres
The vertical interval is 5m

Early Christianity thrived here, too. The great abbey church of St Peter and St Paul **41** was built around 1140 on or near the site of a Saxon cathedral dedicated to St Birinus. The portions you see today survive because, in 1536, when the abbey was dissolved, a 'great riche man' of Dorchester, one Richard Beauforest, bought it and gave it to the people of the parish. Any pilgrims along the Thames must surely pause here, especially for the glory of the 14th-century glass and the unique Tree of Jesse window, where tracery, sculpture and stained glass combine in a masterwork by an unknown hand. The nearby guesthouse, the only remaining fragment of monastic building, houses a museum providing insights into the area's prehistory, right back to the crop-marks of 2500 BC. The High Street offers even more to see, including two fine coaching inns.

But these are diversions. The Thames Path continues under Little Wittenham Bridge and on by the riverside beneath Wittenham Wood, before crossing the meandering River Thame and leading on towards Shillingford. Before the village, the tow-path comes to the site of Keen Edge Ferry, and as you can no longer cross, a diversion away from the river is necessary. Just beyond a brick pillbox, a fingerpost **C** points you, left, to the nearby main road. Cross very carefully to the footway on the far side and turn right. At the crossroads, with The Kingfisher pub on one corner, turn right into Wharf Road, the charming village street of Shillingford. Immediately on the right is Wisteria

A tiny church and pretty thatched cottages hide in the trees at Clifton Hampden.

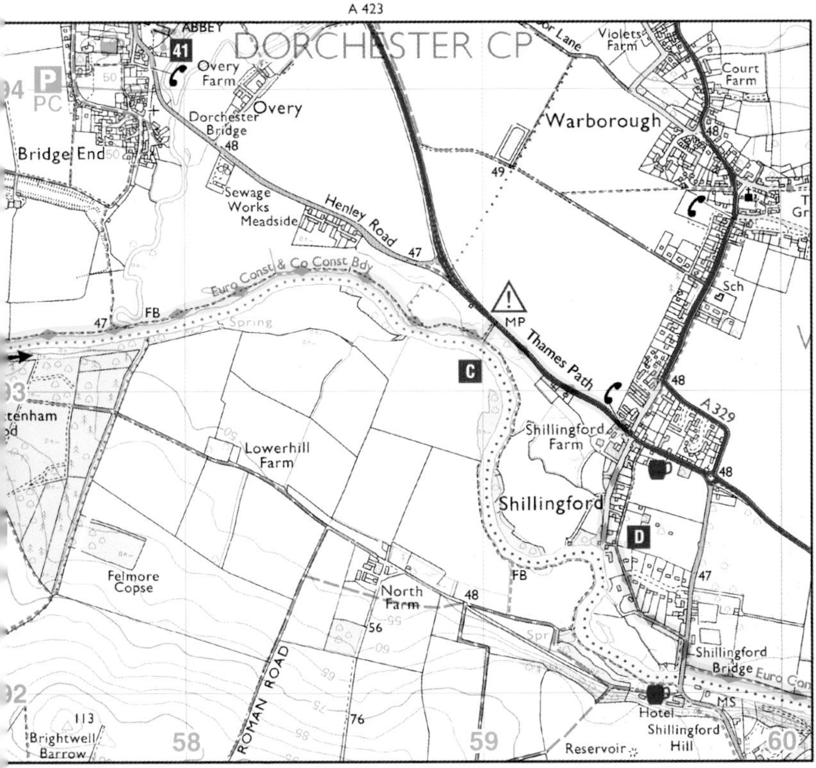

ntours are given in metres
he vertical interval is 5m

Cottage, well named because its wisteria is some 50 yards long, stretching way beyond the cottage to take over a nearby barn as well. Where the road ends at the Thames is a memorable spot with, on one side, a thatched boathouse, and, on the other, the stone and brick of Shillingford Court. There are even benches where you can sit and watch the river flow by.

Just before the corner of Shillingford Court, your way goes left on a narrow path between walls **D**. On the corner itself, there are plates recording the historic flood levels here, the highest, in 1809, being above head-level. Joining another path at a T-junction, turn right, still keeping the Court wall to your right, pass the entry gates, carry straight on through a kissing-gate and turn left up a drive to a busy road. Turn right in the road, but soon, just as you reach Shillingford Bridge, cross to drop down to a path leading to the river, then turn left on the towpath again.

Pause for a moment to look back at the elegant, three-arched bridge in its park-like setting. Carrying on, you will soon come into open fields with the distant line of the Chilterns escarpment way ahead. Around one more bend, you will see the moored craft of Benson cruiser station. Walk on over a small side stream and through a gate into the marina and caravan area, all the time keeping near the riverside. Eventually you join a drive to skirt round a slipway. As you pass their sheds and cross grass, look out for a useful cafeteria on the left. Another gate leads into a tiny public garden, where you turn immediately up to the road; Benson and its church are just across the junction.

Take the little lane that forks right here, and follow it towards Preston Crowmarsh. After some 300 yards, you will see a 'footpath to the river' sign on your right; ignore it. Another 150 yards further on, with the sound of thundering water to guide you, turn right through a gate **E** leading directly to a footbridge over a millstream, and then to the crossing of the spectacular Benson Weir. Over the weir, a perfectly clear path continues ahead over the lower lock gates. On reaching the far bank, go left for 30 yards and cross the ditch by a wooden footbridge, then turn left and follow the river along a broad path, fenced off from the adjacent meadows.

In the past there was serious erosion along this bank, and the path you follow today had to be created on a new line, further back into the field. Ahead, a distinctive church spire seems to be imitating the line of poplars that frames it. This is St Peter's **42**, which was given its open-work spire in the 18th century by Sir Robert Taylor. On sighting this, you know that you are approaching Wallingford.

Soon, to your right, fragments of stonework on a grassy bank appear, all that remains of Wallingford Castle. It declared for the king in the Civil War, and was finally taken and demolished on the orders of Oliver Cromwell. Just short of the bridge, the towpath turns up right between walls, then left to the foot of the High Street, with The Town Arms on the corner.

It seems that even prehistoric man forded the Thames here at Wallingford, the lowest point where it was possible to cross at any season. The first bridge at Wallingford we are sure about was completed in 1141, and Henry II granted the first charter in 1155 to a town already important enough to house a royal mint and boast of at least ten churches. A short walk up the High Street brings you to the town museum in Flint House, a medieval hall-

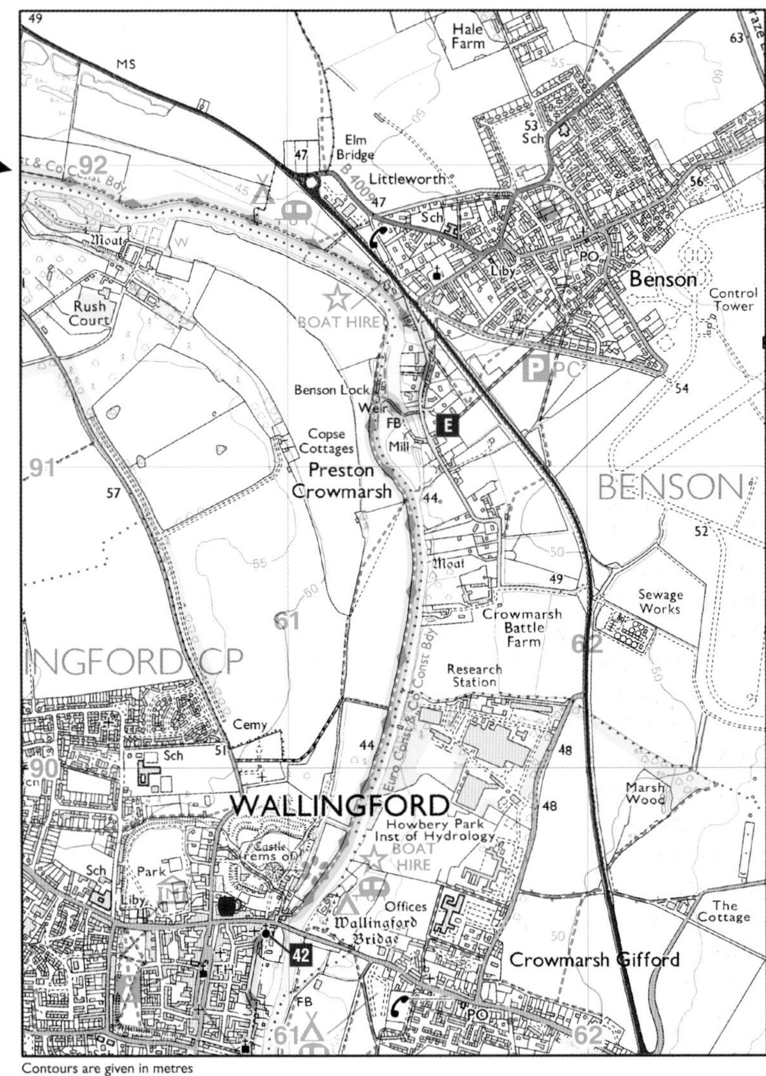

Contours are given in metres
The vertical interval is 5m

house, and opposite, on the open space called Kinecroft, you can still see the 9th-century earthworks that surrounded the Saxon town. Just past the fine 16th-century George Hotel with its courtyard, St Mary's Street leads left out of the High Street to the Market Place and the Town Hall, which dates from 1670. It houses the Tourist Information Centre, and is very much the heart of Wallingford. *The buses stop here.*

Looking down to Day's Lock and Weir, from the viewpoint of Wittenham Clumps.

The Thames Path turns right up the High Street, but very soon turns left into Thames Street, following it to the end where stands St Leonard's, oldest of the Wallingford churches with much Norman work in its flint and zig-zag stone courses. Just before the church, your path leaves on the left to skirt the churchyard, crossing a tiny brook to go through a terrace of cottages into a lane. Bear left here, and, at once, you are back by the Thames again. Where the lane stops, your path continues, coming to the grass of a boatyard area. Keep by the waterside, go around the slipway and return to the grass. Then go through a gap in the fence and continue on a paved path just a few yards back from the river, out into the open fields.

Under the new bypass bridge, the towpath goes confidently on, across lawns, by meadows and through tree-belts – a tranquil stretch with the Chilterns now a continuous line beyond the river. A grove of trees and traces of a landing stage across the Thames announce the location of Littlestoke Ferry, one of those points where our towpath once crossed to the far bank. An ancient track, the Papist Way **F**, comes down to the Thames on our bank. The Thames Path continues through the nature reserve by the river here, *but for Cholsey station turn up the track, now called Ferry Lane. Keep straight ahead at the crossroads for a long half-mile, turning left at the next crossroads by The Walnut Tree pub.*

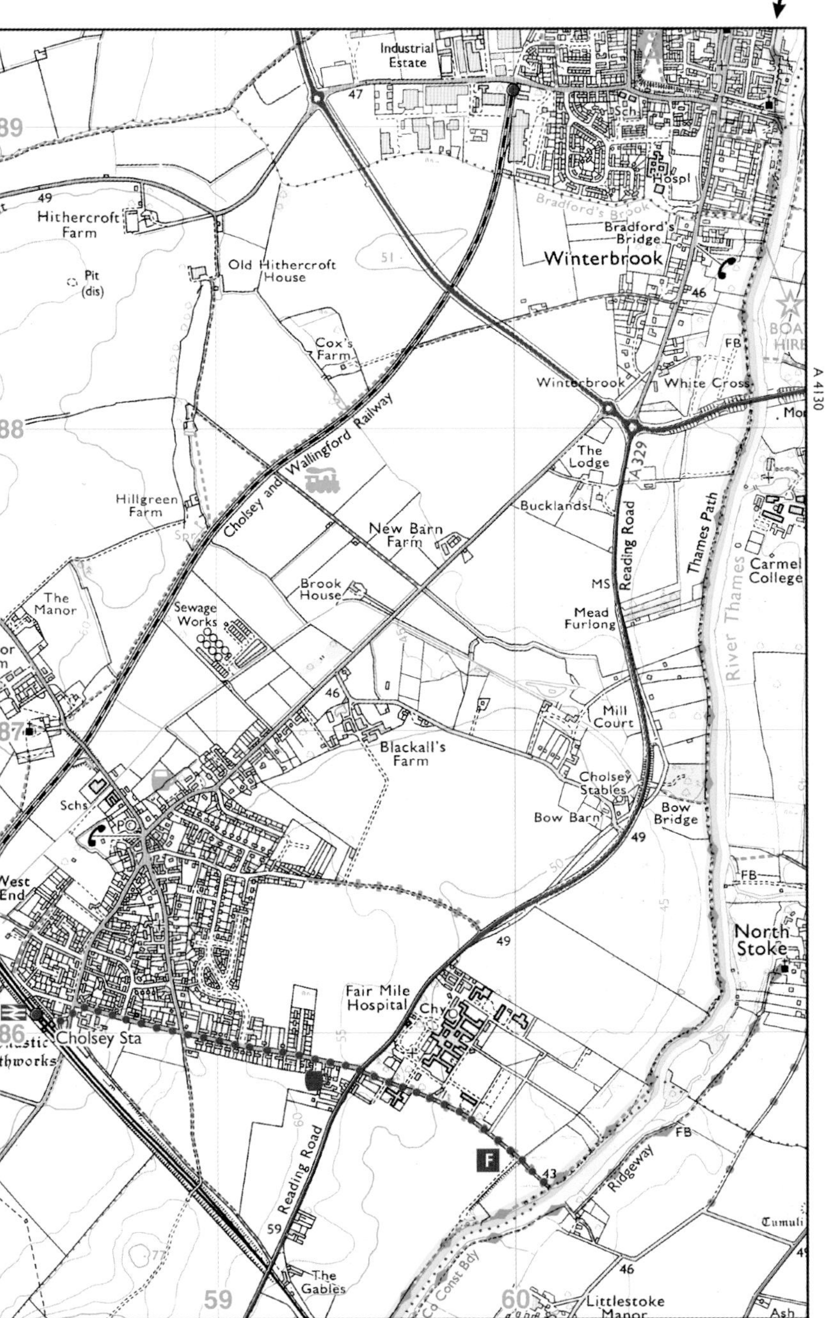

ontours are given in metres
The vertical interval is 5m

7 Cholsey to Tilehurst

11¾ miles (18.9 km)

Transport Options

Short walks are easy to plan along this section. There are handy rail connections at Goring & Streatley after 4 miles (6.4 km), and Pangbourne after another 4¼ miles (6.8 km), the same trains serving Tilehurst at the end.

Between the old Littlestoke ferry point and The Beetle and Wedge, that errant towpath escapes to the other bank, so a walk via Moulsford is necessary. From the ferry, the Thames Path keeps by the river, through the greenery of Cholsey Marsh Nature Reserve until a wooden causeway takes you under the railway viaduct. Truly there are two almost identical bridges here; the upstream one, Brunel's creation, is a superb example of skew brick construction. A farm track continues on, bearing right at a fork, up to join the A329 at Offlands Farm. Turn left here into Moulsford, a straggle of attractive cottages along the main road.

After the first terrace, you glimpse the little church of St John the Baptist (not as old as it looks) down its drive by the river **43**. When rebuilt in 1846, the wall facing you was the only fragment to be retained from what was possibly a 12th-century chapel. As the village ends, go left down Ferry Lane **A** to reach the river

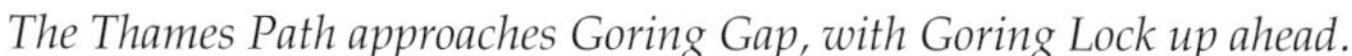

The Thames Path approaches Goring Gap, with Goring Lock up ahead.

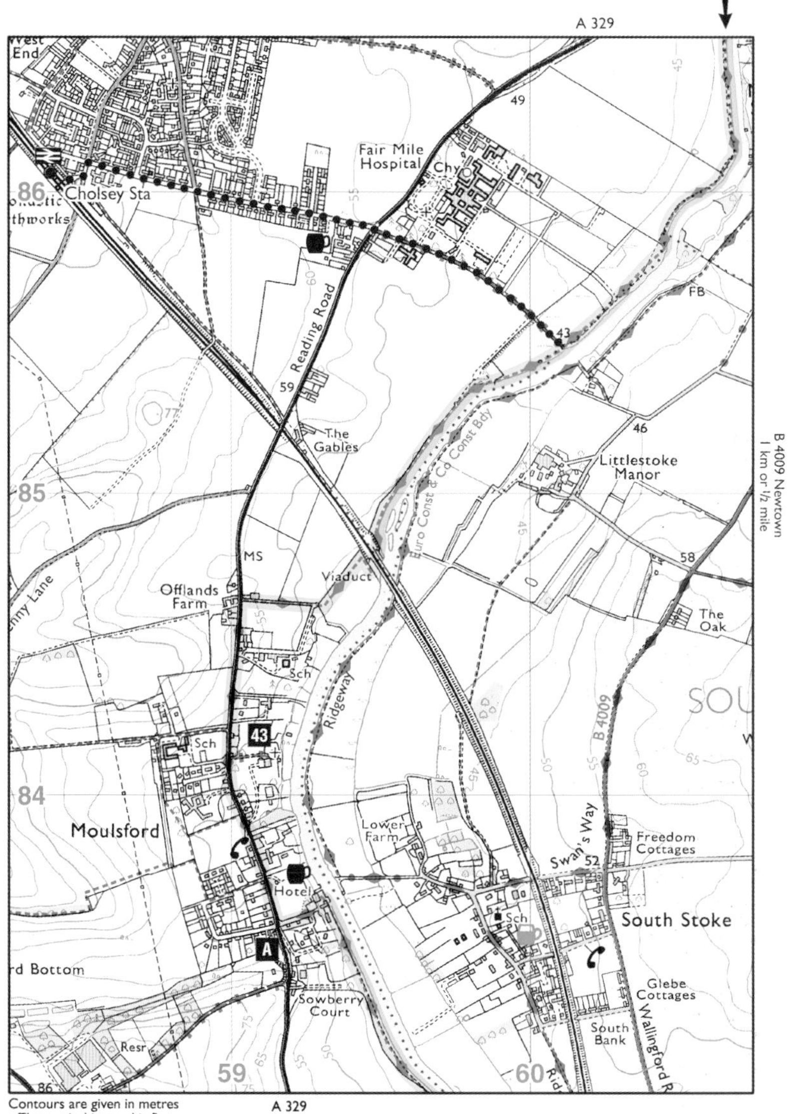

again, bearing left via The Beetle and Wedge, an inn with literary associations. The name derives from the mallet and wedge used in wood-splitting, the tools depicted on the inn's sign.

At the river, turn right, then continue by boat moorings and via a familiar brown gate onto the towpath again. Soon you are in open meadows, the tower of South Stoke Church across the river. Beyond Cleeve Lock, the walk is wooded for a

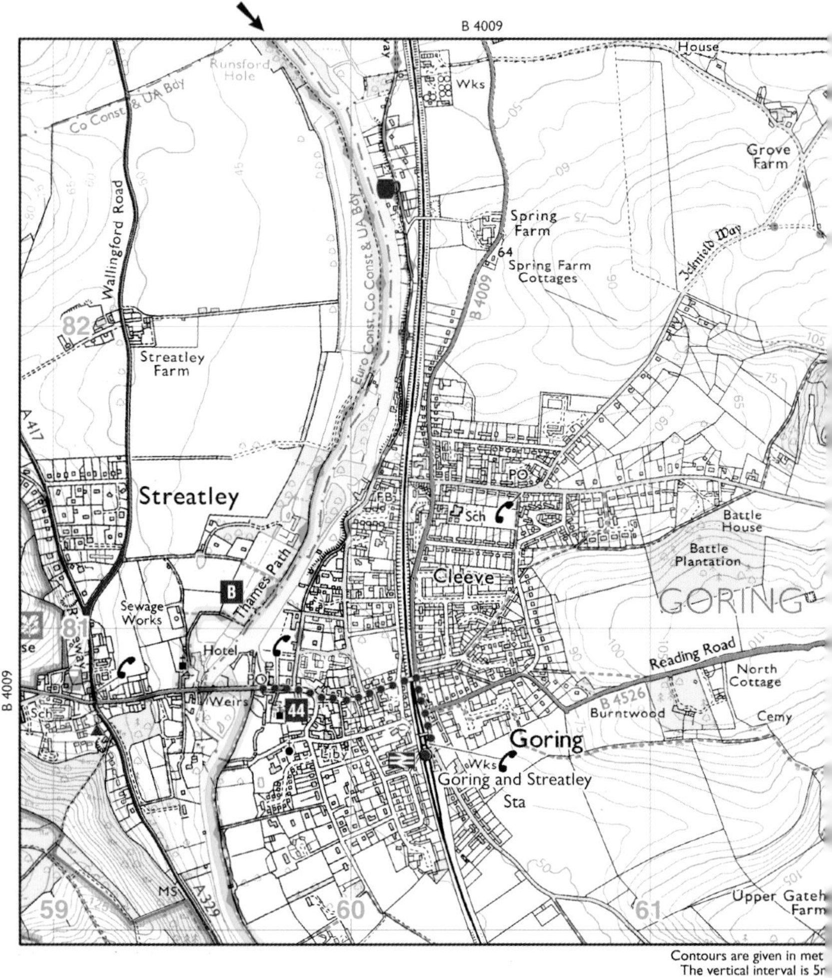

the walk is wooded for a while. Then it opens up to a vista of hills framing the white lock house of Goring Lock. In the last field before the lock, the path goes diagonally right **B** over concrete stepping stones leading to a wooden footbridge and a path beyond, which soon becomes a narrow tunnel between hedges. It joins a gravel track running past white cottages, twisting right and left around Streatley Church to reach the road. Turn left now, and over the Thames to Goring.

Two ancient tracks, the Ridgeway and the Icknield Way, once came down to the ford here, where the river flows broad and shallow; later a Roman causeway crossed here, then a ferry.

Today's long sequence of bridges and causeways, although mainly concrete, retains the character of an old trestle bridge on this significant line. Here you meet up briefly with another National Trail, the Ridgeway, which crosses the Thames before setting off along the Chilterns escarpment to Ivinghoe Beacon. *For Goring and Streatley station, keep ahead through Goring, over the railway line and turn right.*

Coming to the Goring bank, opposite the handy Riverside Tearooms, go down the steps on the right and return to the river, turning left onto the towpath again. A footbridge over the millstream gives the briefest view of Goring Church **44**, then tree-clad hills descend to the Thames, and you are into the Goring Gap, where, back in the Ice Age, the river cut itself a new channel through the chalk hills. To the right, the dramatic slopes of the downs are high above you, but in contrast the Chilterns, with their characteristic hedgerows and beech-clad summits, only come into view to your left as you walk on into open meadows. Under the railway bridge – one of Brunel's Great Western masterworks – a fenced length of towpath leads to Gatehampton Ferry Cottage, one more point where the old towpath crosses to the far bank beyond our reach. So, turn left over a footbridge **C** and, by a fence on the left, go up to a track and turn right. The track climbs slowly, clinging to a steep, roughly wooded bank, treating you, at one clear spot, to a surprise view of the Thames and the distant downs.

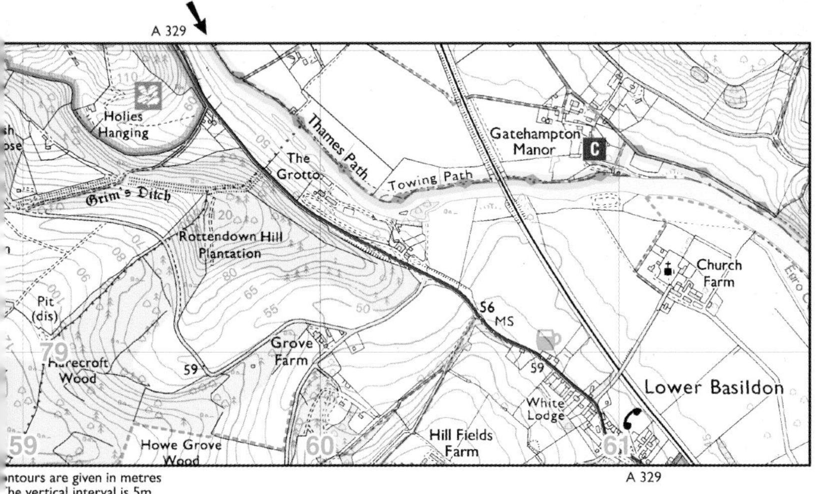

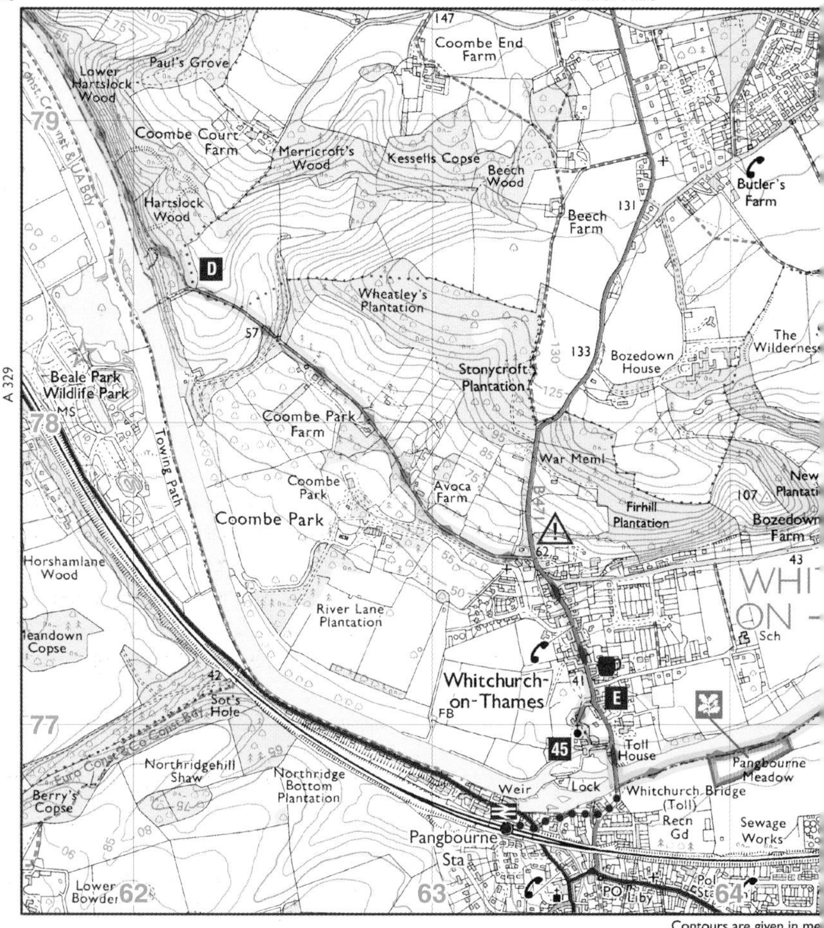

A chalk cliff requires the track to swing left and climb to the edge of the wood **D**. What follows is a pure Chiltern interlude, the hedged track dropping down steps into a typical dry bottom, then rising steeply up more steps on the other side to join the drive from Hartslock Farm. The broad drive ahead leads down to the road to Whitchurch. Turn right here and take care as you follow the road towards the Thames again.

The village street leads directly to the bridge, but the path turns right **E**, 75 yards beyond The Greyhound pub, onto the drive to the church. Take the little path to the left of the lych-gate, cross the churchyard grass, and follow the path between walls until it comes out at Whitchurch Mill **45**. Turn left here to walk past the pretty Church Cottages, turn right past the Toll House, then continue over Whitchurch Bridge. This is the second of two remaining toll bridges on the river, but there is no need to fumble for coins – pedestrians go free.

If you look back as you start across the bridge, you will see one of the picture-book Thames views – church, mill and cottages, ranged on the far side of the millpool. Coming to the Pangbourne side, walk on to the end of the white railings, then cross, go through a gap and turn left to cross a car park, and continue towards the National Trust-owned Pangbourne Meadow. *For Pangbourne station, keep on up the road from the bridge and take the path to the right, which crosses the Pang, and gives a close-up view of the weir. On reaching a road, the station is to the right on the opposite side.*

As you set forth from Pangbourne, the Thames takes a vast, majestic curve, which terminates at Mapledurham Lock. On the way, look out for a fleeting gap in the trees opposite, where the gabled Tudor mansion of Hardwick House **46** can be seen over its lawns. Mapledurham itself **47** is a delightfully time-passed-by little community gathered around the Elizabethan mansion of the Blount family, but it can only be glimpsed through trees on the far bank.

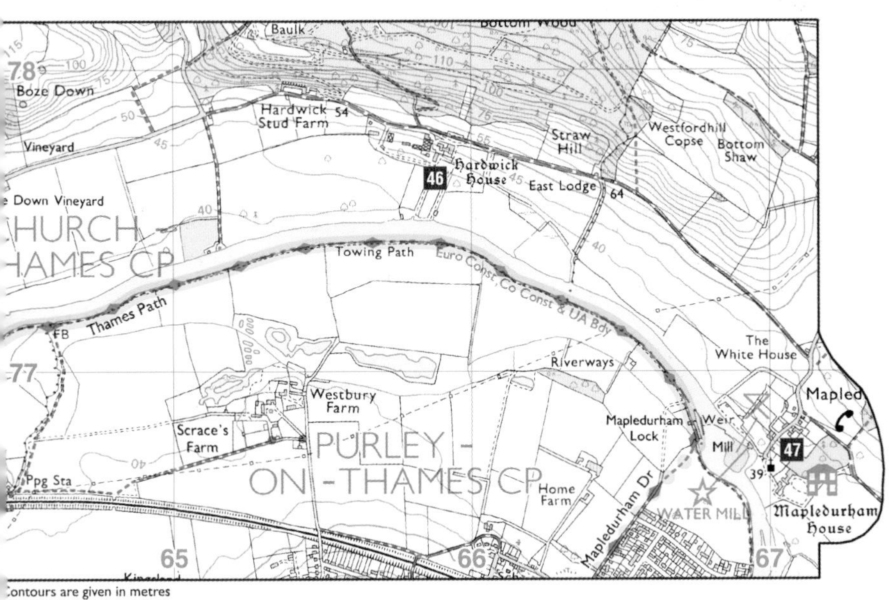

Contours are given in metres
The vertical interval is 5m

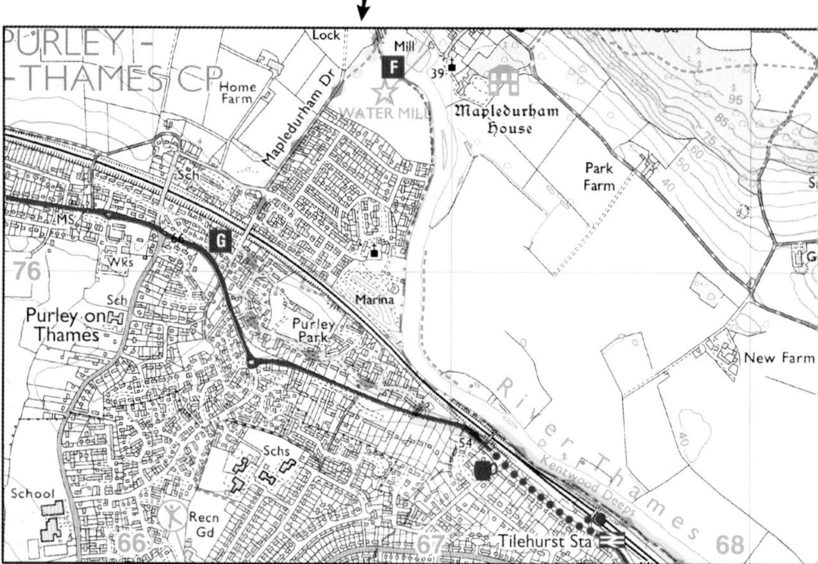

The tower of St Margaret's Church can be seen from some distance over the lock, then the corn mill, happily restored and working again, on its backwater. Beyond the lock, the great house can be sensed rather than fully seen through a veil of greenery. Mapledurham Lock is a delight, especially in summer, with its lovingly tended flowerbeds; there is also a gallery of Thames scenes painted by a local artist, and an adjoining tea hut which, happily, is often open. A sign on the lock island tells you that it is 78½ miles (126 km) to London, just in case you feel lost.

Through a gate beyond the lock **F**, turn right along the field edge, then via another gate continue along a track, with the houses of Purley to your left. Follow this track, Mapledurham Drive, to its end, then continue up New Hill, just to your left. Once over the railway bridge, turn left into Hazel Road **G** and follow it through the new housing of Purley Park, up and down and around bends, eventually turning right into Skerrit Way. Where this road ends, concrete steps on the right lead up to the A329 road. Turn left and follow the pavement to a large inn. A path to the left, just by the hotel entrance, leads over a railway bridge and steeply down to the towpath to continue the walk, *but for Tilehurst station simply carry on along the road.*

The locks, with their neat cottages and lovingly tended flowerbeds, add to the pleasure of walking the Thames in summer. Goring Lock, seen here, is typical.

8 Tilehurst to Shiplake

10 miles (16.1 km)

Transport Options

From Tilehurst, a 3½-mile (5.6-km) stroll brings you to Reading with all its transport connections. Sonning, 3¼ miles (5.2 km) further on, has buses Monday to Saturday into Reading or on to Henley, Marlow and High Wycombe. Shiplake, at the end of the walk, has train services on the Henley branch to Twyford.

Beside The Roebuck at Tilehurst, a path **A** leaves the A329 to cross railway lines and drop steeply to the Thames and its towpath below. Just to your left, the old towpath ends at the gate of Roebuck Ferry Cottage, a reminder that it has just spent a mere quarter mile on the far bank, a manoeuvre that involved two ferries and hours of delay to the barge traffic, thanks to the cussedness of an 18th-century Purley landowner. Turn right now. 'Welcome to Reading' proclaims the sign, but Reading will not intrude for a while yet. Indeed, you seem to be alone here with the Thames and the Chiltern Hills across the water, blissfully unaware of the main line high on the bank above you.

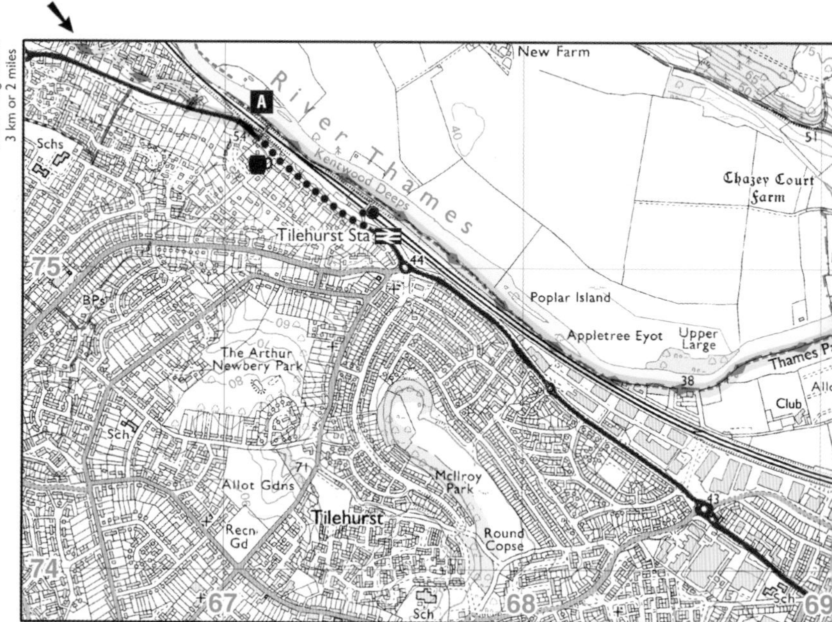

Crossing the forecourt of a marine services depot, you leave the railway and swing left with the river into open fields. Enjoy them while you can; Reading is around the corner, and soon the signs of civilization – benches, litter bins and tidy grass – tell you that you have joined the Thames Side Promenade. Now Caversham Bridge is in view, and across the river, lawns rise to Caversham church **48**, the tower you can just see amongst the trees. Keep along the surfaced path on the riverside past a big rowing clubhouse, and The Three Men in a Boat tavern, and go through a tunnel under the bridge.

Reading is an odd town, in that it stands on the Kennet rather than the Thames, and has never quite worked out a relationship with the river. Between the two bridges of Reading, industry has now given way to a pleasant mix of old and new housing, so your walk is enjoyable enough, taking you on to pass under Reading Bridge by a causeway built out into the water.

For Reading station, go under the bridge, turn right up the steps to the road and go ahead via pedestrian crossings to walk under the railway bridge. On the other side, paths lead up to a footway that crosses the main road alongside the railway lines and continues into the station foyer.

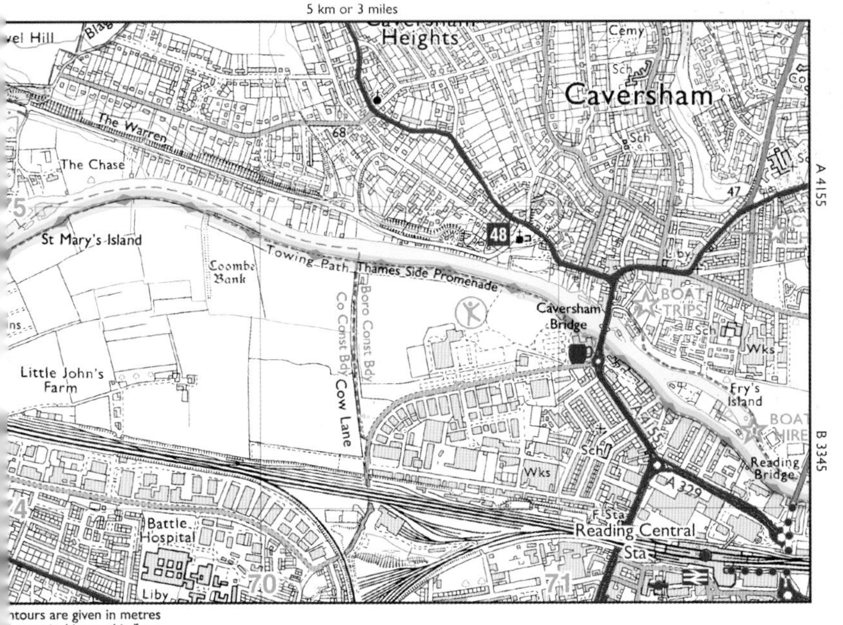

Beyond Reading Bridge, take the tarmac drive which leads past Caversham Lock and out into the expanse of King's Meadow. The sense of escape here is a little premature, as Reading still has a supermarket and a mighty gasholder to contribute to the Thames environment. But beneath the gasholder, you come to that significant spot where the Kennet enters the Thames, and your towpath crosses it via the gaunt old Horseshoe Bridge **49**, until recently a slatted horse bridge, but now redecked and more comfortable for our feet. For years, this spot, Kennet Mouth, lay under the threat of road schemes that would have swept the Horseshoe Bridge away and blighted the Thames hereabouts, but a famous victory in 1993 saved it. Two major walks meet here, and, via the well-restored towpath of the Kennet and Avon Canal, you could explore the 87 miles (140 km) via Bath to Bristol, and carry on to the Bristol Channel. The canal route was created in 1810, when two river navigations, Kennet and Avon, were linked. Though it fell out of use, a Trust has restored it magnificently, and today's towpath walk is, once more, by a working canal.

Beyond the Kennet, walk on by the riverside, trying to ignore the new office developments that come painfully near. Then, as the open meadow ends, you come to a wetlands nature reserve, with paths wandering off around its ponds, returning to the

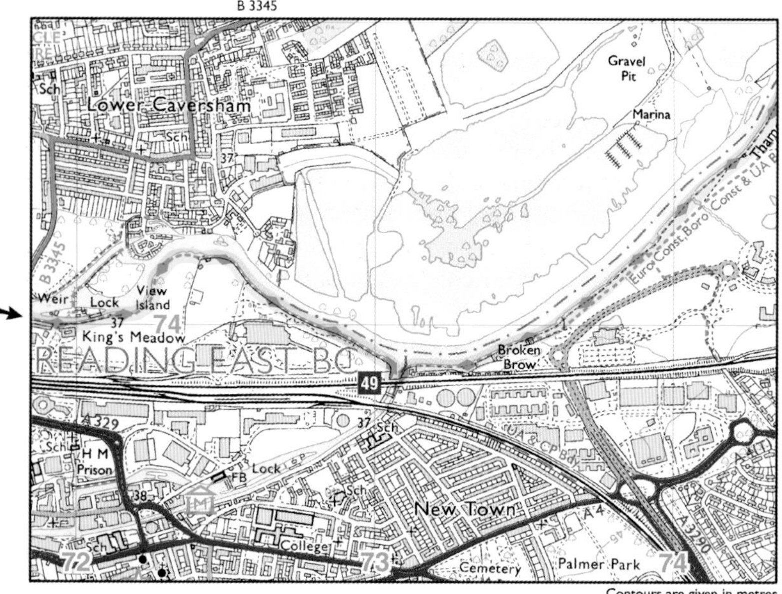

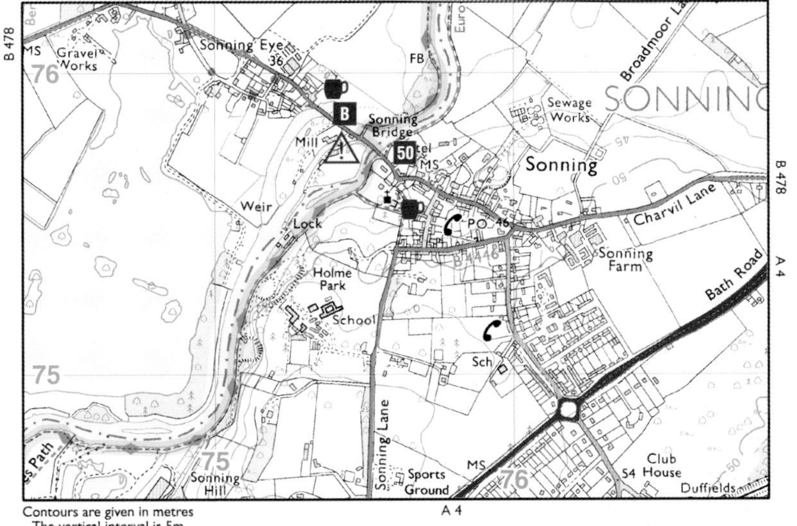

Contours are given in metres
The vertical interval is 5m

A 4

towpath a little further on. Once into the trees, you have the grounds of Reading Blue Coat School above you, and surprising glimpses of skimming sails and lagoons across the river where flooded gravel workings have been put to new use. Then, carry on past Sonning Lock, a pretty, tree-circled location with urns and flowerbeds to admire, and continue by the access road to Sonning Bridge.

Before the bridge, you might be tempted to follow the path to the right, which passes the church, taking you into Sonning village by the attractive Bull Inn. If you do walk through the churchyard, note the massive buttressed walls of mellow, Tudor brick – all that remains of the palace of the Bishops of Salisbury, which once stood here. Like many Thames villages, Sonning has grown around an ancient crossing point, a big well-preserved village with several fine hostelries, well worth exploring. But it is the old, red-brick bridge **50** in its lovely setting which draws the village together. A boundary plate on the centre arch confirms that it spans a county boundary, one half being in Oxon, the other in Berks. This may explain its quirky construction – eleven arches, all of different sizes, spanning the main Thames channel.

The Thames Path turns left across the narrow, humpback Sonning Bridge, and again watch out for the light-controlled traffic-flow here. On the north side, take the big concrete bridge on your right over a weir stream **B**. Some of this water once powered Sonning Mill, an 18th-century flour mill now converted to a theatre and restaurant, and worth a stroll up the road to view. Below Sonning, the towpath is just a simple country way for a while, with loops and verdant backwaters of the Thames creating a constantly changing scene – a fine stretch.

A distant line of high ground comes gradually to the river, and when they meet you will know you are at Shiplake. A gated footbridge takes you in front of a handsome boathouse to a little lawn where you will often encounter the boys of Shiplake College and their boats. Shiplake itself **51**, just a cluster of cottages around the church, is high above you, and can be reached by a path just beyond the footbridge, which goes left by the boathouses, then steeply up the chalky bluff to the top.

But the towpath continues over the grass and by the riverside; above, in the trees, are the college buildings (built as Shiplake Court in 1905). Now, you are approaching Shiplake Lock along a meadow sloping to the water's edge. A kissing-gate takes you into a metalled track leading up from the lock, where you turn left (the footbridge on the right leads only to the lockside). Coming into a lane, turn right for just 25 yards then left onto a temporary route along a field path **C**, continuing with a fence to your left. As the field ends, the path wriggles to the left through a gate, then crosses diagonally over the corner of another field before reaching a gate and steps up into a lane. Turn left here over a little bridge, then right in the road to walk on via Lashbrook to Lower Shiplake. While passing the cottages of Lashbrook, you

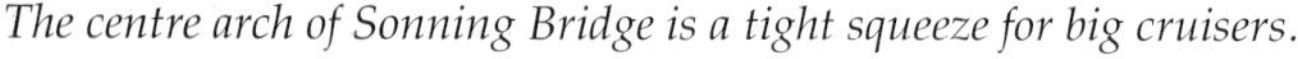

The centre arch of Sonning Bridge is a tight squeeze for big cruisers.

A4155 Henley-on-Thames
3 km or 2 miles

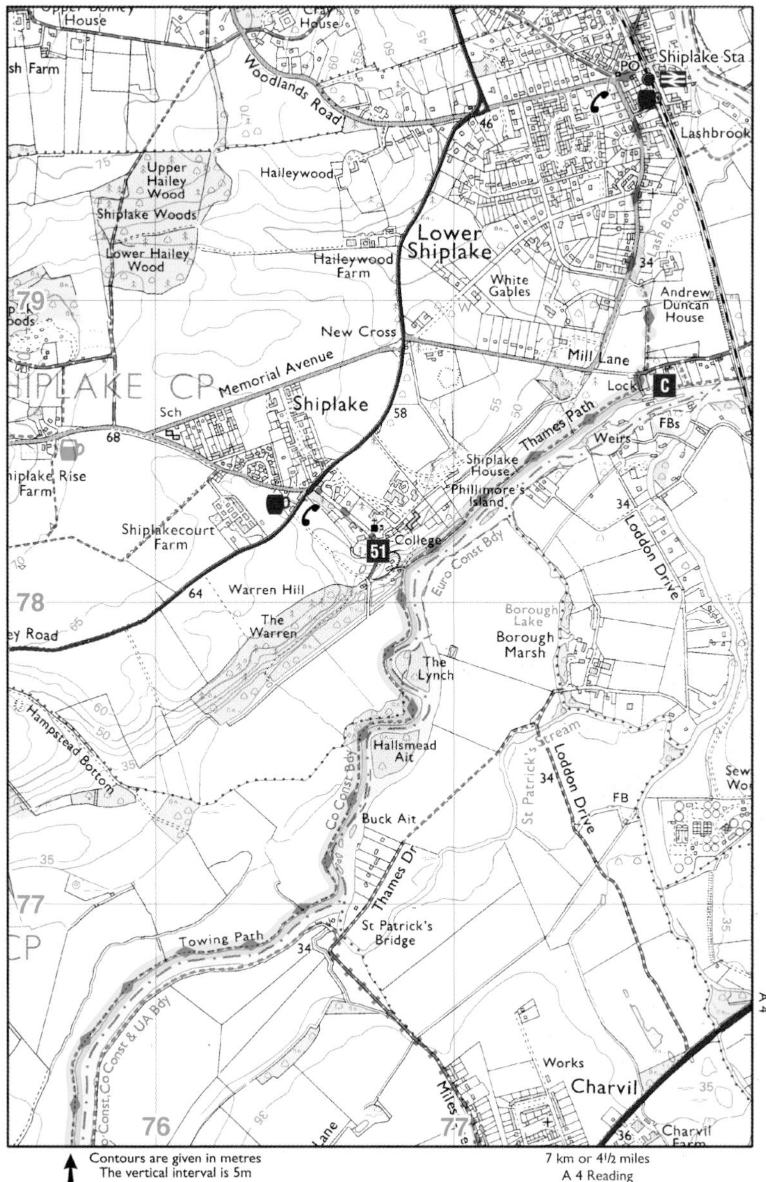

Contours are given in metres
The vertical interval is 5m

7 km or 4½ miles
A 4 Reading

may notice, down a drive to the right, a white, boarded, barn-like building with a simple cross over the door – the Lashbrook chapel. The road comes to a crossroads with The Baskerville Arms on one corner *and Shiplake station just to your right*.

9 Shiplake to Marlow

11 miles (17.7 km)

Transport Options

From Shiplake, you pass Henley station in 2¼ miles (3.6 km); then another 2½-mile (4-km) walk brings you to Hambleden Lock, where, from Mill End, there are bus services every day back to Henley and Reading, or on to Marlow and High Wycombe. Another 3¾ miles (6.0 km) brings you to Hurley, from where occasional buses run into Henley or on to Maidenhead. Marlow has train services on its branch line to Maidenhead.

At Shiplake, your truant towpath crosses to the other bank at Lashbrook Ferry, returning again via Bolney Ferry after less than a mile, and as we cannot follow it, a diversion away from the river is necessary. On the east side of the level crossing at Shiplake station, a grassy path **A** sets off between the railway and house gardens. After 150 yards, where a path comes over the line to join yours, bear right through a kissing-gate, and follow a path between gardens to a road, where you turn left. Along this attractive, tree-lined way, you can admire some impressive houses; those on the right are actually on the Thames.

The road bears right and you come to some gates, at which point a footpath **B** continues to the left, fenced off from the drive and from open fields. Beyond the drive, a miniature railway runs by the garden edge – it even has a miniature station. The path continues, still fenced, over a crossing track and a footbridge into riverside meadows, where you bear left. This is the site of Bolney Ferry, so the towpath returns to our bank, and you can follow it to Marsh Lock. Iron studs were placed along this meadow in 1903 to define the 14-foot (4-metre) width of the towing path. Only one seems to have survived, tottering on the river's edge as an indication of the extent of bank erosion here. Across the river, the grounds of Park Place rise and display odd features, including a cyclopian bridge of huge rocks, which you can see on the estate road up from the Thames **52**.

Marsh Lock is oddly situated in midstream and you reach it via a long, wooden causeway, which is obviously a favourite seagull perch. Then, go past the Georgian lock house (very handsome with hanging flower baskets), and back to the bank again by a second causeway leading to pretty cottages at the foot of Mill Lane. By the riverside now, past the Old House, you enter Mill Meadows, a popular promenade with all the usual accessories of memorial seats, bye-laws and doggie bins galore. There is a refreshment chalet across the grass to your left, toilets in the sports rotunda, and also the River and Rowing Museum, where you can find out more about the Thames. Henley seems constantly abustle with every activity connected with boats, and they are moored in rows as you pass the landings of Hobbs & Sons – 'Waterman to HM the Queen' as their sign proclaims. A walkway is clearly defined along the waterfront until The Angel on the Bridge blocks the way, by

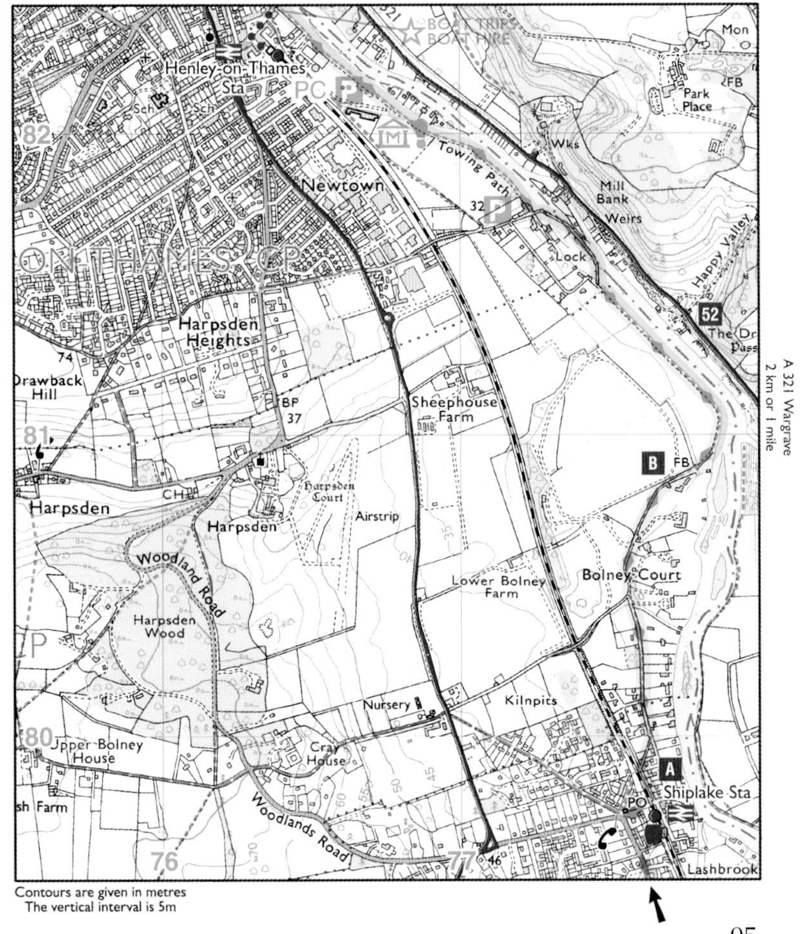

Contours are given in metres
The vertical interval is 5m

which time you are at Henley Bridge. To explore this bright, little town, turn up Hart Street to the Market Place with its Victorian town hall.

Henley looks its sparkling best from the other bank, and the Thames Path crosses the elegant 1780s bridge, allowing you to enjoy the view of the bridge, river front and the tall, 16th-century tower of St Mary's **53** – a much-photographed Thames view. Over the bridge, cross at the pedestrian island and walk 25 paces on to the path that turns sharply back to the riverside **C**. You are now looking down the Henley regatta course: 1 mile 450 yards (2 km 21 metres) of remarkably straight Thames, descended upon by the rowing world every year, in the first week of July. For some weeks either side of the Royal Regatta week, the stands and hospitality marquees transform this reach, and your riverside path may be diverted to a line back from the river. If you aim to enjoy the beauty of Henley Reach without diversions, best strike these weeks out of your diary.

But it is worth noting that the first Oxford versus Cambridge race was rowed along this reach in 1829, before moving to the familiar course from Putney to Mortlake, which you will encounter later. Sensing the town was on to a good thing, a public meeting in Henley Town Hall established the regatta 10 years later. The towpath has a metalled surface for part of the way, provided for the coaches of rowing crews to cycle along. Then the meadows open up, and a pretty string of brick cottages is followed by the low, flint tower of Remenham Church appearing over the trees. You can visit by means of a gate into the lane opposite the church, but ahead, the long regatta reach is terminated by a tiny temple on an island **54**. It is actually a fishing lodge with a cupola on top sheltering a nude lady, and was built as a landscape feature to enhance the view from nearby Fawley Court, but the naked lady's view up to distant Henley must itself be breathtaking.

Beyond Temple Island, the river bends sharply towards Hambleden Lock, soon passing, across the river, the grounds of the Italianate mansion of Greenlands **55**, built in 1853 for W. H. Smith, the bookseller, who became Viscount Hambleden. Then a wicket gate takes you along the lockside, with views across the series of weirs to Hambleden Mill **56**. The big weatherboarded mill, so accustomed to the clicking of appreciative tourist cameras, was driven by a water turbine, and only ceased working in

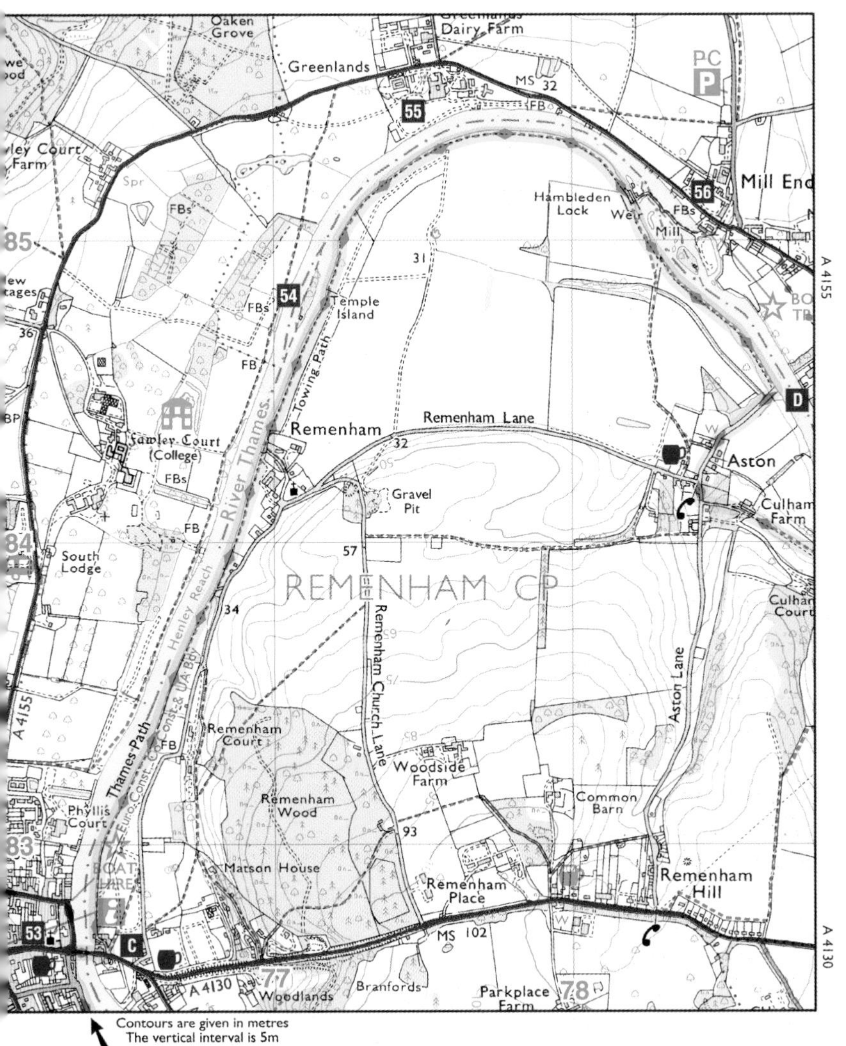

Contours are given in metres
The vertical interval is 5m

1955; now it is divided into flats. For a closer view (or to reach the Mill End bus stop), a right-of-way crosses the lower lock gates and the spectacular white water of Hambleden Weir.

Beyond the lock, follow the access road for a short way, then leave it to go through a gate, and continue by the riverside to Aston Ferry. Here, by the ferry landing, the towpath departs for the other bank for a while, so turn right up Ferry Lane **D** to The Flowerpot. This inn has an Edwardian feel to it, the bar full of fish in cases, and often with anglers too, and the legend outside

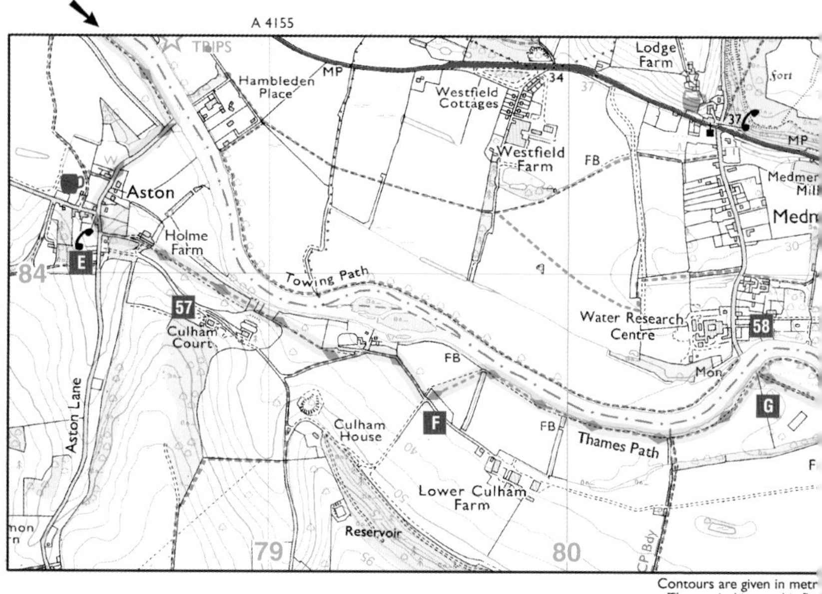

Contours are given in metr
The vertical interval is 5m

announces: 'good accommodation for fishing and boating parties'. Pass the inn, carry on up Aston Lane for 75 yards, then turn left along a drive **E** that climbs past Holme Farm until, where it turns right, your path keeps ahead into an open field. From the clear path, there are magnificent views to the left over the Thames Valley, and ahead, to the red-brick, 18th-century Culham Court on its rise **57**. The path goes below it via kissing-gates, then ahead over an open meadow, at first with a high wire fence to your right. Coming to another fence, go through a gate which leads into a track, where you turn left for 100 yards towards cottages, then right along a gravel track. When this track comes to a farm road at a corner, go half-left over a field **F**.

Once more, you are back by the Thames, and you can follow the bank via several more gates and footbridges for a long half-mile until, just to your left, you can see traces of a ferry landing stage. You have reached Medmenham, and just across the river, best viewed from a few paces on, is Medmenham Abbey **58**. With its hint of romantic ruin, and scandalous associations with Sir Francis Dashwood and his Hellfire Club, the label 'picturesque' could be used with justification here. But there is little left of the original building; what you now see is mostly an 18th-century Gothic creation.

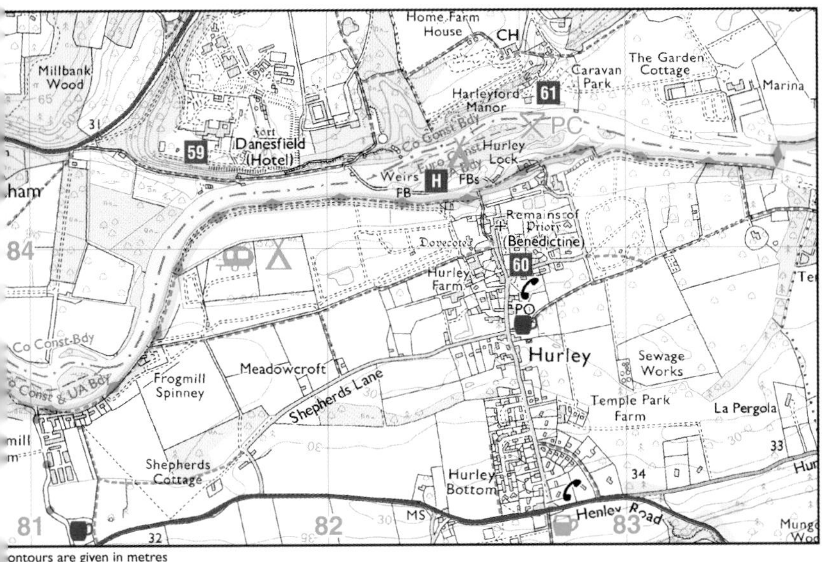

ontours are given in metres
The vertical interval is 5m

From the ferry landing, the Thames Path takes a short-cut along the track that heads off diagonally across the fields **G** and through a gate to rejoin the towpath. Ahead are the big barns of Frogmill, residential now, but characterful with their stone-and-flint patterning. The waymarked path keeps by the water's edge until it is forced to join a gravel drive past bungalows before reaching open meadows again. The big, white, castellated mansion ahead, gazing down in proprietorial fashion from its high, chalk cliff, is Danesfield, built around 1900, and now a hotel **59**.

Approaching Hurley, the riverside in summer tends to be overpopulated by picnic parties, but as the picnic meadow ends and its access road swings away, a weir signals the close presence of Hurley Lock. Your path continues by the river's edge. When you come to a rustic bridge over the lock cut, go left onto the lock island **H**. Another path on the right leads, rather delightfully, over a stream, past cottages into Hurley village **60** just a few minutes away.

Here is a little parcel of green with, on the right, one of Hurley's two tithe barns, which has been converted into a house with a circular, 14th-century dovecote alongside. The second barn is just along the village street and a little further up is the marvellous Olde Bell, which claims to date from 1135. A priory

Temple Island is the starting point for the Henley Regatta races, facing up the long Regatta reach, with the Chiltern Hills rising in the distance.

was established here in the 11th century, and traces remain on the other side of the green. The parish church of St Mary the Virgin, with its long, narrow nave, was the priory chapel, and the quadrangle beside it contains parts of the refectory block.

Having crossed the rustic bridge, you can roam the lock island at will; this is an open picnic area with toilets behind the lock cottage. Beyond the lock, a second rustic bridge returns you to the riverbank. As you walk on, look back to see Harleyford Manor **61** – a handsome little house built in 1755 – just glimpsed between islands, where it now serves as a clubhouse for the marina.

Ahead now, Temple footbridge spans the Thames **I** on the line of the ferry that closed in 1953. This graceful 150-foot (46-metre) wooden arch was opened in 1989, very effectively solving one of the Thames Path's crossing problems. Cross it gratefully, and walk on, past Temple Lock and the modern housing that replaces the mills on Temple Island, with a clear path ahead to Marlow.

Soon, Bisham Abbey makes a mellow composition across the river **62**. Most of what you see is the Tudor house built here by Sir Philip Hoby using fragments of the original abbey, but now it has a new life as Sport England's National Sports Centre. Then comes Bisham Church with its late 17th-century tower right by the waterside, adding to the river scene. The last bend brings Marlow into view, the pinnacled church spire and delicate line of the suspension bridge **63** making another classic river view. William Tierney Clark was commissioned to design the bridge after his success with the earlier Hammersmith Bridge, and it proved to be his masterwork; it was opened in 1832. Rather than replacing it in the 1920s, its ironwork was renewed in steel and its masonry towers restored.

Walk right up to the bridge and admire its detail, then turn left up the slope to the main street. If you walk into Marlow now you will quickly come to some gates on the left that lead into Higginson Park with toilets to your right and a refreshment kiosk ahead. *For the station, cross by the park gates and walk down Station Road opposite. At the Marlow Donkey pub (the affectionate local name for the branch line shuttle), go half-right down Station Approach to the well-hidden platform.*

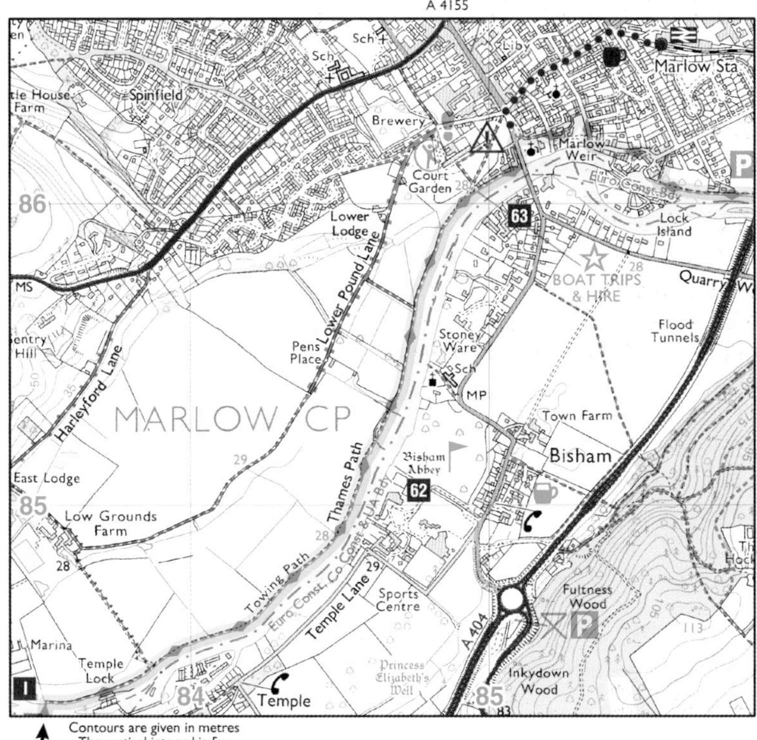

10 Marlow to Windsor

14¼ miles (23 km)

Transport Options

From Marlow, you pass near Bourne End station after 3¼ miles (5.2 km), then Cookham after another 1¼ miles (2 km); both are served by the Marlow branch. Maidenhead is then a 3¼-mile (5.2-km) walk on and has rail and express bus connections to London. Windsor, at the end, has two stations, offering a shuttle service to Slough or a direct service to London Waterloo.

From Marlow Bridge **63** down to the lock, there is no towpath, and barges had to be manhandled or hauled on a long towline while their towing horses were led round on a tortuous path. So, keeping to the tradition, the Thames Path sets off along that odd route, known locally as Seven Corner Alley, for reasons that will soon be obvious. From the bridge it crosses the road to the fence on the north side of All Saints Church, then crosses the corner of the churchyard **A** to emerge in St Peter Street opposite the charming Two Brewers pub.

A few paces to the right, the path continues, bending this way and that between walls to reach a busier road where you turn

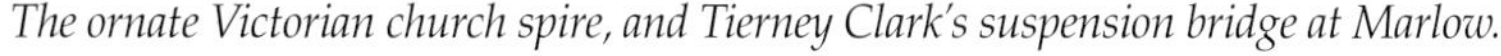

The ornate Victorian church spire, and Tierney Clark's suspension bridge at Marlow.

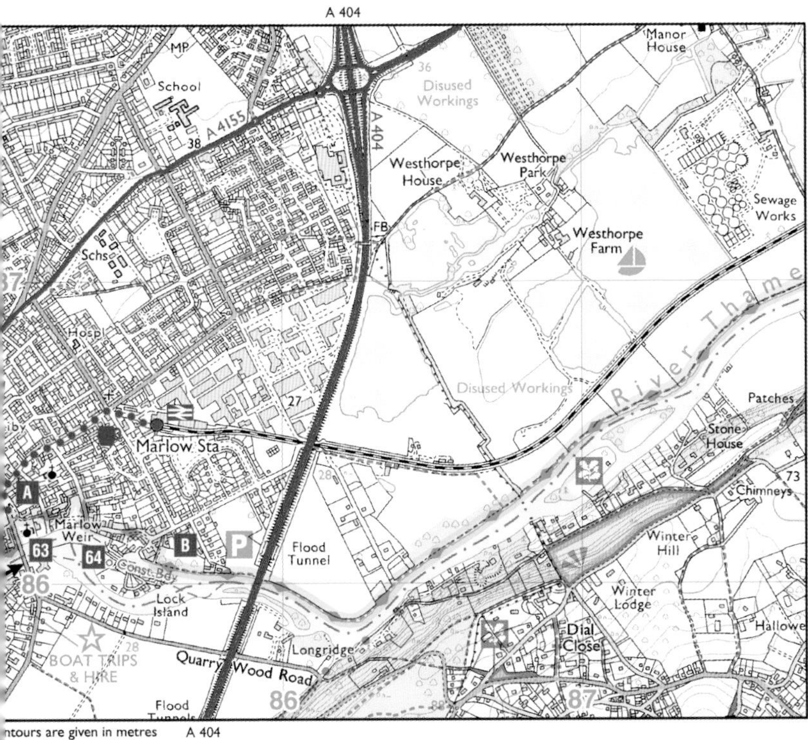

right to the riverside. Although your route now follows the road for a while, it is well worth turning aside briefly on the path to the right, signed to Marlow Lock **64**, to enjoy the classic view of church and bridge over the weir. Downstream, you cannot miss the striking, angular roofs of the weatherboarded housing on the site of Marlow Mill, its mill-like ambience still retained.

Walking on along the road, you pass the mill housing, then, around a left-hand bend, a gravel path to the right leads to the Thames **B**, where it turns left to go to the river side of houses, and then under the bypass bridge. Now, the great, beech-clad rise of Quarry Wood blocks the way, and the Thames turns aside to skirt the foot of Winter Hill. There are boathouses by the waterside and villas climbing the slopes. One property on the bank is a genuine mini-castle with turrets and battlements, a cheeky but perfect complement to its dramatic river setting. As you come onto grass, a magnificent poplar avenue screens playing fields, and picnic benches invite you to linger. Then you are into open meadows, with the slopes of Winter Hill, bare now, falling back from the river. On the opposite side, the very last white cottage is Spade Oak Ferry Cottage, yet another old towpath crossing.

On the near bank, a level crossing over the little branch line leads past the spruced-up Spade Oak Farm and, just around the bend, a useful hostelry, but your way continues on a broad track just back from the Thames. Bourne End ahead is a favourite reach for dinghy sailing. White gates lead you onto a paved path across the Upper Thames Sailing Club lawn, and on past the handsome clubhouse. Then come moored motor cruisers, and a gravel walkway past housing, leading to a small marina with a restaurant over its office. Briefly you join a road, but where it turns away left, a narrow path continues between garden fences towards the railway bridge you can see ahead.

A gate on your right leads to a footbridge attached to the railway bridge **C**. *For Bourne End station, go under the railway bridge and turn immediately left on a path to the station car park.* Cross the footbridge, turn and walk under the railway bridge, and go through a gate into the National Trust-owned Cock Marsh. This expanse of marshland and grass between Winter Hill and the Thames has been common land since 1272, and is still grazed in the traditional manner. Your path keeps to the riverbank through the open meadows until a bend brings Cookham Bridge into view. Go through some gates, walk across another sailing club area into a public open space, and, when the tidy grass ends, just short of the bridge, turn right into Cookham churchyard **D**. The path goes to the right of the sturdy 16th-century tower of Holy Trinity **65**, and on through the old gravestones to a group of white buildings beyond. This is Churchgate, where you bear left, then right in the main road to the village centre.

On a corner across the road, you can see the Tarry Stone, a big chunk of sarsen stone, the subject of many local tales. Where the roads meet, the turning to the right leads past The Bell and Dragon Inn and the creeper-clad Royal Exchange, out onto the open common, Cookham Moor. Facing you is the Wesleyan chapel, reopened in 1962 as a memorial gallery for the work of Stanley Spencer, the artist who immortalised Cookham and drew a lifetime's inspiration from the village and its people.

Spencer was born in a nearby house, Fernlea, and used his 'village from heaven' as the setting for many New Testament studies. He portrayed *Christ preaching at Cookham Regatta*, and his *Judgement Day* had Spencer and his friends rising sleepily from

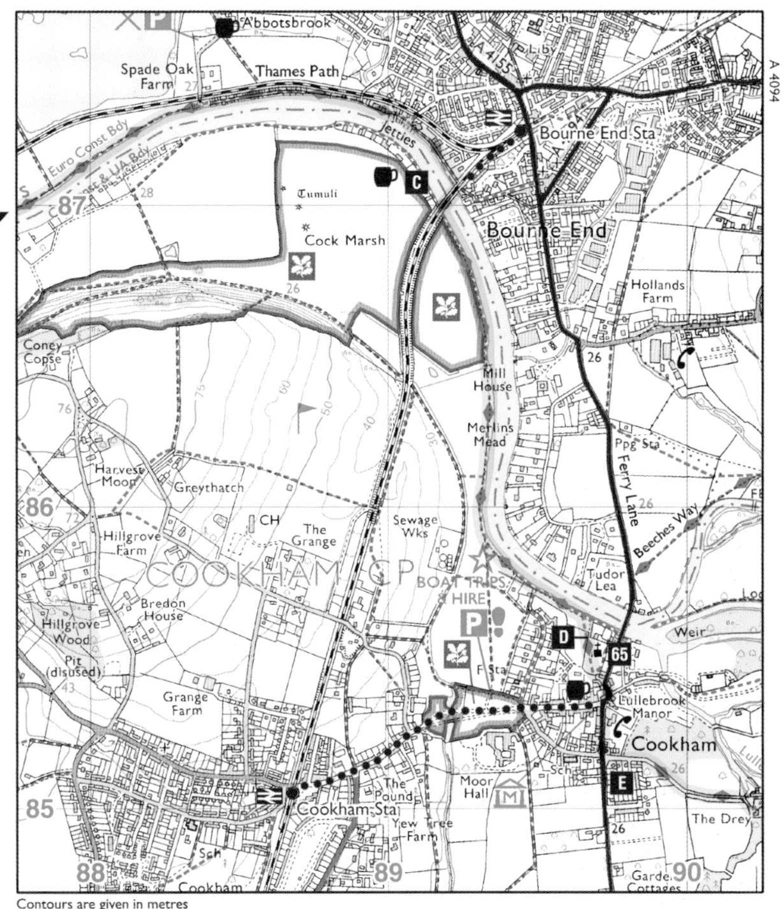

Contours are given in metres
The vertical interval is 5m

those graves you passed in Cookham churchyard. In the gallery, open daily in summer but only at the weekends in winter, you can even see the ancient pram he pushed around with all his painting gear aboard. *For Cookham station, follow the High Street on across Cookham Moor and straight on through the newer houses of Cookham Rise.*

Just below Cookham Bridge the Thames blossoms into no fewer than four channels, two of which enclose Formosa Island. Three ferries were needed to get the towpath past all this, so understandably you have a diversion away from the river here. Leave Cookham along Sutton Road to the left of the gallery, turning left after 200 yards down Mill Lane **E**, which quickly brings you into open fields. Arriving at houses again, the path goes right between hedges, curves round a property, crosses a drive, then continues as a woodland way with open fields just to the right. Keep by the field edge around several bends until the path, with a touch of drama, suddenly comes to My Lady Ferry. Across the river, the beechwoods rise steeply. At your feet are the last traces of the ferry landing and, opposite, the elegant estate cottages and well-tended lawns of the Cliveden estate. This reach can be magnificent in autumn, the hanging woods reflecting in the water to create a sheer wall of colour.

Walk on a little and you should be able to look back to Cliveden itself – commanding on its hill-top platform **66**. Designed by Sir Charles Barry in 1881, it was bought by William Waldorf Astor in 1893 and gained a colourful reputation for political intrigue and scandal, especially in the 1930s, when it hosted the 'Cliveden Set', and in the 1960s, when the Profumo affair focused world attention on one of those innocent riverside cottages.

Approaching Boulter's Lock **67**, with thundering water across the Thames, civilization returns to the near bank in the shape of lawns, landing stages and smart cruisers at their moorings. Follow the lock cut up to the road, then continue along the pavement to Boulter's Lock. Back in the Edwardian days of punts and parasols, this was the most fashionable spot on the Thames, especially on Ascot Sunday, when as many as a thousand small craft would parade through beneath an admiring audience.

By the lock, a bridge leads over to Ray Mill Island, 4 acres (1.6 hectares) of public garden, and to the hotel, which was once a flour mill – indeed, the millrace still rushes underneath. Boulter is a milling term, and the earlier name here was Ray Mill Lock. Walk on along the promenade beside Ray Mead Road until it ends and you have to cross to the pavement side. There is a refreshment hut and toilets in a little public garden along this road. Approaching Maidenhead Bridge, you can recross and take the path over another public garden to the bridge. *For Maidenhead station, do not cross, but turn right up Bridge Road, the A4. At a big roundabout, turn left into Forlease Road, then second right into York Road, at the end of which bear left along Queen Street to the station. The bus stops are down the first turning on the right off York Road.*

Cross Maidenhead Bridge by the upstream pavement, turn left on the other side and immediately left again through gates into a boatyard **F**. Go under an arch of the bridge and along the

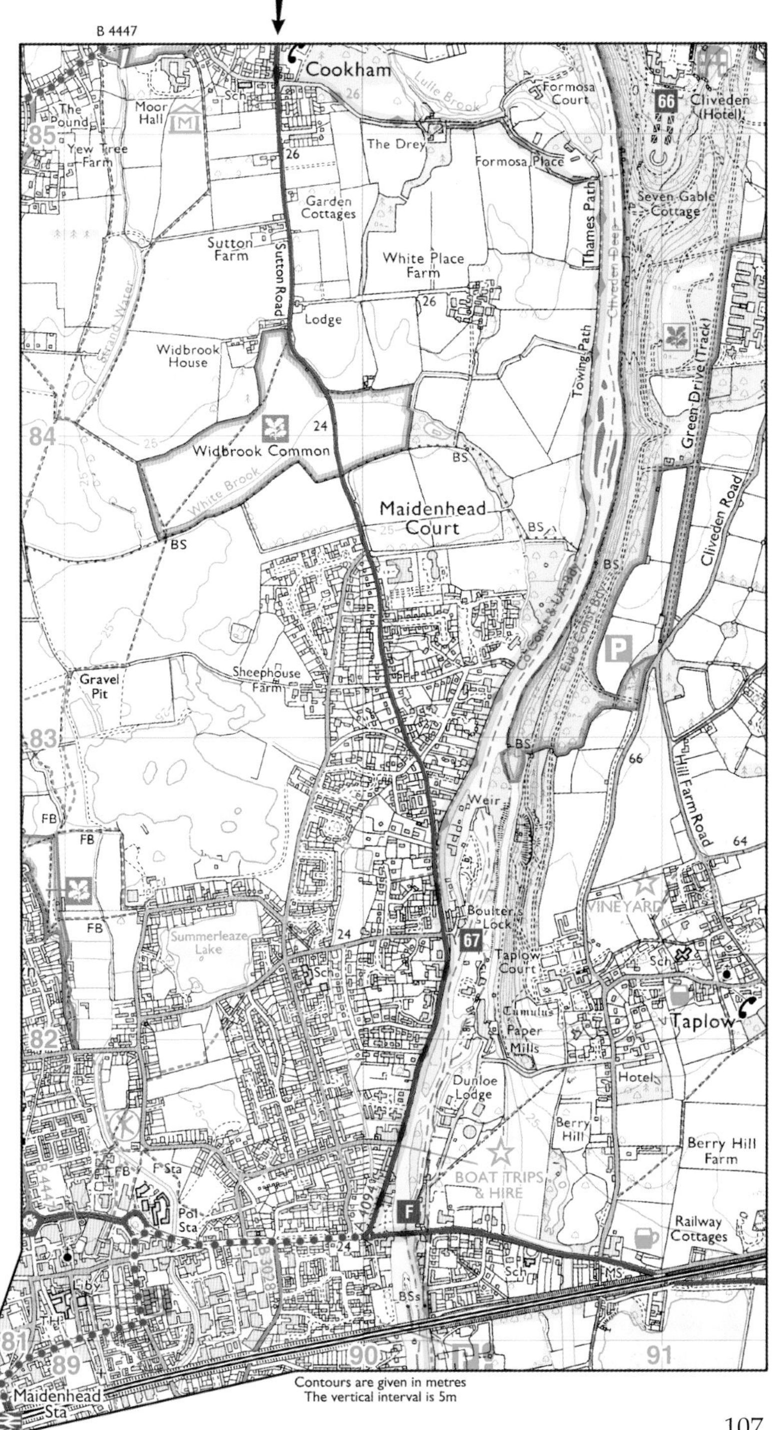

Contours are given in metres
The vertical interval is 5m

concrete wharf on the other side. Beyond a boathouse development, turn up through a car park to Riverside Road and follow it, to the right, towards Brunel's masterpiece of a railway bridge **68**. The famous Victorian engineer designed it in 1839 to carry his broad gauge line to the West Country. When challenged to span both towpath and navigation channel together, he responded with what are still the widest, flattest brick arches in the world: 128 feet (39 metres) across with a rise of just 24 feet (7.3 metres). Critics believed it could not be done, but the expresses still thunder over it, just as they did in Brunel's day, when Turner captured the drama in his famous study: *Rain, Steam and Speed*.

Beyond the bridge, you are on a riverside road for a while, then, when it turns away, your footpath continues, green and pleasant, past Bray Lock and under the M4 motorway bridge. For a while, the path is well preserved across the grass at the bottom of the some large gardens. Now you come to a footbridge over the Thames, substantial but puzzling, as it does not serve any obvious purpose. But Summerleaze Bridge has a secret – a concealed conveyor belt – and its cunning role, when opened in 1996, was to carry gravel across the river. Do not cross it, but continue, soon reaching the great open field of Dorney, Thames Field. Along its near edge, a path offers a tempting diversion to

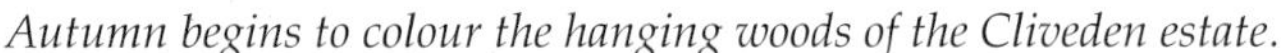

Autumn begins to colour the hanging woods of the Cliveden estate.

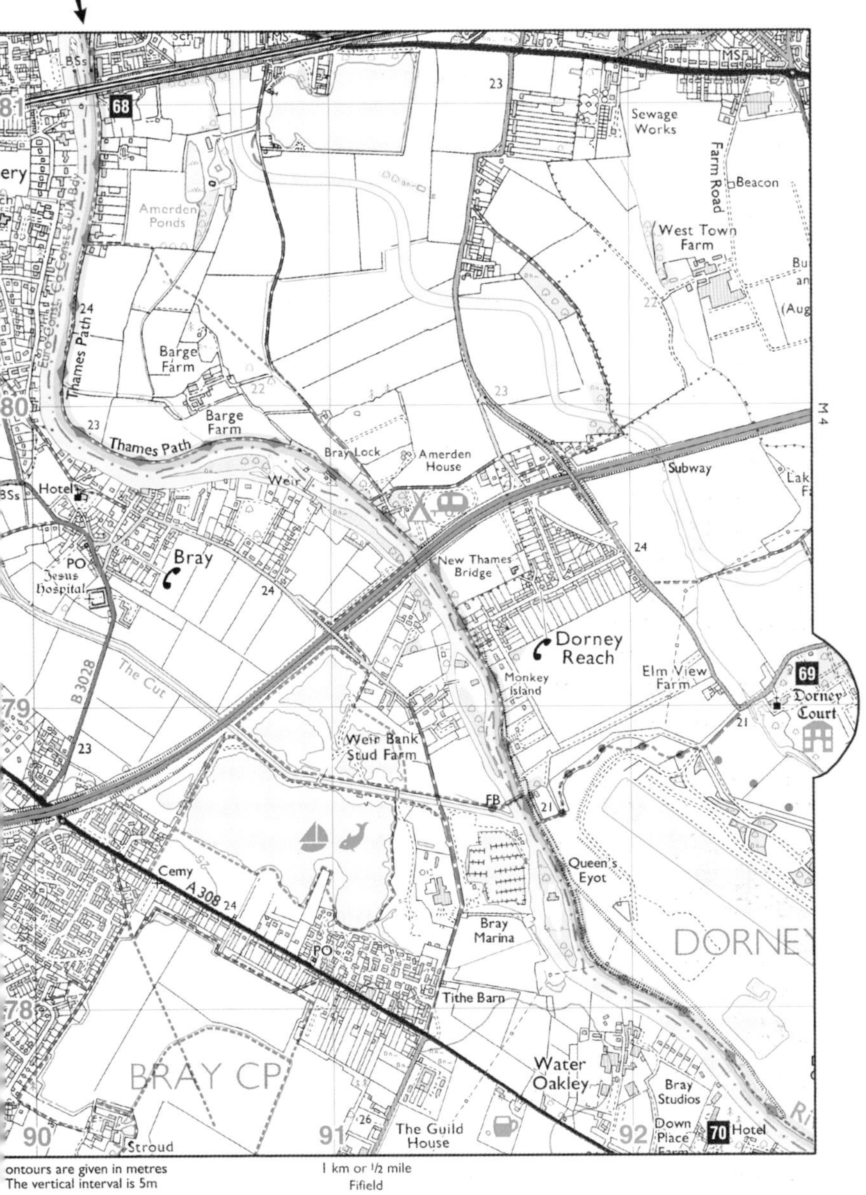

the delectable grouping of Tudor Dorney Court and the church of St James, hiding peacefully together, near the river **69**.

The ancient landscape of Thames Field is now transformed by the Eton College rowing lake, soon to become familiar as one of the 2012 Olympic sites. Across the river is Oakley Court **70**,

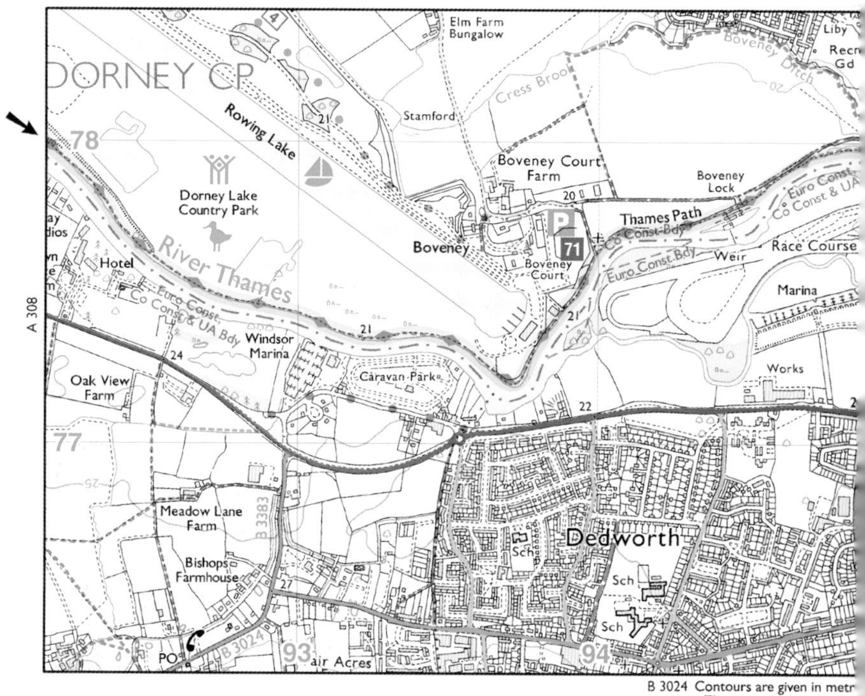

high Victorian Gothic with towers and fanciful animals crouching on the roofs. With a puff of dry ice it could well serve as Dracula's Castle, and indeed probably has.

Around another bend, passing one of the college boathouses, you come to the simple little chapel of St Mary Magdalene, Boveney, in solitude by the river **71**. Rubble chalk courses are well buttressed and crowned with a clapboard belfry, sitting at a rakish angle. The earliest parts are 12th and 13th century, and it probably served a wharf here, shipping timber from Windsor Forest. Boveney hamlet itself, just up the path beyond the chapel, has several well restored, timber-framed Tudor houses.

Your way is on now, by Boveney Lock, the houses of Eton Wick across the expanse of South Field to the left, and Windsor Racecourse across the river. Along the track here, you will pass a featureless platform with a bench and a low tablet, which tells you that this, believe it or not, is Athens, traditional bathing place for the boys from Eton. Quoting from the rules, it states that: 'boys who are undressed must either get at once into the water or get behind screens when boats containing ladies come in sight'.

B 3022

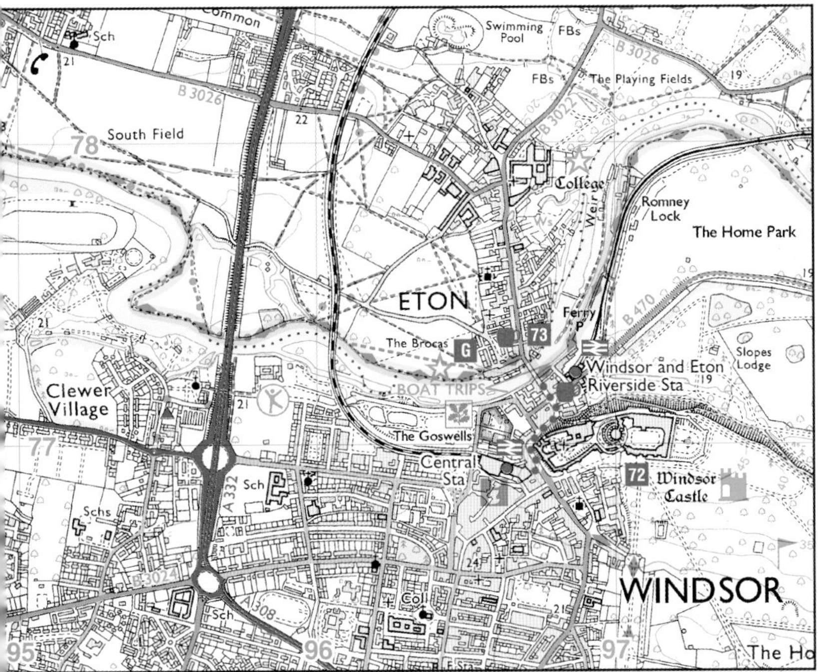

ontours are given in metres
The vertical interval is 5m

Over a footbridge, the path follows the grass bank around a river loop. Then, it continues under a road bridge and a railway bridge, its long viaduct bringing the line along from Slough. You then enter the Brocas meadow. You may already have had glimpses of Windsor Castle, but now it is there in all its majesty, towering over the town **72**.

Leave the Brocas by a gate **G** to the left of a white house on the riverside, go to the right of The Waterman's Arms and out to the foot of the narrow and decidedly picturesque Eton High Street. The college buildings are up to the left, while the path goes right, over the pedestrians-only bridge **73** into Windsor.

As companies competed for royal patronage, Windsor gained two substantial railway stations. *For Windsor & Eton Riverside station, go down the steps on the left over the bridge, walk along the riverside for 70 yards and turn right. For Central station, walk ahead from the bridge and bear right with Thames Street beneath the castle ramparts. The grand station entry is down a turning on the right just beyond the castle entrance.* The information office is a few paces further up the High Street.

11 Windsor to Shepperton

13¾ miles (22.1 km)

Transport Options

From Windsor, a 2-mile (3.2-km) stroll brings you to Datchet; then it is another 6¼ miles (10.1 km) to Staines. Both points have convenient connections to the same trains that serve Windsor & Eton Riverside station. From Staines, it is another 6¼-mile (10.1-km) walk on to Shepperton, where there is another rail connection.

From Windsor Bridge **73**, take the steps down to the riverside promenade on the downstream, Windsor side, and walk past Salter's office, where their riverboats, which offer trips to Runnymede and Staines, are often moored. Ahead, a narrow spit of land called The Cobbler separates weir stream from lock cut, carrying a section of the old towpath that ends rather forlornly in midstream. Just beyond The River House pub, go ahead through gates onto Romney Walk. Soon, you are bearing left along a broader drive that leads to Romney Lock. Go to the right of the red-brick tower of the Victorian waterworks and enter a boatyard.

Your route is at most times fenced-off from the working area, and heads left towards a footbridge leading to the lock. Bear right before you reach it, to a kissing-gate **A** into open fields. Walk on with the lock cut still to your left, then under Black Potts railway bridge and out into the open area of The Home Park. Windsor Castle, beyond the playing fields, provides the distant backdrop.

Ahead now is Victoria Bridge **74.** The towpath ahead is closed for security reasons, so your path changes to the other bank. First, bear right over the grass to a point where the white railings of the bridge approach road end. Cross the road here and go left over Victoria Bridge on the downstream pavement. Once over the river, go down the steps **B** and follow the path until it leads away from the river and back to the road. As there is no footway on the near side, cross the road with care and turn right towards Datchet. *Soon, two road turnings lead into the village centre, and the second, the High Street, also passes the station.*

Just beyond the High Street, you may notice the Old Bridge House. Looking to the Thames across Datchet's tiny riverside garden, it is difficult to believe there was ever a bridge here. Yet, old Datchet Bridge was demolished in the 1850s and two new

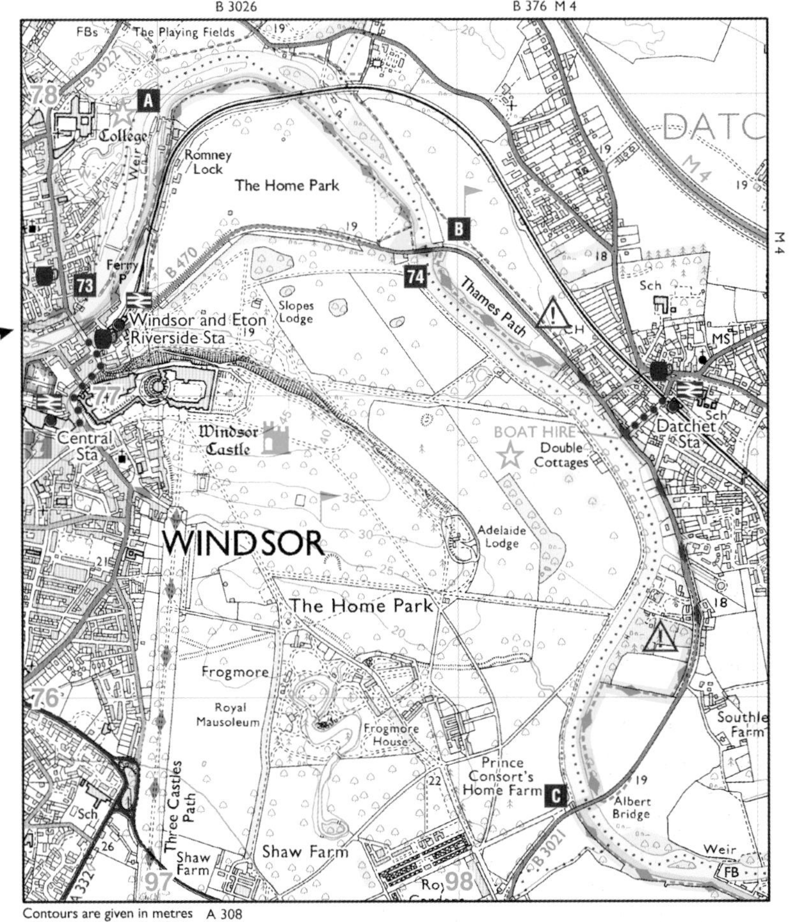

bridges were built – Victoria and Albert – in order to create a private riverside park for Queen Victoria. No trace of the bridge remains, but by all accounts it was a strange affair. The boundary between Berkshire and Buckinghamshire ran through the centre of the span and when, in the 1830s, urgent repairs were needed, Berks rebuilt their half in iron while Bucks merely repaired theirs – in wood.

Follow the road until, just beyond the last riverside properties, you can cross carefully to a plank footbridge. Once over it, a fenced path follows the road, then turns right to the riverbank. Walk under Albert Bridge, up the slope to cross the bridge and turn down the steps **C** to rejoin the towpath. Soon, the true channel of the Thames turns away to the left, but you must continue along a lock cut on a path that joins the drive to Old Windsor Lock. Half a mile (800 metres) beyond the lock, you pass the river frontage of two apartment blocks, then on a path between river and road, eventually coming to the roadside. Soon the path **D** leaves the road to follow the river past the French Bros boat landing, and out into the meadows of Runnymede **75**.

Immediately to the right here are two of the Lutyens gatehouses; the one across the road houses a popular tea room, with toilets nearby. Lady Fairhaven, who gave these historic meadows to the National Trust in 1931, commissioned Sir Edwin Lutyens to design the two sets of lodges as appropriate entrances. Just ahead of you, a display panel by a car park entry locates the Runnymede memorials: the domed Magna Carta temple of 1957, designed by Sir Edward Maufe for the American Bar Association; and the John F. Kennedy memorial of 1965, by Geoffrey Jellicoe, standing on an acre of land given, in perpetuity, to the United States. Both are within easy reach of the Thames Path, while in the trees, on the skyline high above Runnymede, can be seen the tower and terraces of the Commonwealth Air Forces Memorial of 1952.

Halfway along Runnymede, be careful not to follow the riverside too closely into a 'dead end' spit of land, but be guided by waymark posts nearer the road. Across the Thames, the wooded banks of Magna Carta Island conceal the scant traces of the 12th-century nunnery of Ankerwycke. Exactly where, however, King

Swans preen by the Brocas meadow, with Windsor Castle in distant view.

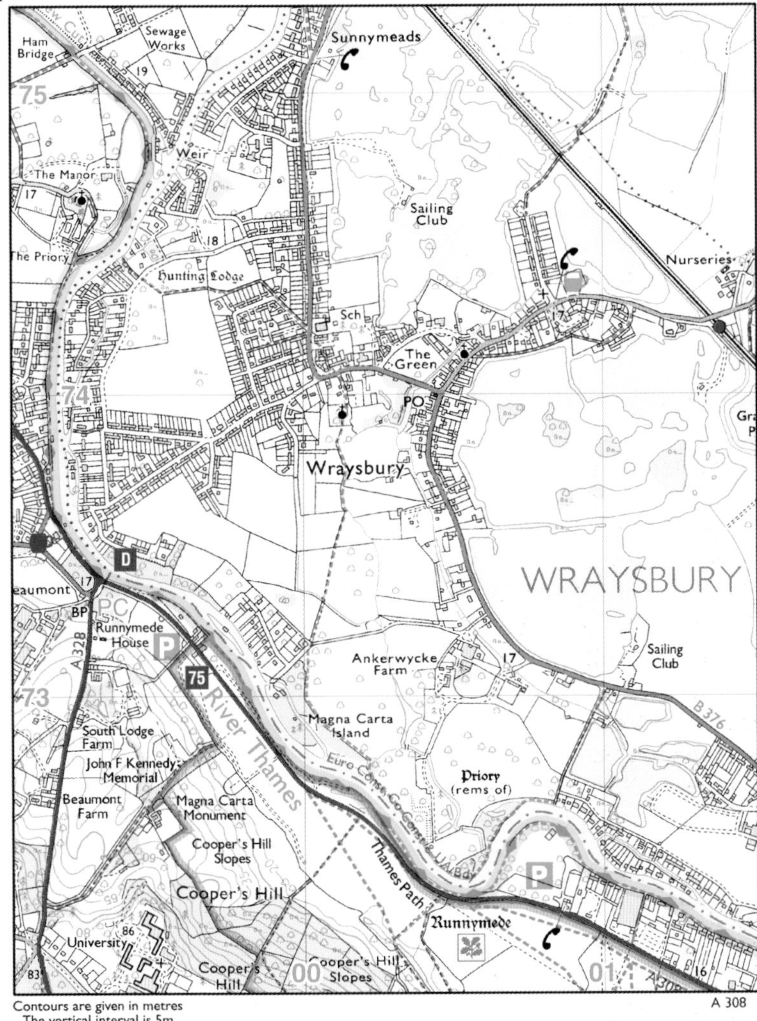

Contours are given in metres
The vertical interval is 5m

John set his seal to the Great Charter in 1215, no one knows for certain. Try to ignore the picnic parties and the traffic, and respond instead to the ambience of those great historic moments which still lingers in these meadows by the Thames.

As the river curves to the left, go through a squeeze gate and follow it. Ahead, near the roadside, are a tea hut and more toilets, but the Thames Path, keeping close by the riverbank, now heads for Staines. You pass charming bungalows, their tubs and flowerbeds a glory of well-tended colour in summer. Go

The historic meadows of Runnymede, with Cooper's Hill on the skyline.

past Bellweir Lock and carry on under the double motorway bridge. To many, the thunder of M25 traffic overhead carries the sure message that you are entering London. But there are other clues to a boundary crossing nearby. A short way on, as you pass a superstore car park, you may spot a white, iron post by the towpath. This is a 'coalpost', one of many that ringed the entries to London to warn merchants that, under an act of 1831, they were now due to pay a levy on coal. And, almost hidden by trees on the far bank, there is a replica of the London Stone **76**, placed here to mark the upstream limit of the City of London's jurisdiction over the Thames, which lasted from 1285 to 1857, when the first Thames Conservators took over.

Ahead now is Staines Bridge. Under it the towpath leads to the Hythe, a little Thames-side community with some pleasant cottages and pubs (Hythe means a landing place). The Thames Path, however, turns right up the slope to cross Staines Bridge on the upstream pavement, then continues down the steps on the other bank to a car park area. Walk back beside the bridge to rejoin the Thames and turn under Staines Bridge to walk downstream again. Cross the River Colne, then, coming to a small garden with fountains, spare a minute to divert up a path on the left to the little market square with its pretty town hall, all yellow brick and white stone, the date AD 1880 below the clock tower.

The river walk continues until, where the new garden promenade ends, the Thames Path joins the road, and turns right. But during daylight hours you can continue through gates here, and along the river front of the Thames Lodge Hotel. By either route, right beneath Staines railway bridge you find the start of the towpath again. The stone slipway here was the 'shut-off' point at which horse teams were detached and led up to Staines Bridge, from where the towline was floated down to pick up the barge.

From Staines railway bridge, the towpath continues as a broad, metalled path past riverside houses **E**. *For Staines station, keep on along the road and take the third turning on the left, Gresham Road; the footbridge at the top takes you into the station yard.*

Along Riverside Staines, the little houses, in their infinite variety, still reflect the joy of simply living by the Thames. Too many have recently given way to out-of-scale apartment blocks, but the affection still felt by locals for their riverside is evident in the number of dedicated seats along it; 'Cli and John welcome you' is the message on one little two-seater.

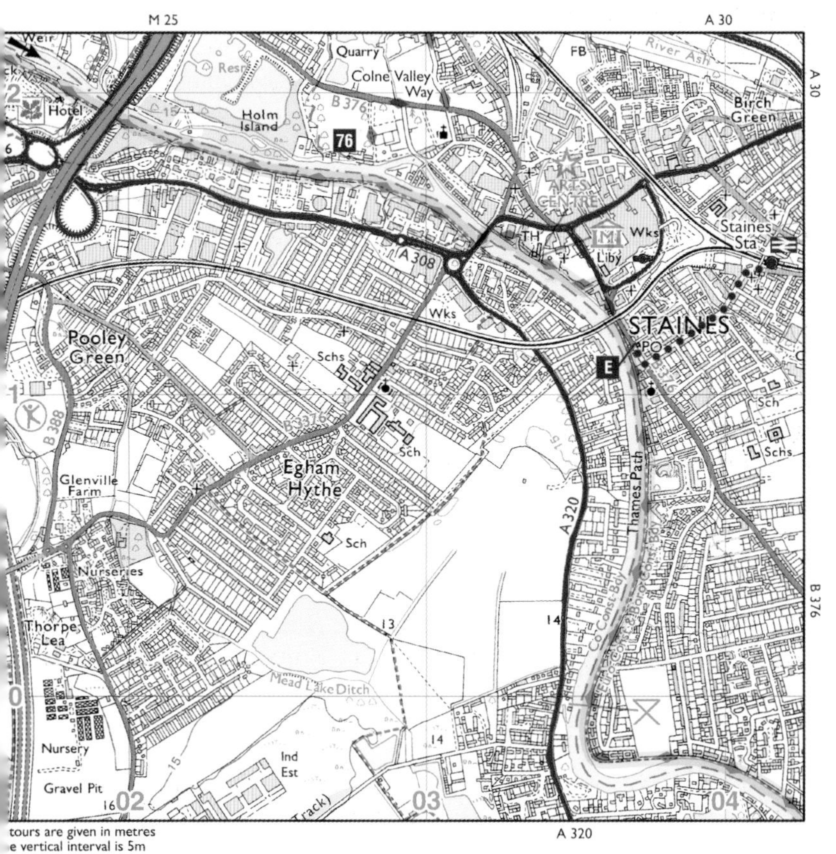

For a short distance you will take paths over an open grass area before a broad, gravel track leads on to Penton Hook Lock. The Hook **77** is surely the most impressive river loop along the whole Thames. Early in the 19th century, its narrow neck was broken through by flood waters so regularly that barges took a 'short-cut'. The first lock was built here in 1815 in recognition of this, and today the island, managed by the Environment Agency, has the feel of a nature reserve. It was built up with spoil from dredging, but has now been reclaimed by ash, hawthorn and elder, and presents a fine, wild aspect. If you have time, cross either of the lock gates and the main weir beyond, and try the paths around the island.

Beyond Penton Hook, now on a road, you cross the intake to Thames Water's vast Queen Mary Reservoir. In another half-mile (800 metres), a turning up Blacksmiths' Lane leads directly

A grassy towpath invites you to stroll by this typically tranquil stretch of the middle Thames, just downstream of Albert Bridge.

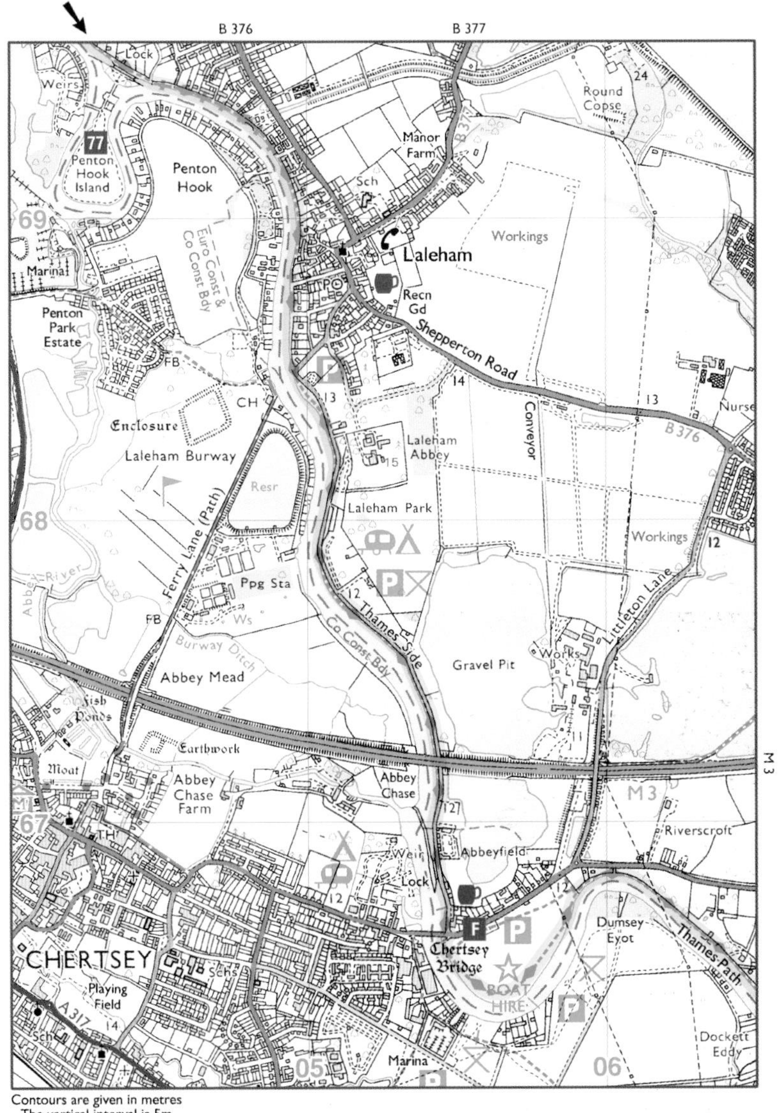

Contours are given in metres
The vertical interval is 5m

to Laleham Church and, for refreshment, two nearby pubs. Otherwise, the path continues over grass along the riverside past Laleham Park, an extensive open space. As the Park ends, you can hear the thunder of traffic from the M3 motorway bridge ahead. Beyond the bridge is Chertsey Lock, from where the path continues to Chertsey Bridge. Go under the bridge, then through a kissing-gate **F** to follow the riverbank through open meadows.

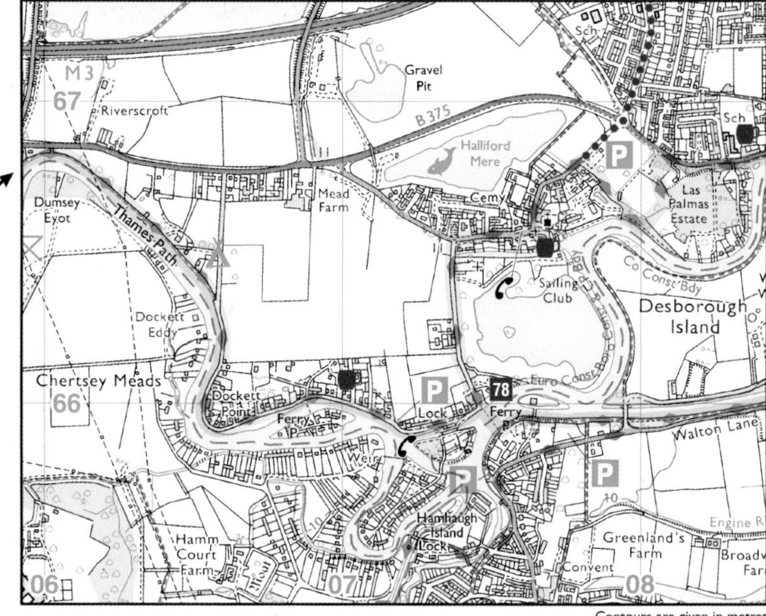

Contours are given in metres
The vertical interval is 5m

As Chertsey Meads open up on the further bank, you have the traditional Thames watermeadow scenes around you for the last time. Where the meadows end, another kissing-gate leads to a broad, grass path by an assortment of moored boats, all very domestic and, indeed, one among them could best be described as a 'floating house'.

Again, you join a riverside road and find yourself walking, wherever possible, along grass strips by the water's edge. You may notice that the bungalows across the river depend on boat links to this bank, as indicated by landing stages, postboxes and even the occasional bell to signal, 'please come and collect me'.

Soon, you will be looking across the Thames to Shepperton Weir, with the spire of Weybridge Church just visible beyond. Then comes Shepperton Lock, where a little refreshment hut is often open on the island, which can be reached over the lock gates. At the bottom of Ferry Lane just beyond, the Thames Path uses one of the few remaining ferries **78** on the river to take you to the Weybridge bank. *For Shepperton station, turn up Ferry Lane, turn right at the top and follow the road for half a mile (800 metres). At the war memorial roundabout, carry on up the High Street; at the traffic lights the station is just to your right.*

The American Bar Society's Magna Carta memorial on Runnymede reminds us that events of world significance happened in these Thames meadows.

12 Shepperton to Teddington

11 miles (17.7 km)

Transport Options

From the Shepperton to Weybridge Ferry, it is a 6¼-mile (10.1-km) walk to Hampton Court, where there are buses to Kingston and elsewhere; there is also a rail service from Hampton Court station. From there on, you have an easy 3-mile (4.8-km) stroll to Kingston Bridge, with Hampton Wick and Kingston stations nearby, or a 5-mile (8-km) walk past Kingston to Teddington which has another station connection.

From Shepperton Lock, you have two options. The old towpath used to cross to the Weybridge bank at the ferry point **78**, just downstream, and this is the one point on the Thames Path where you can do as the barge teams did – cross by a ferry that still operates. When the ferry is not running, the Thames Path takes an alternative route on the north bank to rejoin the towpath at Walton Bridge.

The ferry route

The ferry can be summoned by ringing the bell on either bank. It runs quarter-hourly but only at scheduled times: at weekends from 9am (10am on Sundays), to 5pm (5.30pm from May to August). To confirm, ring the ferry office on 01932 254844.

Having stepped off the ferry onto the south bank, turn downstream and follow the broad, surfaced track, which soon passes a private footbridge over to an island with a chalet-like house, usually known as D'Oyly Carte Island. Now the old Thames channel can be seen looping away to the left, while the Thames Path goes under a road bridge and straight on beside the Desborough Cut.

The Cut, only completed in 1935, was dug in order to improve the flow, and was named after Lord Desborough, longest-serving chairman of the Thames Conservancy. If you have time to spare, the towpath walk around the old loops of the river is far more rural, even if longer. Just take the steps up on the right to cross the road bridge **A**, then carry on by the river to rejoin the Thames Path after crossing the bridge at the far end of the Cut.

Beyond the Cut and approaching Walton Bridge, the riverside widens to a popular grass strip where a refreshment hut is often open.

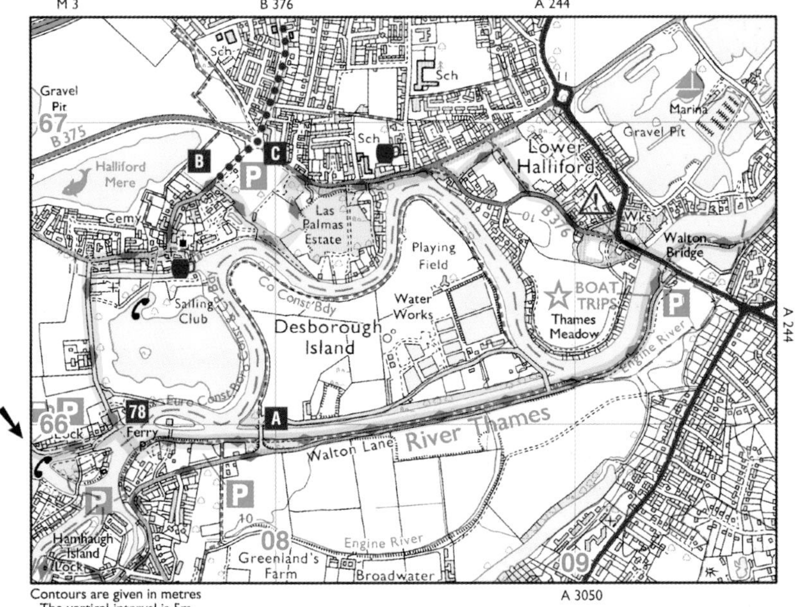

The alternative route

To follow this option, walk to the ferry point and turn left up Ferry Lane, using the verge where possible in order to avoid the traffic. Turn right at the top and follow the main road past the little Church Square of riverside Shepperton, then right again after another 400 yards to cross a car park area **B** on the edge of the public gardens. Walk on with a brick wall to your right, keeping by the wall on the enclosed path until it ends, and you can bear right to the riverside. This idyllic spot is one of the Shepperton Loops, no longer the main channel but still navigable. Turn left along the riverside, but look back for a delightful view of the Manor House and its lawns by the Thames.

This is but the briefest of encounters with the river, so after 130 yards, turn left into the trees to find a gravel 'bridge' over a ditch, leading into an open, grass area. Walk left across the grass to where a gravel path continues, soon bringing you into another small car park. Bear right out of this on its access drive, but, just before reaching the road, turn right **C** on a gravel path, with a stream between you and the road. Coming to a wooden causeway, your route crosses the stream by footbridge and continues, with the stream now on your right, until you eventually join the road opposite the Ship Hotel.

Cross to the other pavement and pass The Ship and The Red Lion. As soon as you come to open grass, cross the road again and take a gravel path towards a big, white, weatherboarded cottage. Cross a lane and continue along the right side of the green for 200 yards until, just beyond Merlewood House, you turn right **D** into another open field. Now follow the wall on the right, down to a lane. Turning left in the lane, you come to a busy road junction, where you should use the pedestrian islands to reach the far pavement and follow it to the right to cross Walton Bridge. On the south side, take the steps on the left leading down to a path that doubles back to join the towpath **E**.

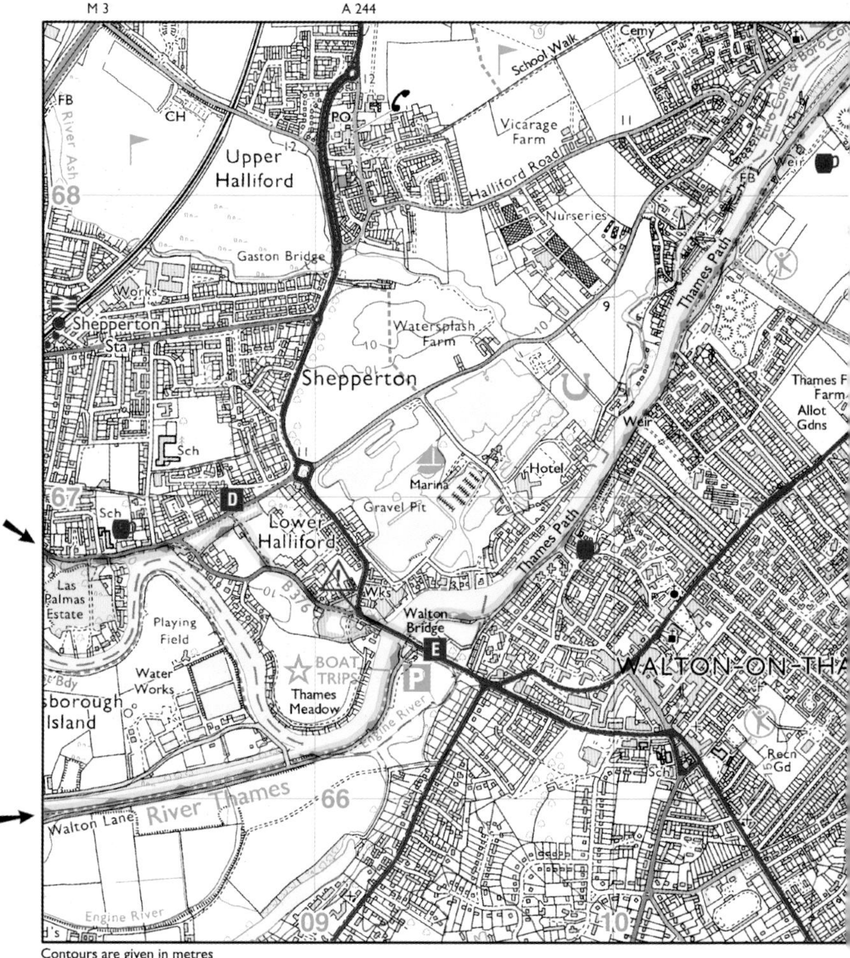

Contours are given in metres
The vertical interval is 5m

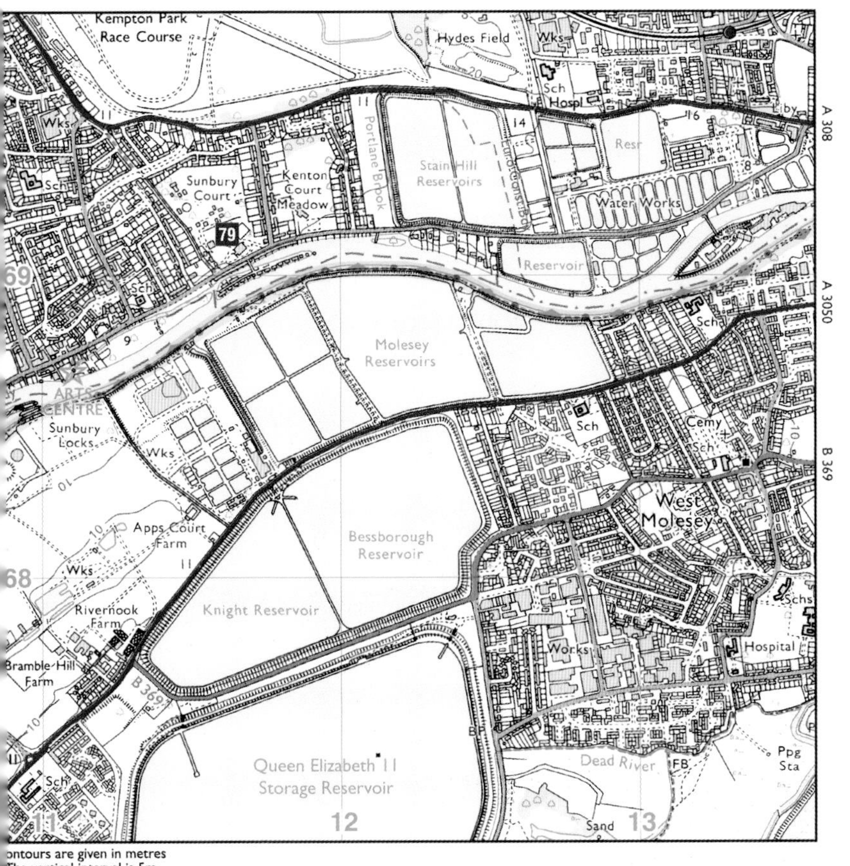

ontours are given in metres
The vertical interval is 5m

Beyond Walton Bridge, the broad track soon continues, over a marina entry and past a couple of riverside pubs. Then comes the big, factory-like block of Elmbridge Leisure Centre, which has a useful public cafeteria. Ahead now is Sunbury Weir and, visible beyond it, the tower and cupola of Sunbury Church. You then pass the original lock house, with 1812 inscribed on its facia tablet. The original lock stood here, but today's Sunbury Locks, two of them side by side, are further downstream.

Along the next stretch, the path is overshadowed by the walls and banks of the Molesey reservoirs, a claustrophobic walk. Some way along, you will glimpse a fine house across the river **79**: Sunbury Court, of around 1770, partly hidden by the bungalows on the island in front. Hereabouts too, you will walk between great concrete blocks, remains of London's anti-tank defences. When the

From the open grass of Hurst Park, the view across the Thames is to the tree-framed early Victorian church of riverside Hampton.

reservoirs end, you will find yourself walking along a gradually widening grass strip – once part of Hurst Park Racecourse.

Across the river is the narrow tower of Hampton Church, built in 1831, and just beyond it, best seen if you walk past Garrick's Ait and look back, is the little domed temple **80** that the actor David Garrick had built opposite his villa to house a statue of Shakespeare. Garrick himself is said to have modelled for the statue. On our own bank, the proclaimed 'swan feeding area' is clearly successful, attracting not only swans, but ducks, Canada geese and pigeons, which feed in amiable family groups.

Several more islands follow, the longest hosting an impressive array of palatial houseboats. Continue now to Molesey Lock, which has public toilets to the right. Just beyond it, there is a gravel path near the riverside, which curves up to the road just before Hampton Court Bridge. *Hampton Court station is across the road to your right here.* Cross the bridge to the north bank, then take the pedestrian crossing to the gates of Hampton Court **81**, and walk back to take the broad track between river and palace.

In such regal surroundings, 'towpath' is too plebian a title, so this next stretch is the Barge Walk, which provides good views of the palace. First comes the drive, with its terrace of 'grace and favour' residences; then the Tudor front of the great house of Cardinal Wolsey's time, the entrance gate flanked by reproductions of the King's Beasts. A little further on, you pass the Banqueting House from William III's reign, which stands out a little from the boundary wall. Then you find yourself looking through panels of the superb 18th-century screen by Tijou into the restored privy garden. Beyond it, the south wing was designed for William by Sir Christopher Wren. After passing the semicircle of garden terrace, you can take to the pedestrian path nearer the river, and follow it around the great curve of the

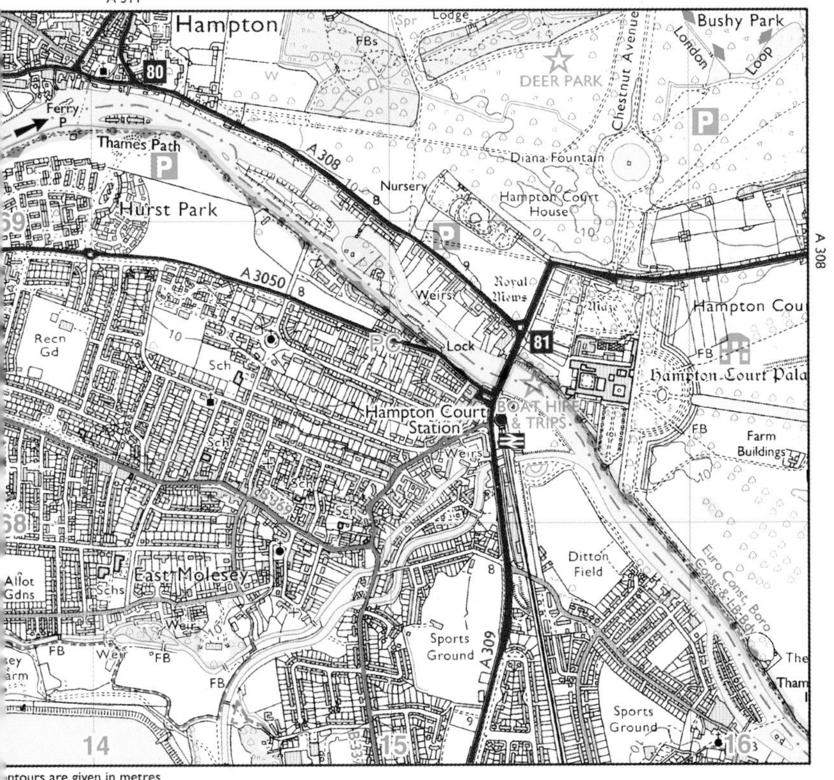

ntours are given in metres
'he vertical interval is 5m

Thames until Kingston Bridge comes into view. Just before the bridge, join the road sloping up to the bridge approach, and cross on the upstream pavement to the Kingston side. *For Hampton Wick station, do not cross the bridge but go over the road and ahead up the High Street.*

Immediately on reaching the south bank over Kingston Bridge, turn down the steps **F** that seem to be taking you into the river; but turn at the last moment onto the promenade. Continue under the bridge. Here there are pubs and restaurants along the riverside. Follow the walkway along the river frontage of the John Lewis store, past Turk's Pier, under the railway bridge and on through the tree-lined Canbury Gardens. The great bulk of Kingston Power Station, with its landmark chimneys, once loomed over these gardens, but all has been demolished. The Boaters Inn here has public toilets inside.

The gardens end at a road **G**, where it is best to cross and take a raised pathway, as there is no pavement on the river side. At the 'Half Mile Tree', the towpath begins again **H**, and soon crosses the boundary into Richmond. Across the Thames, the long run of Teddington Weir begins, leading to the footbridge **82** over to the Teddington bank, a solid, girder affair over the lock cut, but a graceful suspension bridge over the weir stream. *For Teddington station, cross here and walk ahead, over traffic lights and on through the shops to turn left down Station Road.*

The Thames Path passes the rambling Tudor frontage of Hampton Court Palace.

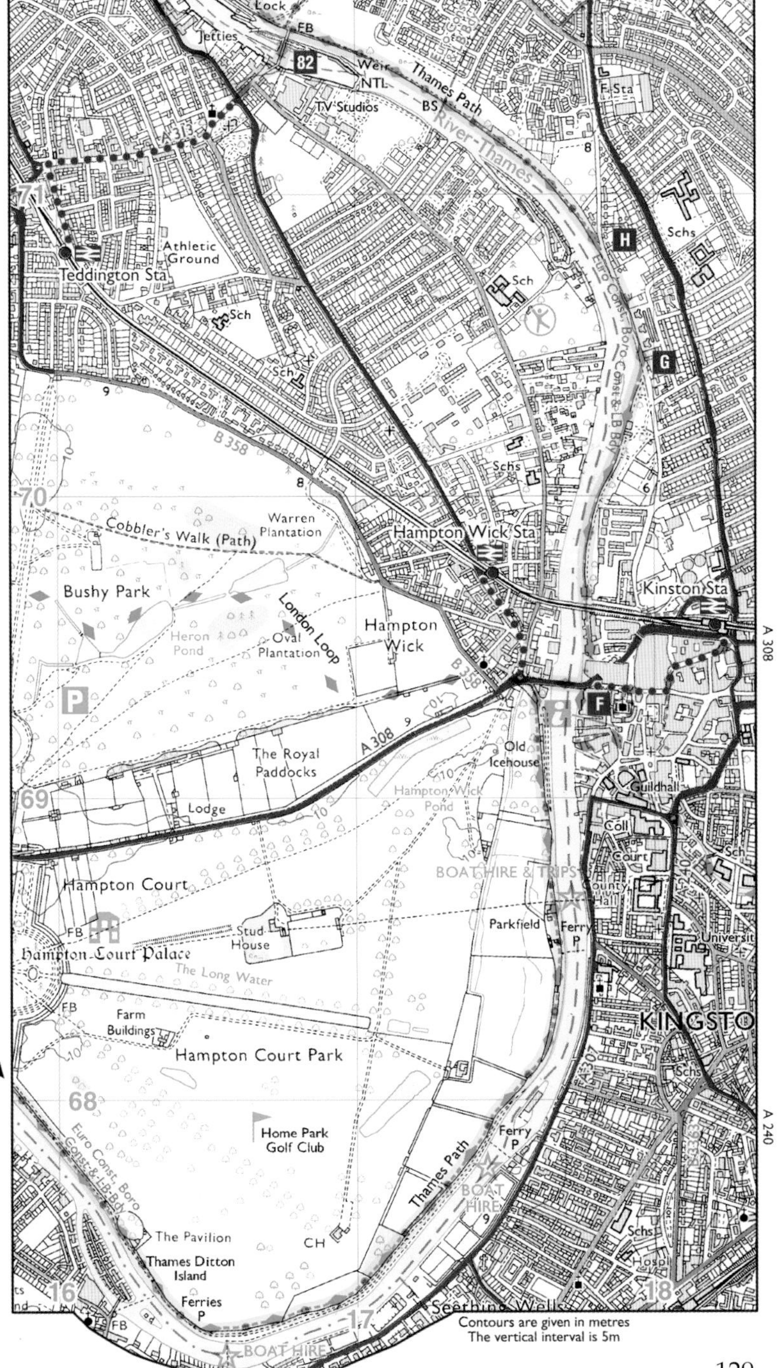
A 307 Richmond
3 km or 2 miles
A 310
Teddington Lock
Jetties
FB
Weir
NTL
Thames Path
TV Studios
BS
River Thames
F Sta
A 313
Teddington Sta
Athletic Ground
Sch
Schs
Euro Const, Boro Const & LB Bdy
B 358
Cobbler's Walk (Path)
Warren Plantation
Hampton Wick Sta
Kinston Sta
Bushy Park
London Loop
Heron Pond
Oval Plantation
Hampton Wick
A 308
The Royal Paddocks
Old Icehouse
Hampton Wick Pond
Lodge
Guildhall
Coll
Court
County Hall
BOAT HIRE & TRIPS
Hampton Court
Stud House
Parkfield
Ferry
Hampton Court Palace
The Long Water
Farm Buildings
Hampton Court Park
KINGSTO
Home Park Golf Club
Thames Path
BOAT HIRE
The Pavilion
Thames Ditton Island
CH
Hospl
Ferries
Seething Wells
A 240
Contours are given in metres
The vertical interval is 5m

13 Teddington to Putney

Transport Options

From Teddington Lock to Richmond Bridge is a 3½-mile (5.6-km), north bank, 2¾ -mile (4.4-km), south bank, stroll, connecting there with National Rail and Underground services from Richmond station. From Richmond, Kew Bridge National Rail station is another 4 miles (6.4 km) along the north bank, or 3 miles (4.8 km) along the south bank. From Kew Bridge, it is another 6¾ miles (10.9 km), north, 5¾ miles (9.3 km), south, to Putney Bridge, where there are British Rail, Underground and bus connections. On the way you pass Barnes Bridge National Rail station and Hammersmith Broadway, with its Underground services, after 2¾ miles (4.4 km), north, 4 miles (6.4 km), south, and 4¾ miles (7.6 km), north, 4 miles (6.4 km), south, respectively.

NORTH BANK

14 miles (22.5 km)

From the Teddington Lock footbridge **82**, the Thames Path continues up Ferry Road **A**, turning right at the crossroads into Manor Road **B**. During daylight hours there is an alternative path you can take here, turning right through a small gate opposite The Tide End Cottage pub, then right again beside a wooden boatshed, down a slipway and left along the riverside. Further gates lead into a tiny public garden. Turn up left, then take the path sharp right into a new development, and thus briefly back to the riverside. Beyond the Wharf restaurant you must turn up to join Manor Road and the Thames Path route.

You now have a mile (1.6 km) of road to walk to Twickenham, so either stride it out or consider using the fairly frequent bus service to the King Street shops. If you are walking, Radnor Gardens offer just one glimpse of the Thames. Beyond a mini-roundabout, go through gates into the gardens, and pass a bowling green to take the riverside path. From here, you see Twickenham Church tower and Eel Pie Island ahead, where your true river walk starts. Nearby is an odd, chalet-like building on the site of Pope's Villa, now a school. The path returns to the road, now Cross Deep **C**, which continues on to the shops and traffic lights of Twickenham.

SOUTH BANK

11½ miles (18.5 km)

As you walk the towpath from Teddington footbridge **82** towards the locks, you have a panoramic view of this elaborate locking system – the biggest on the Thames. From left to right, first you see the seldom-used boat rollers, then the little skiff lock, sometimes called the coffin lock, presumably because that is how you feel if you are in it. Then comes the launch lock, and finally, along the near bank, the barge lock, 650 feet (198 metres) long, designed to take a steam tug and six barges.

Beyond Teddington Locks, the path is broad and rural, a delightfully natural riverbank with willows drooping over gravel beaches, while, to your right, is the greenery of Ham Lands. Soon, on the riverside, you pass the obelisk erected in 1909 to mark the boundary between Thames Conservancy and Port of London Authority jurisdiction. Then, you cross the lock entry into the Thames Young Mariners water **93**. Ham Lands lie to either side, and earlier this century most of this area was quarried for gravel, with this big, man-made lagoon

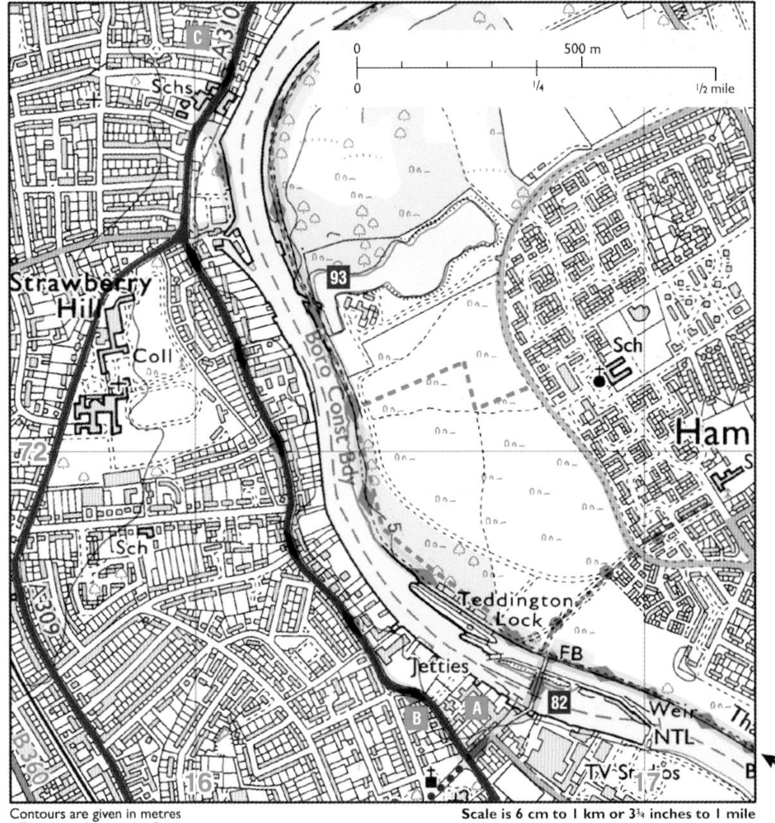

Contours are given in metres
The vertical interval is 5m

Scale is 6 cm to 1 km or $3\frac{3}{4}$ inches to 1 mile from this page onwards

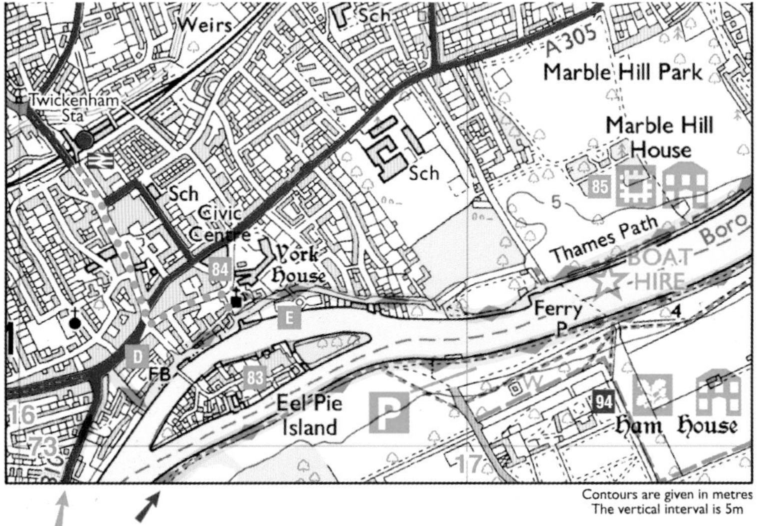

Just beyond the lights, turn right down Wharf Lane **D** and take to the riverside promenade. Thames-side Twickenham retains some fine 17th- and 18th-century houses, and a pub now restored to its familiar name – The Barmy Arms. A plate on a wall offers several theories about the name, while the sign offers an appropriate coat of arms. The footbridge here leads to the exclusive little community of studios and workshops on Eel Pie Island **83**, a name from Victorian days, when crowds came by steamer to partake of ale and the local pies on what was then a popular day trip. Coming to a slipway, the cobbled lane on the left leads to the foot of Church Street, a happily restored village street of small shops. *For Twickenham station, turn left up Church Street, cross the road junction at the pedestrian crossings and walk down London Road.* The church of St Mary **84** has a bold box of a nave with porticos, built in 1714 after the original had collapsed – all tacked on to a 15th-century tower, an odd combination.

Your walk continues via the old, walled lane to the riverside of the churchyard, but linger for a while: there is something rather unexpected here. Enter the little garden area between the lane and the Thames, and go through a gate in the wall on the left which leads onto York House terrace, where, some 40 yards further along, a gate on the left leads to an exotic scene: seven shapely nymphs reclining on the rocks around a fountain, while above them Venus herself rides seahorses. The Indian tycoon Sir Ratan Tata had this seductive scene created while living at York House. Having admired this sight, retrace your steps to the lane, Riverside **E**, and follow it past the fine Dial House, under the footbridge linking the grounds of York House with the river, and on past The White Swan. Just before the inn, be sure to look to the left up the elegant, Georgian terrace of Syon Row.

Round more bends, Riverside comes to Orleans Gardens on the right, where you can turn in and take the path to the Thames. But note that just 100 yards further along Riverside is the entrance to Orleans Gallery, the Octagon Room that survives from Orleans House, presented to Richmond council in 1962 and now a venue for free art exhibitions. As you leave the gardens, you can catch just one glimpse of Ham House in the trees across the river. Then, carry on along the broad promenade, which, before long, passes Hammerton's Ferry, where a reliable service crosses to the south bank, should you need it.

The open grass on the left now is Marble Hill Park, and soon you see, across its lawns, the little white 'dolls house' of Marble Hill **85**. It was built in 1723 for Henrietta Howard, mistress of the future George II – reputedly putting a £12,000 gift to practical use. Beyond the house, a gate gives access to

serving to load barges. Then, in the early 1960s, the quarries were filled in with rubble from London's bomb sites, bringing a rare variety of soils and plant seeds, and creating a very rich plant habitat, which recently recorded 230 species. There are paths along Ham Lands just above the towpath if you want to get the feel of this fascinating area.

Just beyond the car park by the river, an opened-up vista to Ham House **94** has restored its relationship with the Thames. From his proud place in the forecourt, *Old Father Thames* must delight in being able, once again, to see his river sweeping by. We can thank the Dysarts, the Lauderdales, and, more recently, the National Trust, for the lingering magnificence of the house and its collection of 17th-century furniture and decor. Even the gardens have been restored to the formal pattern of paths and clipped hedges of the period. After another 150 yards, you pass the landing steps of Hammerton's Ferry, which runs a regular service to the other bank. Then comes a view across to the exquisite little white villa of Marble Hill.

the park and the Coach House café. From here on, the view across the river is of Richmond Hill, dominated by the Star & Garter home looking, from its heights, out over the open vista of Petersham Meadows – one of the classic Thames views.

Coming to Richmond Bridge, turn up to the left and cross the road at the traffic lights to take the road opposite, which leads to Ducks Walk **F**. *For Richmond station, cross the bridge, turn left at a road junction, then bear right through the shops.* Soon, you are on a paved path, Ducks Walk; continue under railway and road bridges, then by a road towards what appears to be a cream and green bridge across the Thames. This is Richmond Lock **86**, a 'half-tide' lock where the weirs are usually opened for two hours either side of high water, leaving the Thames tidal up to Teddington. It carries a footbridge to the south bank and Old Deer Park.

Coming to a landing slipway, River Lane leads, to the right, up to Petersham. The fine houses of the village are overwhelmed by heavy traffic, but Petersham Church **95** is well worth a visit. To get there, turn right up River Lane, and take the footpath on the left just beyond the Old Stables. The church interior is rather special – near perfect 18th century, with galleries and box pews. It is usually locked, but there are keys at nearby addresses, and a helpful sign guides pilgrims from Canada to the grave of George Vancouver by the churchyard wall.

From River Lane, walk on by Petersham Meadows, where you may still see cows grazing. Despite the concrete flood wall, the Thames is regularly allowed to flood these water-meadows in the traditional way. As the meadows end, your path briefly leaves the riverside (where there are toilets), then passes a three-arch grotto, which provides a useful underpass into Terrace Gardens – should you want to climb Richmond Hill for the view. Then, beyond Richmond Bridge, you enter the newish waterfront **96** opened by the Queen in 1988. Architect Quinlan Terry combined old and new in a striking composition that seems appropriate to the setting. The steps at the end lead up to the Old Town Hall, where there are an information office and more toilets. *For Richmond station, walk under the bridge and up the steps on the right to road level. Walk forward to the road junction, then left through the* *shops, bearing right along George Street, then left again into the Quadrant.*

Follow the cobbled lane past The White Cross pub; you will soon glimpse the elegant portico of the Trumpeters House of 1701, a lovely composition of lawns framed by trees. Then comes the Palladian Asgill House of 1758. The best of Richmond is just to the right; indeed, hereabouts was the river frontage of the royal palace of Shene. Henry VII built his own Richmond Palace on the ruins of Shene, and the traces that remain can be found by taking a detour up the lane by Asgill House, and then following the drive to the right to Old Palace Yard, just beyond The White Swan. Trumpeters Inn on your right is a charming, modern pastiche, but ahead is a little oval of green with, to the left, the palace gateway to Richmond Green **97.** Ahead is the

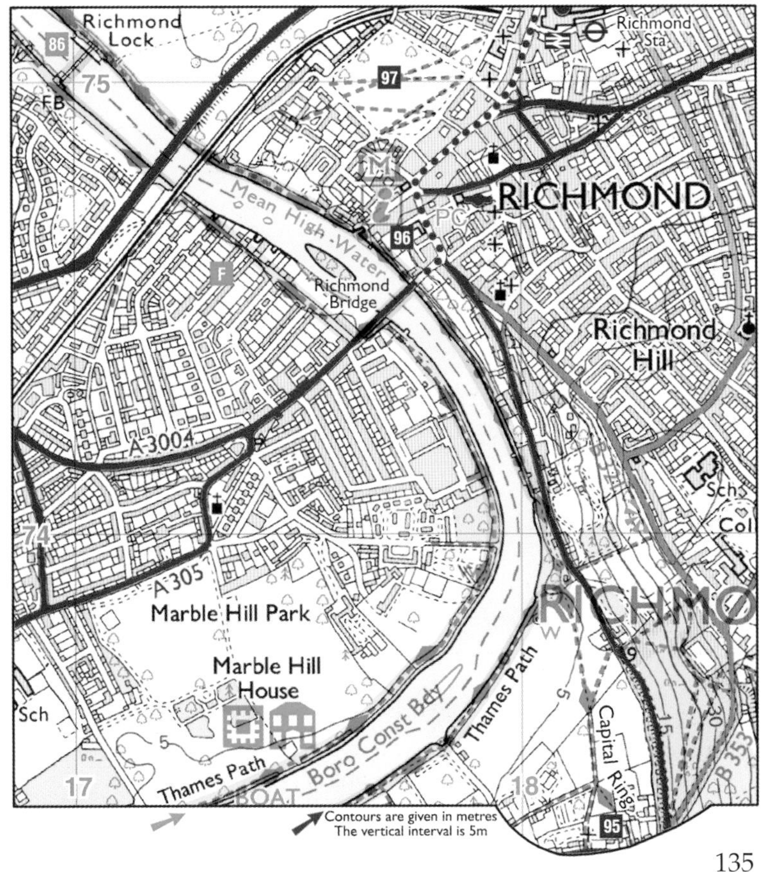

Walk on by a paved path again. Ahead, you can see the flotilla of houseboats and barge conversions moored at Railshead, and Isleworth Ait beyond. Turn up to a main road, bear right over the River Crane, then pass the entrance to Nazareth House, a convent home. Carry on another 40 yards, then turn down Lion Wharf Road **G** to the river. The 'Riverside Walk', signed to the right goes nowhere, so turn left, walk along the riverside past a big, weatherboarded pub, and carry on over a little footbridge with a fine view of the Isleworth riverfront ahead. The walkway goes round a big, preserved crane, continuing by footbridge over the Duke of Northumberland's River, then briefly turning left by the river before turning right into a passage leading through the housing of Bridge Wharf, and again left to the road through their archway. A right turn in the road brings you to The London Apprentice and the attractive houses of Old Isleworth.

The Isleworth Ferry to the Richmond bank runs here at the weekends, from May to September. Keep to the riverside, which just retains a pavement, then by the road, which turns away from the river, to turn right through the gates into Syon Park. Isleworth Church **87** on the corner was gutted by fire in 1943, not a war victim but the target of two schoolboys with a box of matches. A modern church has been built onto the surviving 14th-century tower. Once in Syon Park, you will see a path over the grass that parallels the road, taking you on to the twin lodges that frame the view of Syon House **88**. A Tudor house was built here on the rectangular plan of the original nunnery, but now you see it stone-faced, with superb interiors remodelled by Robert Adam. It still belongs to the Northumberland family, and their stone lion can just be seen on the roof.

warm – and obviously Tudor – decorative brickwork of The Wardrobe. The Tudors seem to have been very fond of their palace at Richmond, and Elizabeth I died here in 1603.

The path continues by the river under railway and road bridges. The open grass to the right is Old Deer Park, now playing fields and a golf course. The two stone obelisks near the river are markers along the meridian line through the Kew Observatory **98** – the white building you may just glimpse through the trees. George III built it to indulge his hobby of astronomy, and to house his collection of timepieces. Beyond Richmond Lock, the walk is remarkably green again, the towpath virtually a causeway, with the Thames to one side and a verdant ditch to the other. As the wooded Isleworth Ait ends, a fine view to Old Isleworth opens up. Just beyond, you see a little white 'temple' that is actually one of the lodges of Syon Park.

Along the Syon reach you are looking across to a rare, preserved habitat, a tide meadow that is flooded twice a day. Then Syon House comes into view, and an open vista into

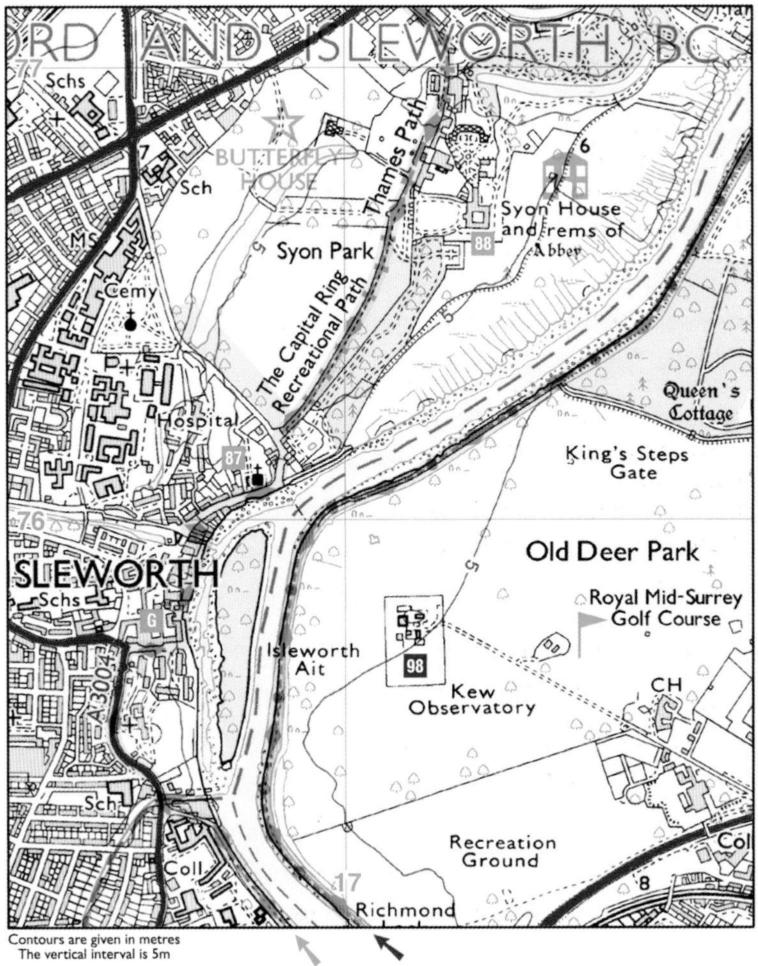

Contours are given in metres
The vertical interval is 5m

Walk on, keeping car parks to your left, past the garden centre, the coffee shop and toilets, eventually to follow a walled path that curves up to Brentford High Street **H**. Turn right now, and after 250 yards cross the Grand Union Canal. A little further on, turn right into The Ham **I**, a sadly neglected little lane that must once have been busy with canal affairs; indeed one building you pass was a school for canal children. It takes you under a one-time railway bridge, beyond which you go over the steps ahead to rejoin the towpath, which soon crosses the canal by a footbridge. Once over it, turn sharply back left and down the steps to the towpath again. Pass the two Thames locks and climb the concrete steps up to road level. At this spot, William Jessop's Grand Junction Canal entered the Thames. In its prosperous days it provided a vital highway for trade up to Braunston on the Oxford Canal, and thus on to Birmingham. Cross over the canal, and follow Dock Road **J** up to the High Street again noting the superb fan patterns in the cobbles beneath your feet.

Turn right along Brentford High Street for just 75 yards, then go right on an enclosed path which soon gives views to a muddy dock inlet. Turning left it takes a promenade past new apartments to reach the Thames. At a wide paved area you detour around the Ferry Quays inlet and continue past further apartments, finally turning left up Goat Wharf to rejoin Brentford High Street. Turn right and in 150 yards go down the wide-spaced steps towards the river – Smith Hill **K**. Go through a blue barrier on your left, then right down a paved path to the walkway on the river side of some offices. Circle up the steps to the higher terrace of the Watermans Art Centre, where a cafeteria and bar is often open; then carry on along Watermans Park to its end. To your left is the tower of Kew Bridge Steam Museum, where the star turns are the vast engines that once pumped west London's water supply.

Where the park ends, you return briefly to the road, only to turn right after a few paces, down Victoria Steps. Nearing the water's edge, a slope leads leftwards up to a new walkway. This takes you on to The Hollows, a leafy, secret little path lined with houseboats. As you come to Kew Bridge, your path goes under an arch of the bridge, up the steps on the other side, then alongside the bridge approach up to a road. *Kew Bridge station is just across the busy road junction from here.*

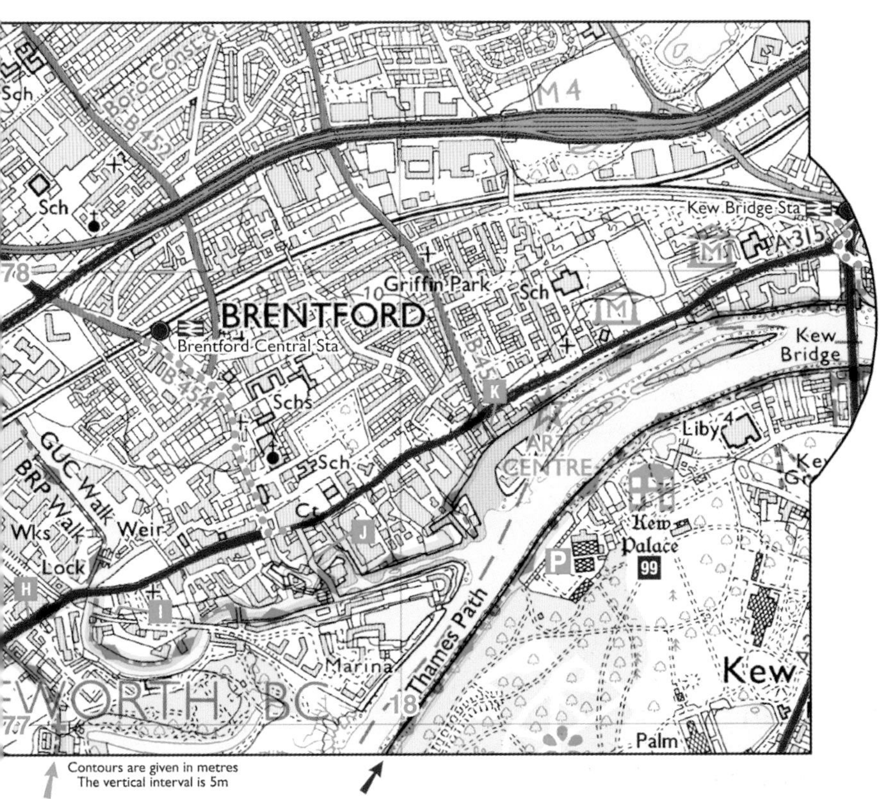

Kew Gardens. Only the tower blocks of Brentford ahead remind you that you are deep into London. Across the river, a couple of barges on the mud, a leaning shed, and an overgrown quayside are the last reminders of the once-busy Brentford Docks, where Grand Union Canal and Thames traffic met. Ahead, beyond a car park, you are looking over a wall to the red brick of Kew Palace **99**, often called the 'Dutch House' because of its gabled roofs. The date 1631 is over the entrance, and royalty lived here until 1818. Now it stands in Kew Gardens. This unique 300-acre (121-hectare) garden, with its 40,000 plant species, needs a day at least to do it justice. To visit the Gardens take the riverside entrance, just to your right, by the car park.

Kew Bridge is ahead now. For Kew Bridge station, go down the steps just before it, then up further steps to cross the bridge. The station is just across the road junction on the north side.

When you come to the road, turn back to the Thames and walk along either its pavement or the riverside garden strips, bearing right on a path signed to Strand on the Green **89**. This miraculously preserved riverside community of houses and one-time fishermen's cottages looks to the Thames over a modest, willow-shaded path. Of special note here are Zoffany House, where the painter John Zoffany RA lived for 30 years; the Dutch House, with its characteristic gables and shutters; and almshouses dating from 1724 – plain but with tiny gardens that are ablaze with colour in summer. Three popular pubs will also tempt you before the path finally comes up to a road.

Walk on along Grove Park Road **L**, bearing right into Hartington Road **M**, now with big houses between you and the river. You could walk straight on now for half a mile (800 metres), but the Thames Path allows one glimpse of the river at Chiswick Quay. Opposite Cavendish Road, turn right down the paved path **N** alongside the access road. When the road bends, keep straight ahead to a broad riverside terrace. Where it ends, cross the lock gates, go left for 40 yards, then right and immediately left to follow Ibis Lane back to Hartington Road again. Carry on now to the main road, where you turn right towards Chiswick Bridge. Here, just before the river **O**, take the steps leading down and under the bridge. You emerge onto the road following the riverside of the open Duke's Meadows, but take the first opportunity to leave it for a newly surfaced footpath nearer the Thames.

Across the river now is the preserved block of Mortlake Brewery, and the tower and bell turret of St Mary's Church, Mortlake. At Chiswick Boathouse turn up through their car park to rejoin the road, following it round several bends, away from the river. Around the third bend, notice the viewing platform on the right for Duke's Hollow Nature Reserve, an unusual wetland environment around the foot of Barnes railway

As you walk under the bridge and past Kew Pier on a wide, gravel path, the view across the river is of the delectable cottages of Strand on the Green. Then there is nothing of further consequence until, walking under Chiswick Bridge, you come to Thames Bank, a fragment of Mortlake riverside with a few houses and The Ship Inn beneath the solid eight-storey block of

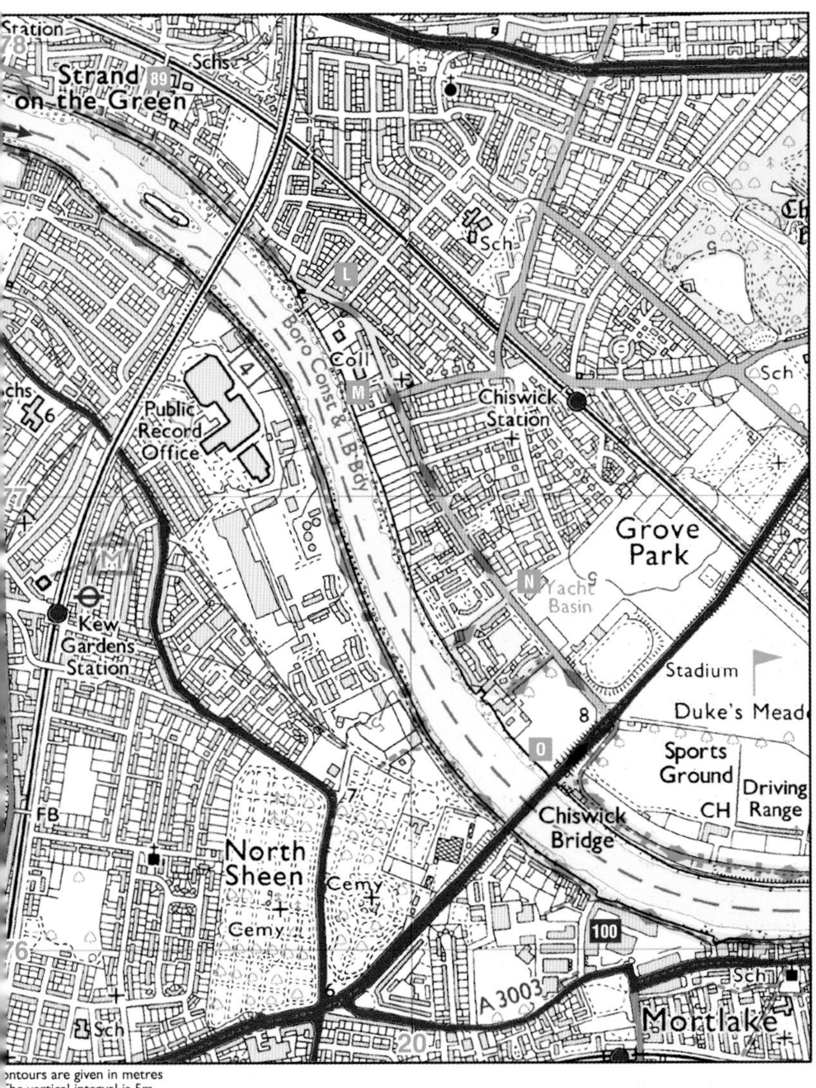

ontours are given in metres
he vertical interval is 5m

old Mortlake brewery **100**. Despite rebuilding, the main building and the riverside walls have been preserved, the cobbled quay and rail tracks beneath your feet retaining a little of the character of old industry. This narrow length of Mortlake towpath often floods, but there are several ways up to Mortlake High Street and back to get around any problems.

bridge. Continue ahead and turn right through the tunnel under the railway, then right again along the road. When it goes left, keep ahead on a footpath and turn left at the riverside to go in front of a boathouse. *For Barnes Bridge station turn right instead to cross the river by footbridge.*

As soon as the road comes to open grass, leave it for a path along the riverside, which passes a forlorn bandstand that seems to have lost its way to the seaside. Keep by the river, briefly joining a metalled cycleway before branching off to go through the wall of new housing, and onto the river terrace. This walkway ends opposite Chiswick Church **90**, with views ahead to Chiswick Ayot and distant Hammersmith Mall.

Turn left to the foot of Church Street **P**, a spot at which to linger. It has several fine houses, especially the Old Burlington, a one-time pub established in the 15th century. Go up the steps into the churchyard of St Nicholas, and a few yards to the left, behind railings, you will find the tomb of William Hogarth.

The Thames Path now follows the pavements past the elegant houses of Chiswick Mall, then a tiny boundary stone outside Cedar House **Q** tells you that you have entered Hammersmith. Briefly, you now part with the river along Hammersmith Terrace **91**, which is favoured with three blue plaques. Of special note is that on the fifth house, where Sir Alan Herbert, 'author, humorist and reformist MP', lived and died by his beloved Thames. When the Terrace ends, return to

Beneath the railway bridge ahead, you pass Barnes Bridge station. Then comes the best of Barnes Terrace: 18th- and 19th-century villas with a happy, 'seaside' feel about their bow windows and balconies. One carries a blue plaque to record that the composer Gustav Holst lived here in 1908, while a second reminds us of Dame Ninette de Valois, creator of the Royal Ballet. Beyond the Terrace, Barnes High Street leads to the green, pond and common – a true village centre deep in London **101**. Not long after the towpath leaves the road, the greenery to your right hides a surprising scene: an ex-reservoir, decommissioned in 1960 and now reclaimed by nature as a local reserve. Gates lead to a path along the waterside – a change from the towpath. Around the Boat Race bend of the Thames, with Hammersmith Bridge coming into view, all the buildings and playing fields of St Paul's Boys' School stand on filled-in reservoirs.

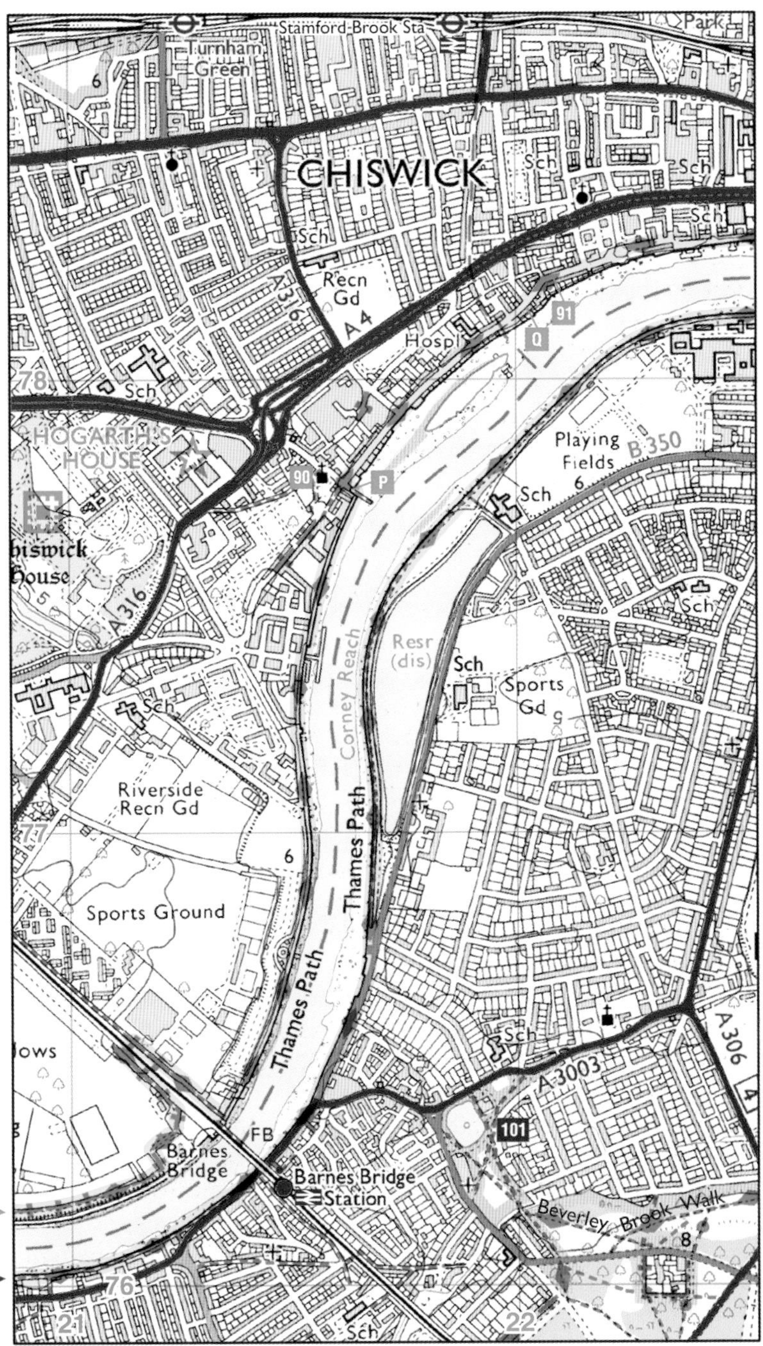

Contours are given in metres
The vertical interval is 5m

the riverside walkway. When Upper Mall ends, a narrow passage, where the famous Dove pub hangs its sign, leads out onto Lower Mall. But, just before the passage, you pass Kelmscott House, where William Morris spent his last years with his printing and design works. He named it after the lovely Oxfordshire manor house you may have passed, way up the Thames, near Lechlade. Cross Furnivall Gardens and continue along the Mall to Hammersmith Bridge.

Walk under the bridge – Sir Joseph Bazalgette's ornate and much-repaired masterpiece. *For transport, turn up left beyond the bridge and walk ahead on the new St Paul's Green walkway, under the flyover. The big block beyond the tower of Hammersmith Church contains both Underground and bus stations.*

Beyond the tiny garden area, turn left away from the river, then right into Crisp Road. Pass the Riverside Studios, an arts centre with a bar and cafeteria which are often open, then immediately right on a walkway that returns you to the riverside again. Now the twin cupolas of Harrod's Depository – a favourite landmark for Boat Race commentators – are in prominent view. Following the river again, a white wall necessitates a brief diversion inland to find the walkway continuing as a fenced path. It crosses the river frontage of Thames Reach, a bravura modern concept of glass and tubular steel. Thames Wharf comes next, then the Richard Rogers' offices, crowned with a giant, curved roof, like a vast, high-tech Nissen hut.

Again you have to leave the river to divert round Palace Wharf and The Crabtree Tavern. Go under the 'rustic arches' of a path **R** just beyond the tavern's garden, and take the narrow path ahead. Carry on beyond a big, iron 'doorknob', then up and down steps to regain the riverside path. Your path continues, pleasant, green and uninterrupted until Fulham Football Club blocks the way. By the club's gates, turn left into Stevenage Road **S**, then pass the stadium frontage, a rather fine, red-brick façade with 'FFC' and 'est 1880' inscribed on plaques. Once past the stadium, turn into Bishops Park, walk directly to the Thames and take to the riverside terrace.

Immediately, you meet the great plane trees of the park, which first line the terrace and, further on, form a stately avenue. Soon, you pass boating lakes, then a play area, aviary

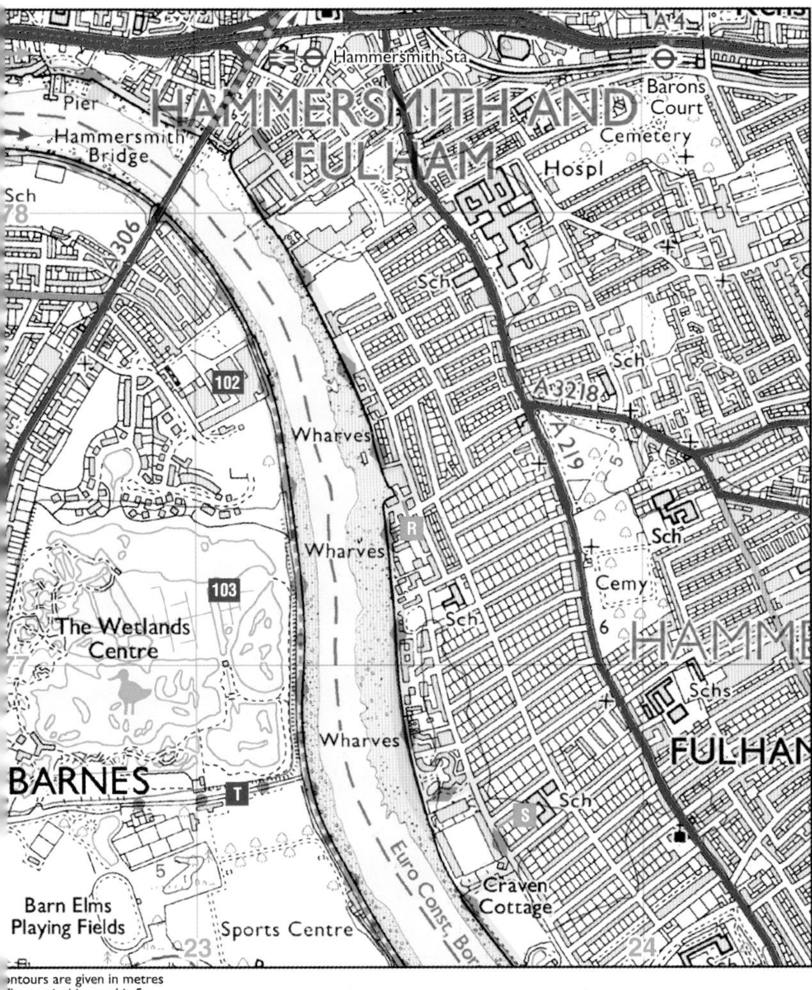

For Hammersmith station, turn up and cross Hammersmith Bridge, then walk ahead under the flyover. The big office block beyond Hammersmith Church contains both Underground and bus stations.

Past Hammersmith Bridge, you are soon in the shadow of that landmark along the Boat Race course, Harrod's Depository **102**, the familiar façade preserved, even though it now fronts apartments. New housing follows, then the open greenery of the Wetlands Centre **103**, where the old reservoirs of Barn Elms have been magically transformed into a haven for some of the and café with nearby toilets. To visit Fulham Palace **92**, the Tudor residence of the Bishops of London, turn left up beyond the play area, and go out via the park gates, where you will see the stone gate pillars of the palace drive on your right. As you approach Putney Bridge, the riverside path passes a rose garden, then a little court with statues depicting *Adoration*, *Protection*, *Affection* and *Grief* surrounding a central fountain. Turn left to a point where you can either climb steps to the road, or take the tunnel under the bridge approach. *For Putney Bridge Underground station and buses, walk straight on beyond the tunnel and up Ranelagh Road. For Putney British Rail station climb the steps, cross the bridge and walk up through the shops.*

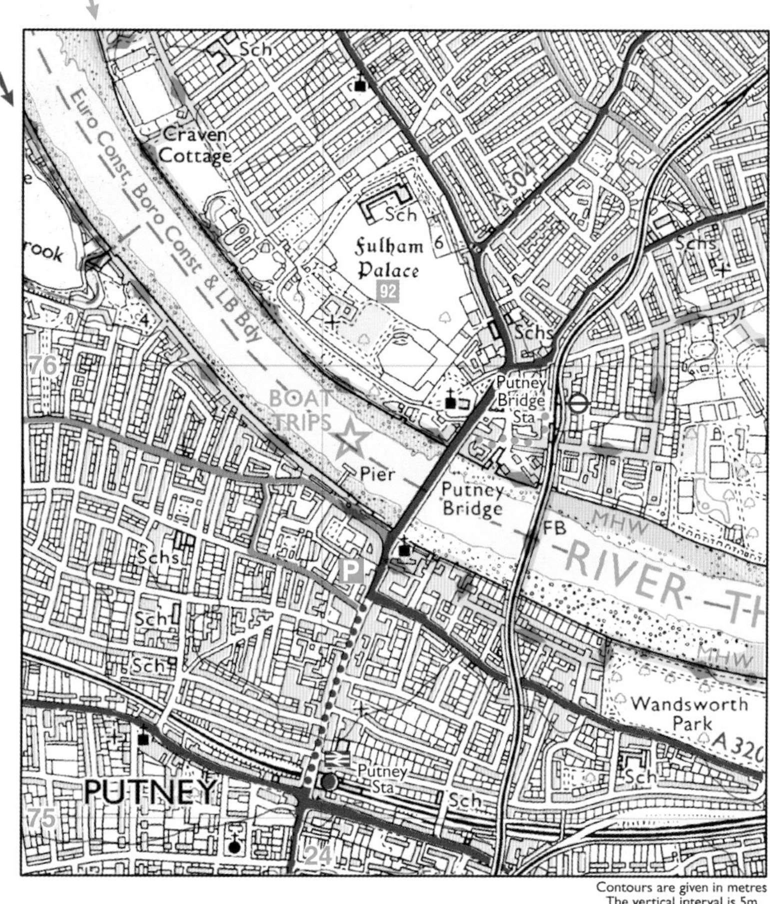

Contours are given in metres
The vertical interval is 5m

The five elegant arches of Richmond Bridge have spanned the Thames since 1777, when they replaced the ferry here.

world's rarest waterbirds. The entrance and visitor centre is on the right, up Queen Elizabeth Walk **T**, but be warned, you need a day to explore here. Crossing the Beverley Brook entry onto the Putney waterfront, you must bid farewell to the old towpath that has served you so well, all the way from Lechlade. As you walk on past rowing clubhouses, you will often find yourself dodging around crews persuading their craft into the water, a reminder that this is the starting point for the Oxford and Cambridge Boat Race. Then, by Putney Bridge, the barge-loading slipway still remains, where many a cargo was transshipped to begin its journey up the river. From here on, the Thames Path will offer a very different range of urban experiences. *For Putney British Rail station, turn right at the bridge, and walk up past the High Street shops. For Putney Bridge Underground station, cross the bridge and turn right.*

14 Putney to Tower Bridge

Transport Options

Numerous bus routes cross every road bridge along this section except Albert Bridge. The north bank route passes Westminster, Embankment, Temple and Blackfriars Underground stations, but the major transport centres are at Vauxhall Bridge after 6 miles (9.7 km), north, 6¾ miles (10.9 km), south, Waterloo and Charing Cross after another 1½ miles (2.4 km), and London Bridge after another 2 miles (3.2 km), north, 1½ miles (2.4 km), south. All offer Underground, National Rail and bus services.

NORTH BANK *10¼ miles (16.5 km)*

Just downstream of Putney Bridge on the north bank, a wide, paved area by the riverside provides the starting point for this stage of the Thames Path. Reach it either via a tunnel under the bridge approach road from Bishop's Park, or by the steps leading down from the road. By either route, go to the riverside and turn downstream, crossing a little dock inlet, and turning left when your way is blocked by the railway bridge. The path leads up to a road *with Putney Bridge station just ahead.*

Turn right to go under the railway arch, following Ranelagh Gardens **A** until, with the gates into the private Hurlingham Park grounds ahead, you must turn left into Napier Avenue **B**. At the top, go right for some 200 yards to gates on the right leading into the public part of Hurlingham Park, with open grass and playing fields. Go through the gates, walk forward a little way along the drive until a gap in the fence on the left allows you to set off diagonally across the playing fields. Walk near the white fence of the running track, then between pitches until you find a small gate leading into the distant road, some 75 yards short of the far corner of the park.

Bear right in the road, Broomhurst Lane **C**, and follow it back to the river. On the way, one building will surely catch

SOUTH BANK *10 miles (16.9 km)*

The towers of medieval parish churches stand on both banks by Putney Bridge, a sure sign that this was an ancient river crossing. For centuries, a ferry crossed, then a wooden toll bridge, and now Sir Joseph Bazalgette's bridge copes with the teeming London traffic. If you are coming up from Putney Embankment, your good friend the Thames towpath regretfully behind, take the pedestrian crossings over to the pavement by the tower of St Mary the Virgin, and turn up Putney High Street **P**. In just 50 yards you can turn left to circuit round the churchyard back to the river beneath a big tower block. Around a dock inlet and past The Boat House pub the promenade continues, turning up to the corner of Deodar Road **Q**. Left here, under a railway bridge. *A footbridge crosses the Thames here, linking with the north bank route and Putney Bridge station.* At the bottom, keep ahead through the arch of Blade Mews, then through the gate in the smaller arch into Wandsworth Park. Follow the avenues of plane trees along the riverside and enjoy the experience of green Thames-side while you can. Most of this day's walk will be very different – palaces, power stations, even a pagoda, but little greenery. The trees across the river belong to the exclusive Hurlingham Club.

When the park ends, keep on by the river through gates onto a new walkway. Beyond a pier, you have to turn right, keeping on up the road, Point Pleasant **R**, away from the Thames. Just

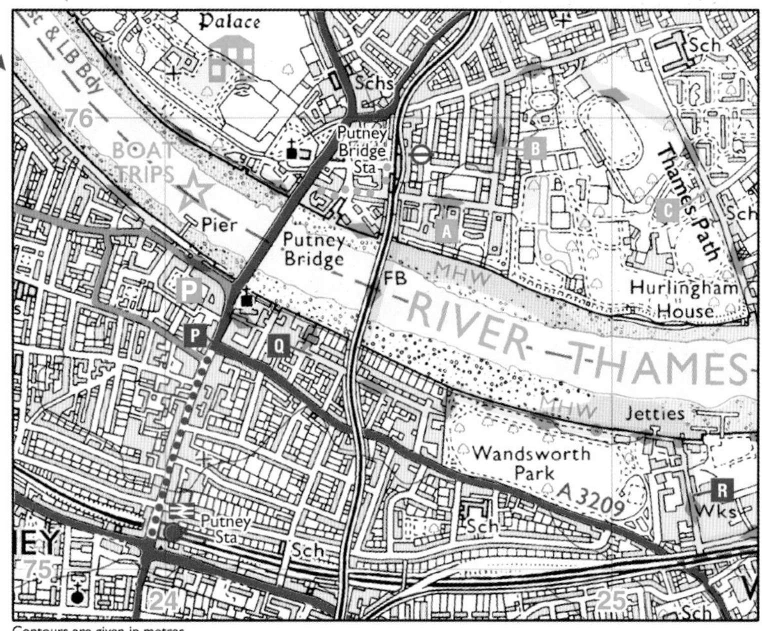

Contours are given in metres
The vertical interval is 5m

your eye, the picturesque 'castle' built, originally as a school, in a jolly, ornate Tudor style in the 1850s. At the corner, you are back on the Thames again, and you can walk ahead beside the old Broomhouse drawdock, now handsomely restored with a pier and boat moorings, onto a riverside walkway. After a while it rejoins the road, now Carnwath Road **D**, but just 150 yards further down, another walkway returns you to the riverside. The promenade here is a broad, sterile affair where the modest attempts at tree-planting do little to breathe life into the scene.

Walk past a Currys showroom and then continue up to Wandsworth Bridge, where you should turn left to join the road. Walk ahead to cross the bridge approach road at the traffic lights, and go down Townmead Road **E** which is opposite. When you reach a roundabout, bear sharp right across the Sainsbury's car park, which will bring you to their river walk beyond.

Turn left now to follow the river past the supermarket, then on past massive apartment blocks in rather aggressive red brick. Through gates, the walkway continues past the open

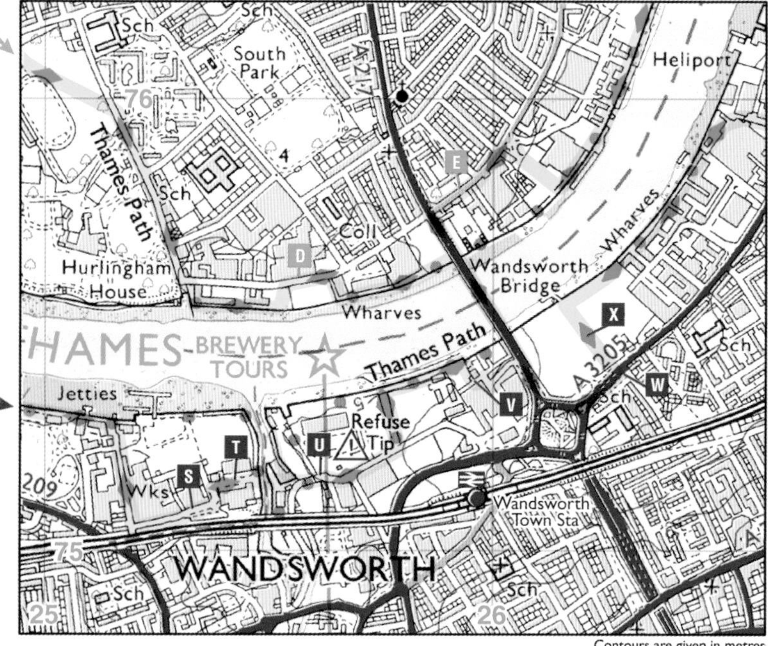

Contours are given in metres
The vertical interval is 5m

before the road goes under a railway bridge, turn left into Osiers Road **S**, bearing left with it, then right into Enterprise Way **T**. At its end, a footbridge takes you over Bell Lane Creek, one branch of the River Wandle, then ahead on a broad walk, The Causeway **U**, with views to Wandle Mouth and the tiny spit of land now restored as a wetland nature reserve. In its day, the Wandle was surely the busiest of all the Thames tributaries. A couple of centuries ago, the waters flowing in leisurely fashion beneath your feet drove over 90 mills along an 11-mile (17.5-km) tumble down from the source springs at Carshalton and Croydon. Ahead, through bollards, The Causeway joins a road that passes the big, red-brick, waste transfer station. This is a busy spot, so watch out for turning lorries.

Walk on past the recycling centre next door to find, rather to your surprise perhaps, a walkway on the left – pleasantly lined by new planting – leading to the river. By the river, you can see, to your left, the most dramatic stage in the waste transfer operation as great gantries lower rubbish containers into waiting barges. The intention is that the Thames Path will eventually go *over* this vast work area – the overhead walkway is already in place, but unfortunately it is not yet open. So, turn right towards Wandsworth Bridge, along Nickols Walk, a promenade where wasteland has been transformed by the vast new Riverside West development with its shops and piazzas. It all leads to The Ship Inn, with a tempting riveside garden. As you come to the pub, turn right over the cobbles and skirt around the buildings into Jews Row **V**. Follow Jews Row around right and left turns, up to the bridge approach road.

Turn right here and take the light-controlled crossing to follow the main road, York Road **W**, as it swings left (there are pedestrian subways a little further on). About 250 yards down York Road, turn left into Juniper Drive **X** and walk on via terraces and gardens back to a riverside walkway. On the right here, you'll note a raised tidal planting area on the river bank. Soon you are passing the impressive Plantation Wharf development, then the apartments on the site of the old Prices Candle Factory. Where the walkway ends, a path neatly defined by 'globe' lighting columns takes you back to the main road again. Bear left, and at the next set of traffic grass of a little 10.5 acre park **F** (this section may be closed after 11pm). Further gates lead onto Imperial Wharf, where The Boulevard greets you with waterfalls and planted beds – not to mention shops and a welcome pub. From here you can walk under the railway lines and out onto the river walk of Chelsea Harbour **104**, crossing the entry into the central marina by a bascule bridge. Until a few years ago, this area was derelict railway sidings around a disused canal basin. Now it stands as a complete up-market township grouped around the marina and the Belvedere Tower, completed in 1989. The moored cruisers have a fabulously expensive look, and there are cobbled paths around the water if you want to drool over them in close-up. But the Thames Path keeps by

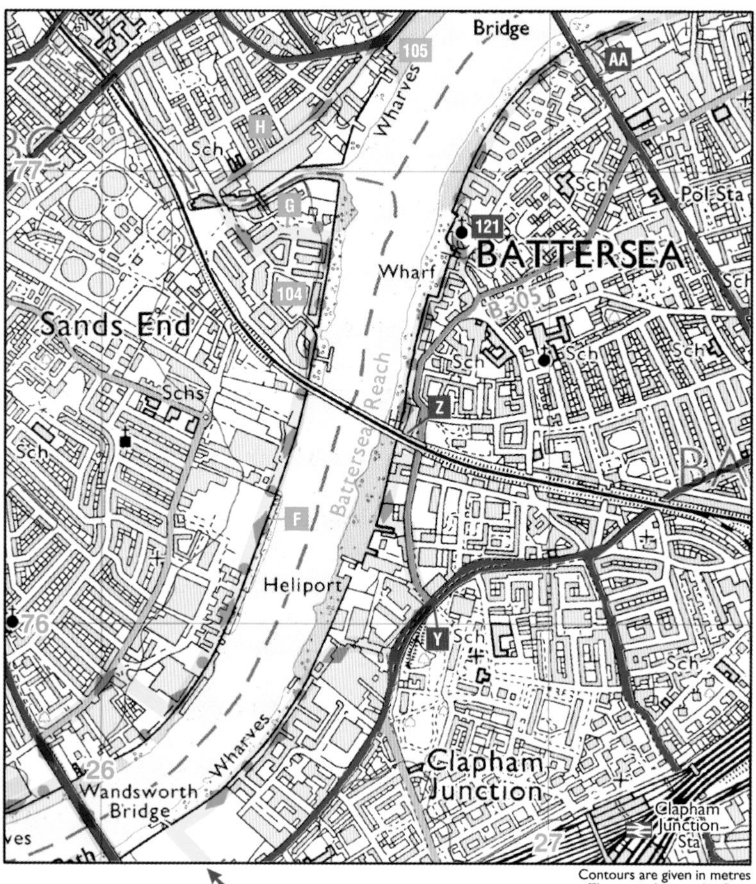

Contours are given in metres
The vertical interval is 5m

the river as far as it can, then finally turns left up a tiled way with the great slab side of Lots Road Power Station abruptly supplanting the lush images of Chelsea Harbour.

Keep ahead along Chelsea Harbour Drive **G**, which bends first left, then right, before leaving over the muddy inlet of Chelsea Creek. Turn right now to follow Lots Road **H**, which begins grimly in the shadow of the power station, but ends charmingly with a colourful terrace of Victorian cottages and then the tiny patch of Cremorne Gardens **105** on the river

lights **Y**, turn left to pass the Battersea Heliport then, immediately beyond the tall blue and glass tower block, a sign directs you briefly back to the riverside. Approaching the railway bridge you rejoin the road to go under it, and back to the riverside again **Z**.

The craft moored on the near bank sport flowerpots and other signs of domestic bliss, while across the river the excesses of Chelsea Harbour contrast with the solid, functional slab of Lots Road Power Station. The Thames Path has some contrasts to offer too, as it continues on, beneath flats, to an unexpected view: the simple little 18th-century church of St Mary, Battersea **121**, which, with neat spire and pillared portico, could easily be Dutch, and with a barge or two on the foreshore, offers a glimpse of a bygone riverside village.

Keep to the river side of a block of new housing, then cross the top of a drawdock and carry on through the gates into the churchyard. Take to the paved path beside the river wall, passing by several houseboats moored alongside, then through a gate onto the handsome Montevetro walkway and on to join an older riverside walk. As you approach Battersea Bridge, the walkway opens out onto a wider concourse with the sculpture *In Town* by John Ravera at its centre. Go up the slope to the bridge approach road, then cross, either directly or via the pedestrian crossing 150 yards to the right, and then down to another river walkway **AA**. On the corner are two swans caught forever at the moment of taking flight – an inspiring vision when the glass of their office backdrop reflects the image of a stormy sky. Take the slope down between the swans, and carry on over the broad new Albion Riverside promenade and over a narrow dock entry by a swing bridge. Albert Bridge is now up ahead.

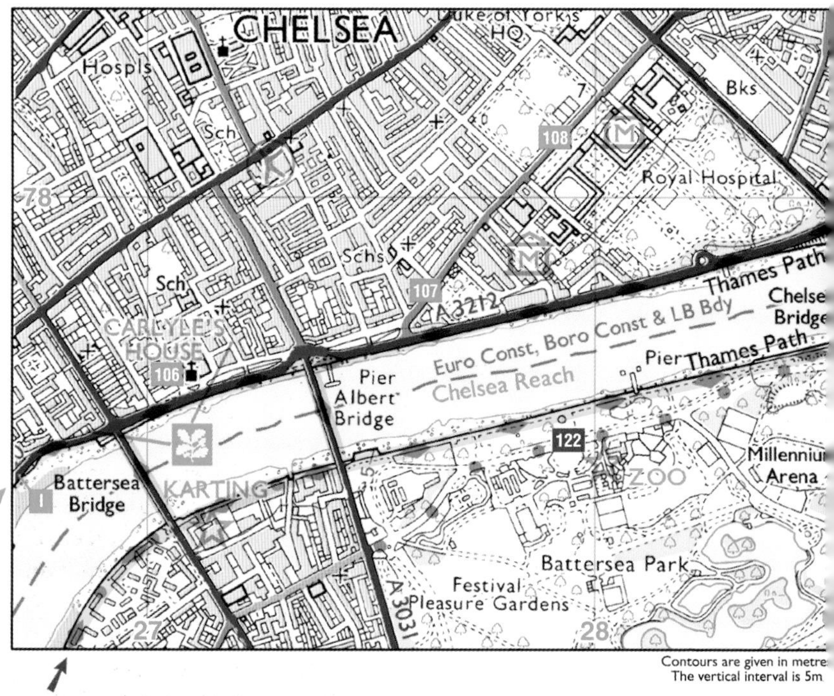

side. Here, the magnificent white gates to the pleasure gardens have been re-erected for you to admire. When the gardens closed in 1877, a local brewery, Bowden's, preserved them and finally returned them to the council for display.

You are now entering blue-plaque country – the famous Cheyne Walk **I** with terraces of the Queen Anne period or later, cruelly cut off from the river and from us by thundering traffic. Until the Embankment was built here in the 1870s, on land reclaimed from the foreshore, the Thames came right up to Cheyne Walk, but today it is almost impossible to imagine the riverside village that attracted so many writers and artists. Whistler and Turner captured local scenes on canvas and their distinguished neighbours included Rossetti, Wilson Steer, George Eliot, Swinburne and Hilaire Belloc. One house proudly boasts two plaques, but perhaps the most famous resident was Sir Thomas More, Lord Chancellor under Henry VIII, who was beheaded in 1535 for rejecting the king's religious reforms. His alarmingly realistic black-robed figure sits in the little garden before Chelsea Old Church **106**, where his chapel survives. The church was damaged by bombing in 1941, but a sensitive restoration has saved many of its monuments, and its atmosphere.

The walkway takes a passage under the pretty Albert Bridge, and very soon there is more of interest to note, across the road. After 200 yards the greenery you are looking at belongs to the 'Botanic Gardens of the Worshipful Society of Apothecaries', or Chelsea Physic Garden **107**, established here in 1673 and the second oldest of its kind, after Oxford. There are shady paths, a water garden, a heather plantation, and, of course, all the medicinal and culinary herbs you would expect. If you are fortunate enough to be here on a summer afternoon, when it is open, you will find the entrance off the delightful Swan Walk. But next, a grander scene opens up, as, across open playing fields, you catch sight of the elegant vista of Wren's Royal Hospital **108**, founded by Charles II in 1682 as a home for old soldiers. The Chelsea Pensioners live here, easily recognised in their 18th-century-style uniforms, scarlet in summer and blue in winter.

This prettiest, most delicate of Thames bridges was built in the 1870s on a rigid-rod principle, the weight being carried by the diagonal stays of wrought iron radiating out from the towers. In white with inset panels of pastel pinks, greens and gold, it could grace a giant wedding cake. But the bridge is also weak, and as your path squeezes up to the road beside one of its four little toll kiosks, you may notice the sign ordering that 'all troops must break step when marching over'. A few paces to your right, there is a traffic 'squeeze point' where you can cross safely and take the gate into the riverside walk through Battersea Park. This was one of the great Victorian parks, laid out in 1854 on marshy land built up with earth from the newly excavated docks downstream.

In addition to the park's welcome greenery, another surprise awaits you: the London Peace Pagoda **122**. This was the seventieth pagoda built worldwide by the Buddhist Nipponzan Myohoji Order. It is over 100 feet (30.5 metres) high with wind-bells on every corner and gilded statues of Buddha in its four niches, portraying his birth, enlightenment, first sermon and passing away at Kushinara. Ahead is the last big obstacle along this stretch: the empty shell of Battersea

At Chelsea Bridge, cross at the traffic lights, then go under a railway bridge with the green aspect of Battersea Park across the river giving way to the industry of Nine Elms Reach, dominated by the assertive Battersea Power Station. You can still admire the scale of this great temple to power, and the vigorous statement it makes with its four corner chimneys, although from some angles you can see right through it – the great building is just an empty shell. Interest wanes for a while now, and the pavement leaves the riverside, making only brief contact in the little Pimlico Gardens **109**. But, before you leave the gardens, spare a moment for William Huskisson, Statesman, who poses here, in appropriate stance, in a toga. Alas, for all his statesmanship, Huskisson's main claim to fame is as the world's first victim of a railway accident: in 1830 he stepped in front of Stephenson's Rocket.

When you are 250 yards beyond the garden, go right through gates onto the Crown Reach Riverside Walk. From here, you can admire the detail of Vauxhall Bridge ahead, the steelwork of its spans picked out in gaudy reds and blues, and its cutwaters graced by heroic-sized figures symbolizing various worthy causes, such as science, education, arts, engineering and local government. Were you strolling *over* the bridge, you would not realise that all this was happening just below you. The walkway climbs steps up to the bridge approach road, where you walk forward to the complex of traffic lights, cross and return on the opposite pavement, to take the steps down again to another walkway on the office-lined riverside. *Cross the bridge for Vauxhall British Rail station on the south bank, but for the nearest Underground station, Pimlico, keep on across the road junction and up Vauxhall Bridge Road; then follow the signs.*

Power Station **123**, around which the Thames Path must take a detour. Just before Chelsea Bridge, leave the river terrace, cross the park road and take the metalled track that sets off by the gates, just within the park. This joins another track, which you follow to the left, initially close to the park boundary, continuing alongside the paling fence of a wild reserve area, and on to the Queen's Circus Gates **BB**.

Leave the park here, go left around the Circus – watching the traffic with great care – and aim for the road that goes under the railway bridge opposite. This blighted thoroughfare has the unlikely name of Prince of Wales Drive **CC**. Bear left under a second bridge, then go over more railway lines – all leading into Victoria station – and carry on. This stretch offers but one small compensation: you now know where the famous Battersea Dogs' Home is. Take the first turning on the left, Kirtling Street **DD**, and follow it as it crosses Cringle Street and turns right. Some 70 yards beyond the bend, a welcome sign directs you to the left, alongside a once-white wall, to the Thames. There are big stages in the river here, with some very odd craft moored, while upstream you can see the quays and the rusting, abandoned cranes of the power station. The walkway skirts an inlet, then, at the Battersea Barge restaurant, it has to return to the road – but only briefly. Another 100 yards further on beyond a couple of industrial sites, the river walk begins again towards Vauxhall Bridge. Before long, you pass a

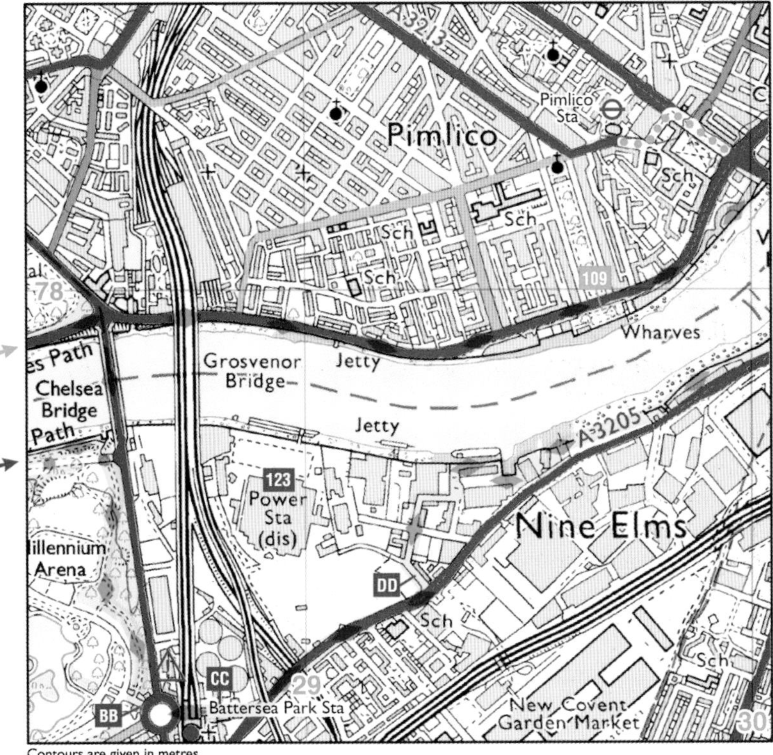

Contours are given in metres
The vertical interval is 5m

Walking on, the little garden beyond the offices contains a giant sculpture, *Locking Piece* by Henry Moore, which is dutifully washed down every minute by its attendant fountains. It serves as an introduction to the Tate Gallery across the road. Then you come to a modern work of a different kind: the recently – and controversially – listed Millbank Tower, with its subtle concave/convex curves of glass. Now, the two Victoria Tower Gardens offer a little relief from the relentless road, so walk beneath their plane trees, up the steps and over the Lambeth Bridge approach to the larger garden, viewing point for the great Victoria Tower, western termination of the Palace of Westminster **110** ahead. There are two sharply contrasted features in the garden: first, a gorgeously ornate 1865 drinking fountain, all intricate stone and enamel; then a bronze of Rodin's *Burghers of Calais*.

Back on the road again, there is almost too much to view. Across the road is the Jewel Tower **111**, one surviving fragment of the old palace, mellow in Kentish ragstone, with a morsel of moat to keep it company. Then, across Old Palace Yard, rise the

bas-relief panel by Stephen Duncan, portraying Father Thames in an unusually macho role, wrestling with serpents, lobsters, and even an octopus. Where the walkway currently ends at a blue hoarding, turn up into Nine Elms **EE**, turn left and bear left again with the traffic in Vauxhall Road **FF**. Soon, just beyond a Tesco Express, you can turn left into a passageway, up steps and on to the riverside walkway of St George Wharf. The Riverside pub stands on the corner, but your route goes to the right and under the bridge approach road. *For Vauxhall Underground station, National Rail and bus stations, take the slope up to the road and turn right.*

At this point, your astonished gaze will fall upon the vast green-and-cream edifice before you **124** – an office block that suggests a child has been allowed to play with a monster set of building bricks. Even while it was still being built, the government bought it as a base for its MI6 security organization, and, whatever its architectural merits, it provides a river terrace. So walk on and follow it past several office blocks on to the Albert Embankment **GG**. A passage takes you under Lambeth Bridge, and thus to one of London's most-favoured viewpoints.

The tourist cameras are, of course, aimed at the Gothic pinnacles and towers of Westminster across the river, but nearer, across the road to your left, stands Lambeth Palace, London home of the Archbishops of Canterbury since the 12th century **125**. Traffic mars your view, but the mellow Tudor brick of Archbishop Morton's gatehouse can still be appreciated. Behind it, you can see the Great Hall, rebuilt around 1660, with a lantern light rising over its high-pitched roof. Beside the gatehouse, tucked in so tightly as to seem part of the same building, is the old ragstone tower of the former parish church of St Mary at Lambeth. Fallen out of use, it was rescued by the

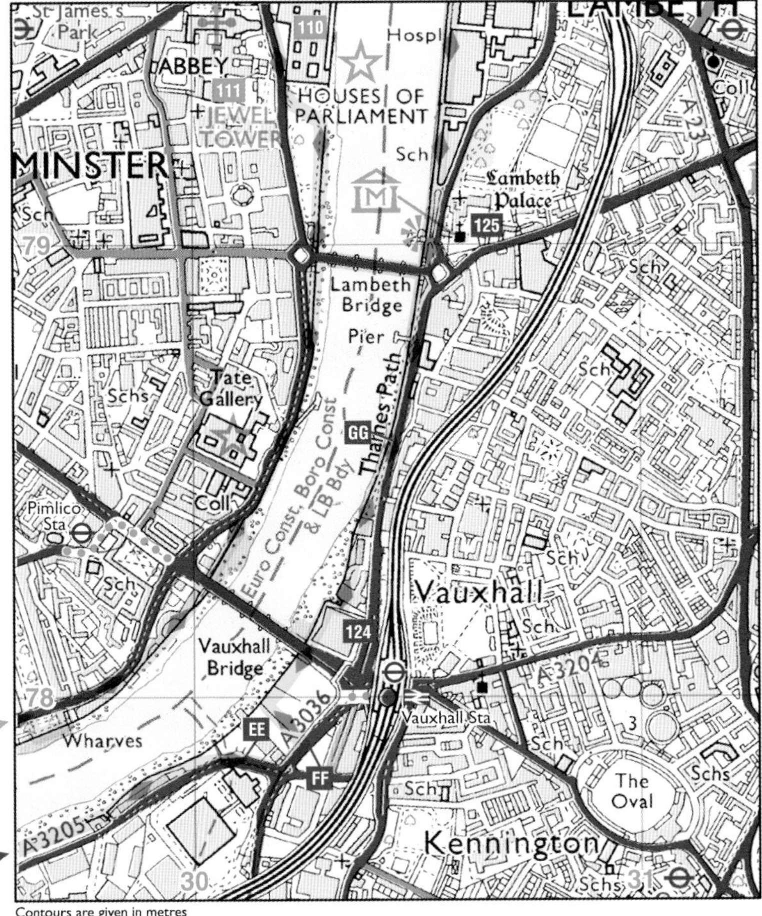

Contours are given in metres
The vertical interval is 5m

great flying buttresses of the chapterhouse of Westminster Abbey **112**. Almost alongside, to a very different scale, is the church of St Margaret's **113**, all in stone as befits its distinguished company. It has served the good folk of Westminster for many centuries as their parish church. On the near pavement the crowds queue endlessly to witness the affairs of state conducted behind the Gothic façade of Sir Charles Barry's Houses of Parliament. His design won the competition in 1835 for a new palace after the earlier building had been almost destroyed by fire. The organisers specified that entries had either to be in the then fashionable Gothic style, or Elizabethan. There is no question as to which style Barry opted for. When Parliament is sitting, a flag flies from Victoria Tower, Big Ben lights a lamp and, usually, a TV crew will be scuttling around, fixing interviews in one of their favourite locations.

Through all the bustle, follow the pavement on to the crossroads, turn right and cross the road via the pedestrian crossing beneath the tower of Big Ben. Turn right immediately on another crossing to reach the steps leading down to the walkway beneath the bronze statue of Queen Boudicca and her daughters in a chariot. You are now walking along the Victoria

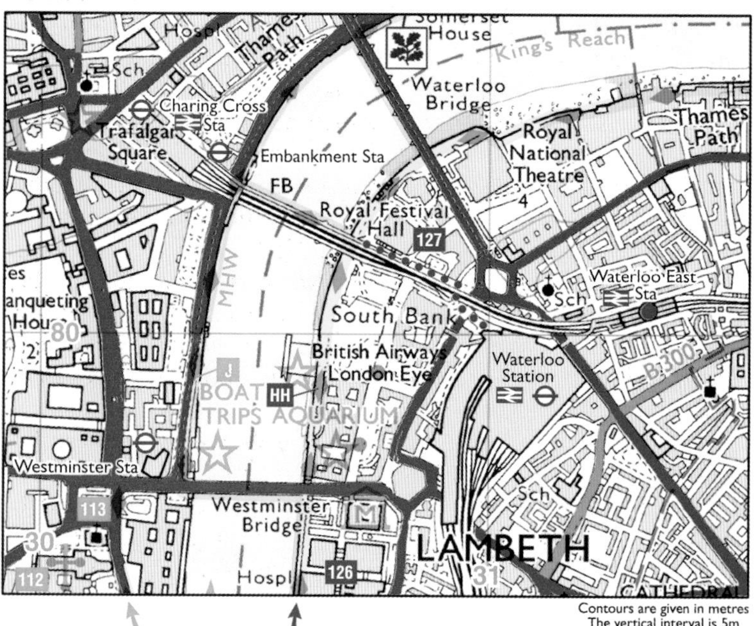

Embankment **J**, the offices of Whitehall to your left and the City skyline unfolding ahead. As you approach the Charing Cross railway bridge, you meet the creator of this walkway, Sir Joseph Bazalgette. His bronze bas-relief by the riverside reveals him as the possessor of a magnificent moustache, and proclaims him to have been the 'engineer of the London main drainage system'– which underplays his achievement. In the 1850s, all London's sewage ran down into the Thames and public opinion held its

Tradescant Trust and now serves as a museum of garden history. The Tradescants, a local family, were royal gardeners, and travelled the world in search of new species. Appropriately, their family tomb stands in a recreated 17th-century garden in the churchyard.

The Embankment walkway now leaves the road, and the buildings of St Thomas' Hospital **126** rise over the wall above you. This famous hospital was established in Southwark 800 years ago, and moved here in the 1860s, into a vast Italianate complex of ward blocks that must have rivalled the Palace of Westminster in scale. Only a fragment remains, just visible amidst a jumble of modern buildings. A pedestrian underpass now takes you under Westminster Bridge, with a friendly stone lion on his plinth above you. Cast in the artificial Coadstone, he once reigned over the Lion Brewery, until the brewery site was needed for the Royal Festival Hall. You are now following the Queen's Walk **HH**, past County Hall, home of the Greater London Council until 1986, its vast bulk now converted to provide restaurants, the Saatchi Gallery and the London Aquarium. Then comes the giant wheel of the London Eye, and beneath it you can marvel at its sheer size.

The walkway passes the Jubilee Gardens, and then goes under Hungerford Bridge to the concrete monoliths of the South Bank arts complex. *The steps up here lead either via the Golden Jubilee footbridges on either side of the railway bridge across to Embankment and Charing Cross stations, or, in the other direction, via walkways to Waterloo station.*

The riverside promenade you are now on was cleared for the 1951 Festival of Britain, the great fun event aimed at revitalizing a war-weary nation, and the Festival Hall **127** in its original form was its centrepiece. Since then, it has been joined by two smaller halls plus the Hayward Gallery, all adding to the bewil-

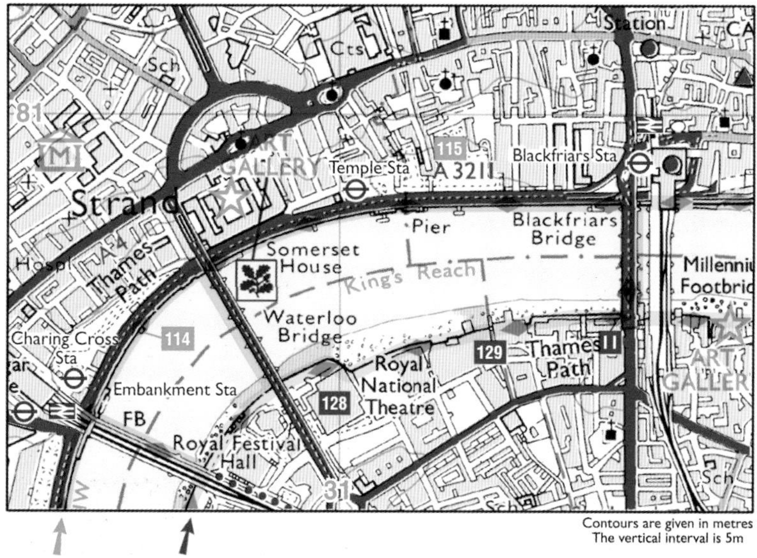

nose and demanded something better. As Chief Engineer to the new Metropolitan Board of Works, Bazalgette offered a bold solution: build up the riverside embankments with main sewers beneath, then divert everything into them, to be carried out to the estuary. In the process, London actually gained land – for example, the Victoria Embankment you are on, reclaimed 37 acres (15 hectares) of foreshore. We also gained London's now-familiar Thames-side scenes, embellished by features such as the lamp columns with fierce dolphins coiled around each base, and the seats supported by strange, winged beasts of cast iron. *Just beyond the bridge, a pedestrian crossing leads to Embankment station. Charing Cross British Rail station is reached simply by walking through the Underground station entrance and on up the road.*

The next riverside feature is Cleopatra's Needle **114**, the great 186-ton obelisk brought here on a hectic sea voyage from Alexandria in 1878. The hieroglyphics running down the column are dedications to various gods, and relate mainly to the time of the Pharaoh Tethmosis III. Two bronze sphinxes sit on either side like serene guard dogs, their bases pockmarked by bomb splinters from, surprisingly, the very first air raid on London by an aeroplane in September 1917. Beyond Waterloo Bridge, you are beneath the fine 18th-century façade of

Somerset House. Soon after, the embankment road is flanked by two rampant silver dragons. They were originally placed over the entrance to the Coal Exchange, but now they welcome you to the City of London. There is one small change you may immediately notice – the winged creatures supporting the embankment seats give way to heavily laden camels. At this point, you are looking left into the Inns of Court **115**, specifically the Middle and Inner Temple. Approaching Blackfriars Bridge, follow the signs directing you down the steps to Paul's Walk. There are toilets here at walkway level, and maps to direct you through the maze of underpasses, should you want to reach the stations.

dering concrete world of steps and terraces. The overall ambience is still unfriendly, until, at dusk, the stark shapes become exciting, and the interiors acquire a kind of magic. Beneath Waterloo Bridge, you can enjoy a coffee, or browse through open-air bookstalls as you pass the National Film Theatre. Then, you find yourself beneath more cascading terraces of concrete – the National Theatre itself **128**, finally settled here by the Thames after many frustrating years of searching for a permanent site. How three different-sized auditoriums have been fitted into this one composition is difficult to comprehend from the outside, but keep it in mind when you come to make comparisons with Shakespeare's Globe, the 'Wooden O', where it all started.

After this overdose of stark concrete, it is a joy to walk on to the cheeky, human scale of Gabriel's Wharf **129**, a little plaza with shops, craft stalls and eating places. The Coin Street Community rescued this site from another bleak commercial fate, and we must be grateful. But do not be deceived by the range of distinguished house fronts behind the little shops; they are painted on plain old warehouse walls. The next bridge is Blackfriars, which you approach beneath The Doggett's Coat and Badge pub. The scarlet coat and badge goes each year to the winner of a single sculls race for apprentice watermen, a Thames tradition dating back to 1715. An underpass **II** takes the Thames Path under the bridge, its white-tiled walls decorated with historical engravings. You can see the alternative designs for the first bridge of 1756, then various stages of construction – an on-the-spot history lesson.

As you walk on, you are looking at Bankside across the river, the rectangles and straight lines of the power station contrasting with the toy-like Globe Theatre a little way further downstream. Continue beneath the broad steps that provide just one 'keyhole' view up to the dome of St Paul's **116**, then, 100 yards further on, you must turn left into Broken Wharf, and then right in a service road, just short of the busy traffic on Upper Thames Street **K**. Follow beside the traffic as it ducks beneath offices, Queensbridge House, then turn right down Queenhithe, a cobbled lane leading back to the river. On the corner, pause to admire one of Wren's churches, St James Garlickhythe, built in around 1680, across the road. The tower has a fine gilt clock standing out from it. Back on the riverside, turn left to walk beneath the portico of Vintners Place. Coming to Southwark Bridge, go left through gates into the enclosed Fruiterers Passage, a public way that turns under the bridge and doubles back to rejoin the river on Three Cranes Walk **L**.

This brings you to the refuse handling facility on Walbrook Wharf, where the way is sometimes temporarily closed while the big container crane is at work. An alternative way of proceeding is to turn left here up Bell Wharf Lane, an unlikely public thoroughfare beneath offices, leading to Upper Thames Street, where you turn right and then right again down Cousin Lane **M**. The way across the dock leads to the foot of Cousin Lane and a riverside pub, The Banker. Just a few paces up away from the

And the lesson continues as you step out into daylight again to be faced with the great crest of the London, Chatham & Dover Railway, reflecting the sheer pride of the company as they took their lines across the river into the new Blackfriars terminus in 1863. Looking closely, you realise that the cast-iron crest is on the abutment of a bridge now dismantled and replaced.

Passing through gates and under today's railway bridge, you arrive on Bankside. The slender line of the Millennium Footbridge leads your eye to St Paul's across the river, but in contrast the mighty power station **130** stands back behind a bank of grass, allowing you fully to appreciate its admirable simplicity – like a giant piece of abstract art. Bankside was designed by Sir Giles Gilbert Scott, and, with its massive single chimney, it is surely a finer creation than his better-known work at Battersea.

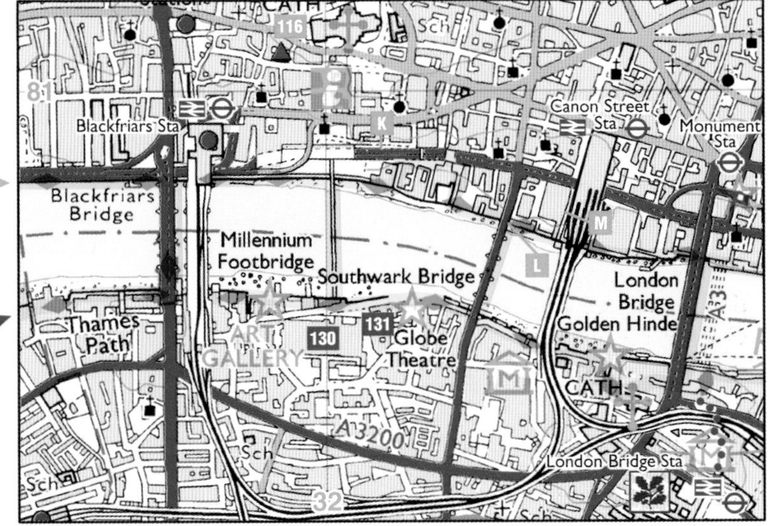

Contours are given in metres
The vertical interval is 5m

Appropriately, it is now home to the Tate Gallery's modern art collection. But in period feel, Bankside truly begins when the tiny fragment of Cardinal's Wharf appears – two charming houses in a cobbled close. The 18th-century Provost's Lodging belongs to the Provost of Southwark Cathedral, while the narrower, older house alongside was reputedly the quarters of Sir Christopher Wren while he was overseeing the building of St Paul's.

Just beyond stands the reason why the crowds are flocking back to Bankside: the amazing sight of Shakespeare's Globe Theatre **131**, reborn. Timber frame, plaster and thatch – all the materials are authentic, the dimensions as accurate as experts can make them. So now the world can come and experience the great tragedies just as the first audiences did, on this very ground. For here, in the late 16th century, with the Rose, Swan, Hope and Globe playhouses all within a tiny radius, occurred the world's greatest outpouring of stage drama. A prudish City Corporation, it seems, required citizens seeking entertainment to cross to Bankside, where the taverns and brothels, the bull- and bear-baiting rings all noisily competed for trade. Incredibly, much of this bawdy revelry was within the Liberty of the Clink, an area administered by the Bishops of Winchester, whose palace stood nearby. It even supported several prisons, including the notorious 'Clink' debtors' prison itself.

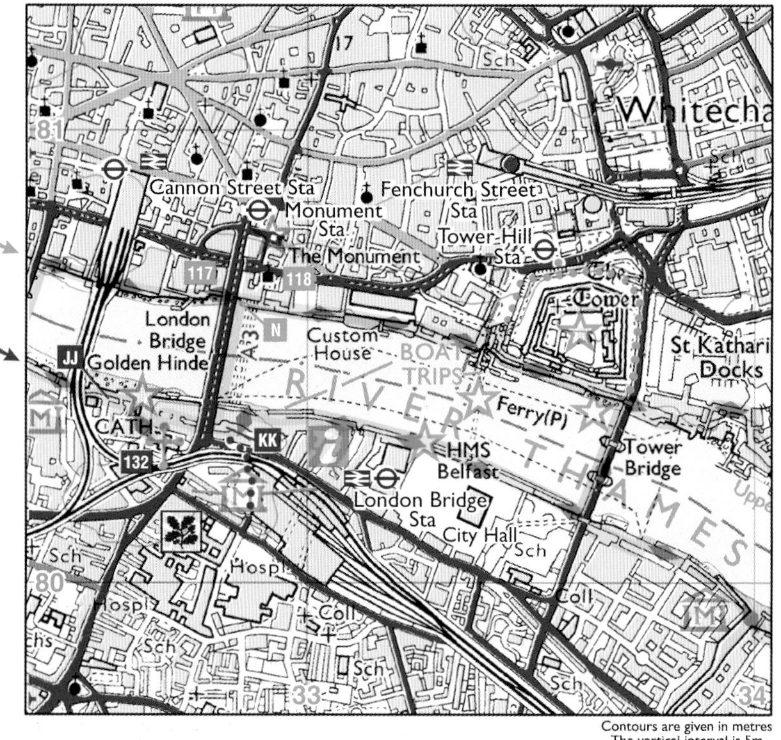

Contours are given in metres
The vertical interval is 5m

Walking on, you pass the cobbled alley called Bear Gardens, at the top of which the original site of the Globe is now under offices. The next turning point is Rose Alley, another reminder of past entertainments. But the river walk continues under Southwark Bridge and on to The Anchor Inn – late 18th-century with a warren of timbered bars within. Go around the inn and under a tall railway arch; you are now in Clink Street **JJ**, which is narrow with grimy buildings to either side. To your right is all that remains of Winchester Palace, so tightly enclosed that you look through medieval window openings to see the fluorescent lights of offices beyond. This was the Bishops' Hall, and the surviving west wall has one superb and unusual rose window, probably 14th-century.

Clink Street leads to the dock of St Mary Overie, which shelters the *Golden Hinde*, a full-sized reconstruction of the 16th-century ship in which Sir Francis Drake circumnavigated river, go right through a passageway beneath the Cannon Street railway line and out onto Waterman's Walk.

Ahead is London Bridge, but before you reach it cross the terrace of Fishmongers' Hall **117**, with its elegant, pillared front much restored after war damage; though, essentially, it dates to 1835. The Worshipful Company of Fishmongers – one of the richest – rated highly amongst the guilds, their hall having occupied this prime site since 1444. Take the steps leading under London Bridge, then keep ahead over a footbridge to follow the riverside, now along Grant's Quay Wharf **N**. A gap in the offices gives a brief view leftwards up to the ornate spire of another Wren church, St Magnus the Martyr **118**. It stands virtually on the line of old London Bridge, and in the tiny courtyard squeezed between its tower and the encroaching offices are a few shaped stone blocks, reputedly from the first arch of the now-vanished bridge. Beyond it you get just a glimpse of the Monument. This simple 202-foot (62.5-metre) Doric column with a flaming gilt urn on top, was designed by Wren to commemorate the Great Fire that broke out in nearby Pudding Lane in 1666.

Follow the riverside up more steps and on to another striking architectural contrast. A new office block presents a vast, blue, glass-clad wall that steps down, storey by storey, to meet its next-door neighbour, the newly restored Billingsgate Market **119** building of 1877. The fish market here closed in

the world. Today's Devon-built version has also sailed the world, and is now open to view. To your left, there is a good riverside viewpoint with a panorama panel, while to the right you come, with quite a surprise, to the east end of Southwark Cathedral **132**. In earlier days this was the church of the Augustinian Priory of St Mary Overie, so the little dock, with its toll-free landing rights, reminds us of an ancient name. Ill-treated as it is by crowding offices and railway tracks, the cathedral has an impressive interior, one that fully rewards any visit. But, having brought you to it, the Thames Path turns sharply left to skirt around the cathedral precinct and follow the road under London Bridge. *For London Bridge station, take the steps on the right beneath Coleford House. They circle up, first to road level, then on to London Bridge Walk, which takes you directly into the station.*

1982, and the river frontage, with its arched colonnade and fish weather vanes, was restored, its brickwork now quite a ferocious yellow. Along the riverside here, since Elizabethan times, have stood the 'legal quays' where goods due for duty had to be landed and checked by customs officers. So, not surprisingly, Custom House Quay is the next site along. Our walkway now goes along its river frontage, neatly confined within blue railings, leading out onto Sugar Quay Walk.

At Tower Pier you turn up to the road and mingle with the myriad visitors to the Tower of London **120**. *For Tower Hill Underground station, walk ahead towards the Tower, then bear right across a broad open area (there are toilets beneath the offices to the left), to take a ramp sloping down beside the castle moat, turning left at the medieval postern gate to go under the road.* To complete the walk, bear right through the gates **O** and go on past the visitor shop to take the cobbled Tower Wharf by Traitors' Gate, the sinister watergate into the castle, to Tower Bridge itself. With the sun gleaming off old stonework and chattering gaggles of schoolchildren filing by, notebooks in hand, it is impossible to associate the Tower with torture, murder and brutal execution, yet all have featured in its bloody history. The ravens remain, but the atmosphere has gone.

To continue the walk, keep on along Tooley Street **KK** until, after another 75 yards, you can turn left into a passage through offices back to the river walk. If you take a few paces to the left, you will be standing on the line of the earlier London Bridge, which was for centuries the only crossing in London. Here, in the late 16th century, you would have been gazing at the Southwark Gate, trying to identify the row of severed heads on display. But today, as you walk to the right, you are in London Bridge City, a redevelopment with Hay's Wharf **133** as its spectacular central feature. Here the warehouses of 1856 have been retained, but the narrow dock between them has been filled in to make a shopping piazza, with the addition of a superb barrel-vaulted roof. Don't miss *The Navigators* at its centre – a delightful ship-fantasy by David Kemp, which bristles with oars, harpoons, paddle wheels and other nautical artefacts that waggle, spin, or just spout water. Visitors seem to have claimed this as a lucky fountain, and the pond around it contains a fortune in small change!

Just down the river, HMS *Belfast*, only survivor of our big-gun warships of World War II, brings a shock of contrast – a reminder of crueller seas, of Arctic convoys and Atlantic battles, all painfully echoed in the chill greys and blues of her dazzle camouflage. Then, a walkway leads on to two contrasting images. First City Hall, the new Greater London Authority headquarters, with its strange, lop-sided tiers of glass. Then the unmistakable shape of Tower Bridge **134**. It rarely has to perform now, but, if challenged, the two great 1,200-ton bascules still rise to allow tall ships to enter the Upper Pool, which was, of course, the very reason for its unique design. Meanwhile, close proximity to the Tower of London justified cladding its steelwork in Gothic-inspired masonry. This 100-year-old triumph of Victorian engineering now has an exhibition to tell its story. The Thames Path goes under the bridge to plunge into the narrow cavern of Shad Thames beyond, *but for Tower Hill Underground station, climb the steps and cross the bridge, then walk on by the side of the Tower moat. Go down the steps to a lower-level footway along the landward side of the Tower, then, when you come to the medieval postern gate, go right under the road.*

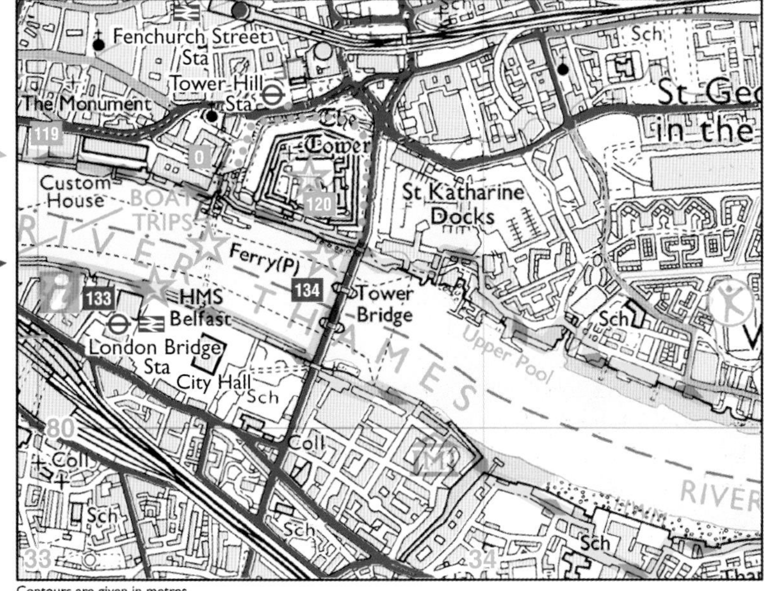

Contours are given in metres
The vertical interval is 5m

15 Tower Bridge to Thames Barrier

Transport Options

The north bank walk passes Wapping station on the East London Line after 1 mile (1.6 km), but more useful connections are made with the Docklands Light Railway at Limehouse after 2¼ miles (3.6 km), Canary Wharf after 2¾ miles (4.4 km) or Island Gardens at the end, all linking back to the DLR terminus at Tower Gateway. The south bank walk passes Rotherhithe station on the East London Line after 2¼ miles (3.6 km), but a 5¾ -mile (9.3-km) walk from Tower Bridge brings you to Greenwich, where there is a National Rail connection, or Cutty Sark on the DLR. After that comes North Greenwich on the Jubilee Line, but Charlton is the nearest station to the Thames Barrier.

NORTH BANK — *6½ miles (10.5 km) to Island Gardens*

The Thames Path follows the promenade to the river side of the Tower of London, from where you walk under the Tower Bridge approach and immediately sharp right to the riverside walkway. As you pass the Thistle Tower Hotel, you can hardly miss the striking bronze water sculpture, *Girl with a Dolphin* by David Wynne, and the great sundial by Wendy Taylor. Then, go over the St Katherine Dock entry by the footbridge and up to the dockside. The temptation to explore is strong here, so pause and get your bearings. You are looking over an entry basin **135**, with larger docks to both sides. To the right is the big Dickens Inn, converted from a warehouse, and, to the left, the little circular chapel, now a coffee bar. This way, you will get a close-up view of a whole string of Thames spritsail barges, superbly displayed against the backdrop of Thomas Telford's great warehouses.

The route goes to the corner by The Dickens Inn, then right to follow the red brick of St Katherine's Way **A**, past Devon House and President Quay. Alderman Steps beyond Miller's Wharf are a rare example today of waterman's access to the foreshore.

SOUTH BANK — *10 miles (16.1 km)*

Butler's Wharf **143**, completed in 1871, was the biggest wharf complex on the river, and its vast warehouse and narrow cobbled lanes provide a dramatic start for the last stage of the Thames Path. Taking the archway under Tower Bridge, you are looking down Shad Thames **K**, a deep, shadowy canyon of a street, crisscrossed by latticed iron bridges at every level. But, before the bridges themselves begin, turn left into the passage called Maggie Blake's Cause, and go through an arch to the riverside. To the right, the narrow way passes a string of restaurants beneath the impressive river front of Butler's Wharf, and comes out on an open quay; ahead, you can see the white buildings of the Design Museum. Pass by a gigantic anchor, then circle around the fascinating 'head' sculpture by Paolozzi. Then, as Butler's Wharf ends, take the footbridge over St Saviour's Dock **144**. Here you can savour just one glimpse of Victorian dockland, the muddy inlet lined with warehouses, the cranes still clinging to their walls. The footbridge leads over to New Concordia Wharf, a one-time flour mill on the corner of Mill Street and Bermondsey Wall West **L**.

The area you have stepped into was known as Jacob's Island, a notorious slum in early Victorian times. But Charles Dickens would find little to recognize today, just a little lane, which you follow, with the Thames just to your left, until, near its end, you turn right, then left into Chambers Street. Coming to new housing, turn left into Loftie Street **M**, bearing right briefly before going left across Fountain Green Square to the riverside. It really does have a little square of grass with a drinking fountain on it.

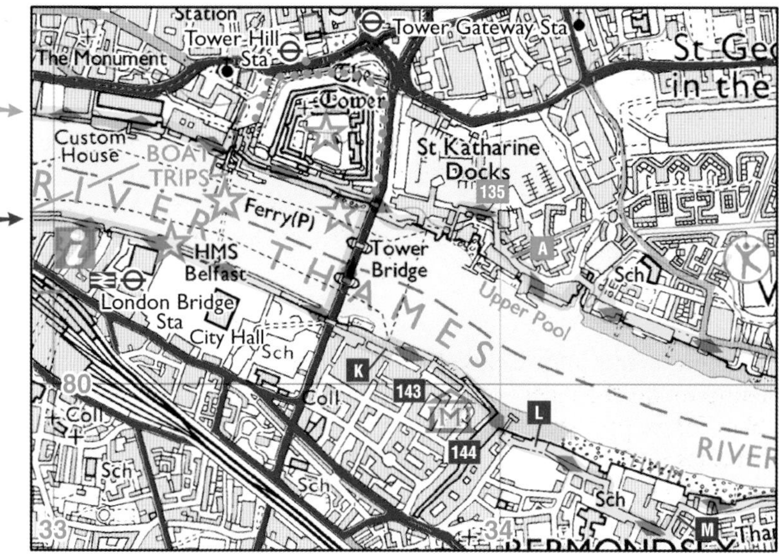

Contours are given in metres
The vertical interval is 5m

Then go immediately right onto a broad river terrace. There are fine views back to Tower Bridge and across to Butler's Wharf, a palatial reminder of the vanished prosperity of the Pool of London. The walkway returns you to St Katherine's Way, which now continues as Wapping High Street **B**. Very soon you meet the surprising little Hermitage Riverside Memorial Garden and paths take you back to the Thames. The memorial is dedicated to the Eastenders who died in World War II. The riverside path continues over a drawdock to pass two big apartment blocks before returning to Wapping High Street.

Going right again, you pass Wapping Pierhead **136** – handsome houses built in 1811 for officials of the London Dock Company. Next comes The Town of Ramsgate pub and Oliver's Wharf, an 1870s bravura exercise in brick and stone. Opposite, down Scandrett Street, is a good example of restoration **137**. The old school of St John of Wapping, 'erected by subscription 1760', was a ruined shell until rebuilt into four town houses. You can still see the stone-swagged entrances for boys and infants, and the niches of the original school once again hold their statues of Georgian-period pupils. The church of St John has been rebuilt as offices, sympathetically retaining the 18th-century tower.

Walking on along Wapping High Street, the little grass area of New Stairs gives a glimpse of the river. It is followed by The Captain Kidd pub with its courtyard entry; *then, in abrupt contrast, comes Wapping Underground station.* Just 40 yards beyond the station, a Thames Path sign points to a riverside walkway. Go up a sloping ramp, through a gate, on along the front of apartments and through another gate onto St Hilda's Wharf. Note here the great anchor found when the site was excavated for housing in 1987. Leave the river again at New Crane Steps (another old access way to the foreshore), walk on along the road, then turn right onto Wapping Wall **C**.

Go right now, on what soon becomes a broad walkway, diverting briefly around Cherry Garden Pier before continuing by the riverside to Angel Wharf, with The Angel pub overlooking the Thames. Here you will meet *Doctor Salter* on his bench by the Thames, waving to his daughter *Joyce* by the river wall. This group by Diane Gorvin is a delightful tribute to a popular local benefactor, a councillor and, later, MP for Bermondsey in the 1920s. On a grass area opposite are the traces of Edward III's

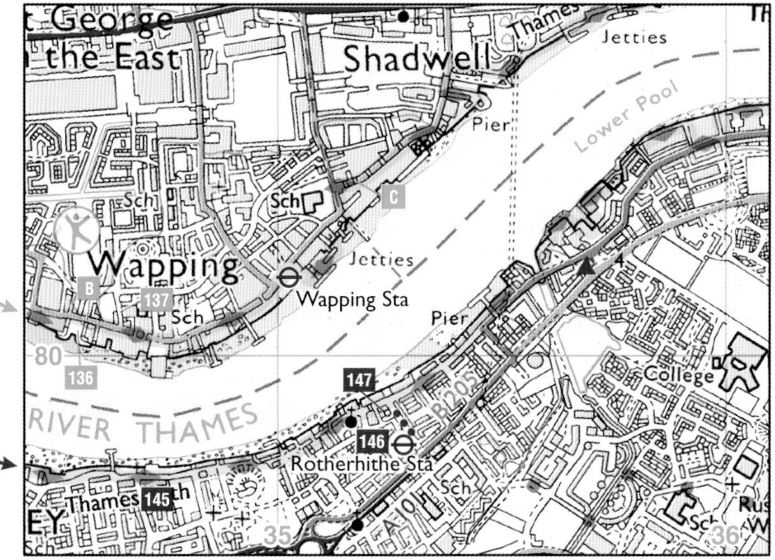

Contours are given in metres
The vertical interval is 5m

moated manor house **145**, built here in 1353 and recently rescued from the foundations of a warehouse. More fragments of river walk follow, then a longer open promenade leading to a passageway beneath the King's Stairs block. Beyond this, go down some steps, turn left, then right into a narrow alley between tall warehouses and out into the best bit of Rotherhithe. To your right is the church of St Mary's **146**. It was rebuilt around 1747 with a great deal of ships' timber being used for the interior. The church had close links with the *Mayflower*. Christopher Jones, the master, and three of the four owners are buried in the churchyard. Opposite, the 17th-century Mayflower pub claims to stand on the site of 'The Shippe', the very spot from where the Pilgrim Fathers set out in 1620.

If you look right across the churchyard, you can glimpse the former charity school with, outside, the two charming carved figures of 18th-century schoolchildren. Then, beyond the church, you pass a little building **147** with a tall, iron-topped chimney. This is the engine house built by Brunel to drain his Thames tunnel, a pioneering venture that opened – after many disasters – as a foot tunnel in 1843, and which to this day takes Underground trains beneath the river. *Just past the engine house, Railway Avenue leads directly to Rotherhithe Underground station.*

Then comes The Prospect of Whitby – tourist Mecca amongst the dockland pubs. Immediately beyond, you can take to the riverside again on a walkway that turns around Prospect Wharf, then has to return to the road because of the Shadwell Basin entry ahead.

Shadwell Pierhead **138** is a canoeing activity centre and you need to walk around it, crossing the big, red lift-bridge and then going almost immediately right again on an enclosed path back to the riverside in King Edward VII Memorial Park. Skirt around a circular, brick tower, an air shaft for the Rotherhithe Tunnel (with its twin on the south bank), and follow the riverside through more gates into a development of vast, red-brick apartments.

Next, you pass the two bays of Free Trade Wharf, built for the East India Company in 1793, and continue via wooden steps over a watergate, then up and rightwards through a tiny garden area to the corner of Narrow Street **D**. Walk on, and in 200 yards you can turn right onto a riverside walkway again, leading to the entry into Limehouse Basin **139**, a dock built to service the Regent's Canal, one of the great arteries of the canal age. An open quayside leads past The Narrow Street pub, once the Dockmaster's House, then steps lead back up to the road.

Two canals still enter the basin, the Regent's branch of the Grand Union Canal, and the Limehouse Cut. Both offer walks along their towpaths, and as the signing now indicates, the Cut even links to the Lea Valley Walk, so from this surprising spot you could, if the mood took you, set out to walk to Luton and Birmingham. *Opposite The Narrow Street pub, there is a link on the left up Horseferry Road to Limehouse station on the DLR.*

Over the entry bridge you can turn down steps to another walkway around Victoria Wharf, but it soon returns you to Narrow Street again. Do not be tempted to follow the 'walkway' sign on Blyth's Wharf – it leads only onto a jetty – but continue past the narrow little Grapes pub and turn into the

Now, as you walk along Rotherhithe Street **N**, you pass a riverside terrace with rope sculpture and then, 70 yards further on, turn onto the walkway along Cumberland Wharf. Here stands the striking group, *Sunbeam Weekly and the Pilgrim's Pocket* by Peter McLean. A 1930s lad reads the story

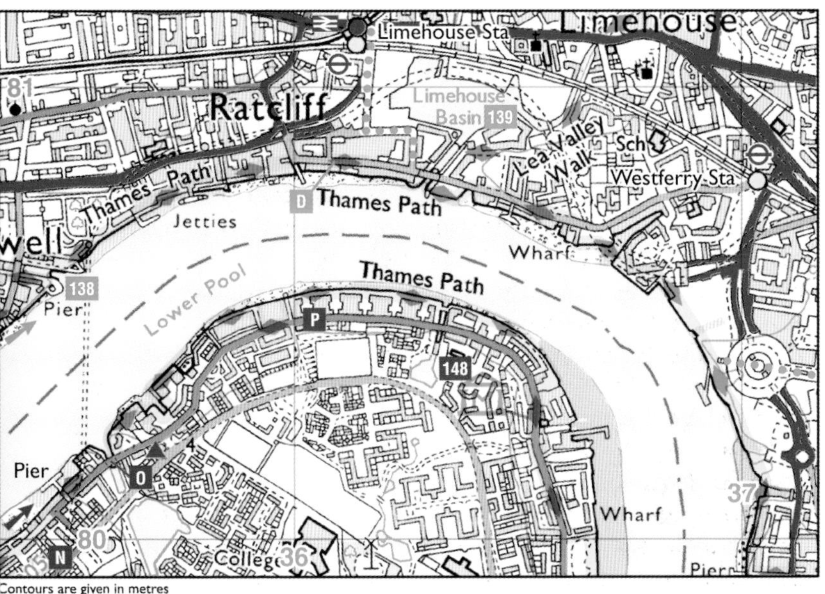

of the *Mayflower*, not only the epic journey, but of all that happened after: skyscrapers, cowboys, Cadillacs and more. He seems unaware of the pilgrim looking, understandably astonished, over his shoulder. Keep by the river, up to a further walkway past a public pier carrying a striking boat/bird sculpture, then down steps back to Rotherhithe Street and over the big, red lift-bridge over the Surrey Water entry. Once across, drop down steps **O** to go to the river side of the big Spice Island hostelry, onto a new promenade. It circuits around one inlet, crosses another, then goes through railings to a further river terrrace. After a while, the massive bulk of Globe Wharf, a one-time rice mill, blocks the way, so return to the road briefly until, opposite The Three Compasses pub, you can turn onto a longer stretch of riverside via Foreshore Steps **P**. Walk past Sovereign Crescent, cross the inlet by a footbridge, from which you will notice, to your right across the road, the pumphouse, built in 1930 to control the water level in Surrey Docks. It now houses the Rotherhithe Heritage Museum. Just beyond it is Lavender Pond Nature Park **148**, squeezing a pond, reedbed, marsh and wildflower meadow into a tiny compass.

entry to Duke Shore Wharf **E**. Cross the car park area and turn left along the riverside, going through a gate onto a new walkway bridging an entry and continuing along the river frontage of the vast Canary Wharf development **140**, with its busy bars and cafés. Above you now loom the soaring office towers, dominated by One Canada Square, Britain's tallest building.

The walkway curves around Westferry Circus, *where the steps up provide the most direct way to the central plaza and Canary Wharf DLR station.* It then crosses another small entry to go to the river side of the Cascades block. Now the walkway continues past several more apartment blocks, going by a tiny garden with a 'twirly' sculpture, then the welcome grass of Sir John McDougal Gardens. Soon after leaving the gardens on a paved walkway, you must go left in Arnhem Place **F**, back to the road again. Rightwards now, you soon pass the delightful Presbyterian Chapel of 1856 opposite Claude Street, an elaborate Romanesque creation in varicoloured brick, with little colonnades of arches and clerestory roof. Now it leads a new life as an arts centre.

By the river now, you are walking along Sovereign View, passing an oddly anonymous column on Pageant Steps, until the warehouse on Canada Wharf blocks the way. Turn right here, back into Rotherhithe Street, to pass the Docklands Hilton, then new apartments on Lawrence Wharf. Where they end, broad steps lead up to the riverside again. You can see a river walk following the stretch you have just tramped by road, but currently a single wall blocks it as a through route. So turn right through the little park and onto the walkway on Trinity Wharf. Where it ends, turn right to the corner of Rotherhithe Street.

On the corner, the animal-decorated gates lead into Surrey Docks Farm **149**. It is closed on Mondays but usually open on other days from 10am to 5pm. If it is open, you can go that way and delight in the sight of children meeting friendly sheep, cows, ducks and goats. The farm also has a homely little café, where your cup of tea will be accompanied by a healthy assortment of farmyard smells. Walk ahead and up a slope on the left to pass to the left of the three-storey central building. Then, go through a gate to the riverside path and turn right to leave the farm via another gate onto Barnards Wharf. There are more animals here, but this time they are bronze sculptures of just the right

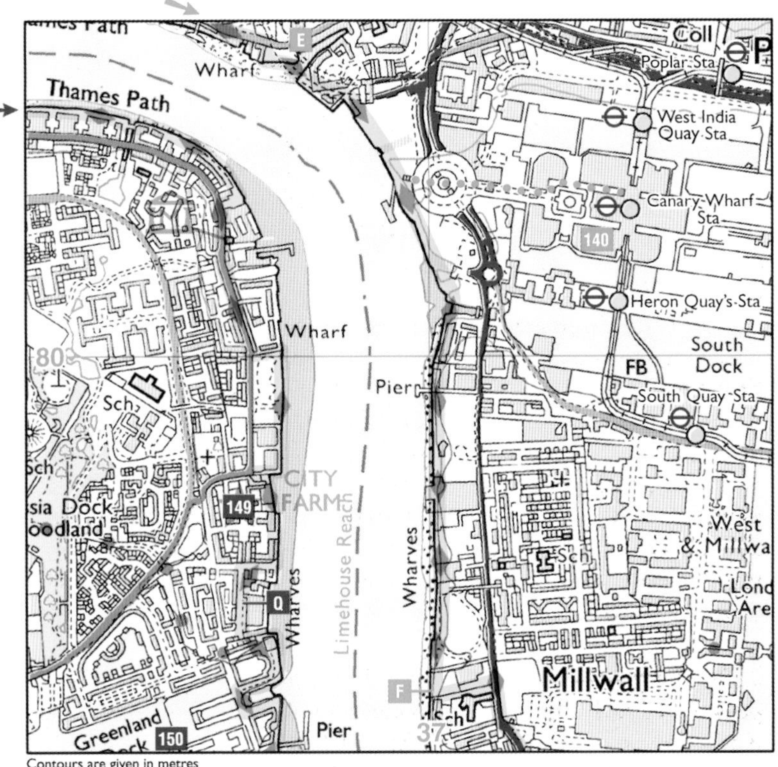

Contours are given in metres
The vertical interval is 5m

size for children to climb on. If the farm is closed, you can reach this spot by turning right by the farm gates at the corner of Rotherhithe Street, then left and left again into Vaughan Street. By whichever route you reach Barnards Wharf, follow it until, just before the big, red crane on Commercial Wharf Pier, you must turn right into Odessa Street **Q** and then left.

Odessa Street takes you past the vast new buildings on New Caledonian Wharf, but when it turns right, keep on across a cobbled area to reach the path called Randall's Rents and turn left to the river again. In the 18th century, Randall's shipyard was one of the largest in London, and its owner rented houses hereabouts to his workers, hence the name. Now you have come to Greenland Dock **150**, the only substantial water area left from the old Surrey Commercial Docks. At the dock entry, turn up to cross the lock swing-bridge, noting the great hydraulic rams that worked the lock gates, powered by high-pressure

At last, 250 yards beyond the chapel, the Thames Path is signed to the right, into a tiled way **G**. Walk up Ferguson Close and under the flats to turn left along the riverside. Across the river are the remaining buildings of the Royal Victualling Yard, Deptford, while ahead you can spot the masts of the *Cutty Sark* on the Greenwich quayside. Walking downstream to the inevitable apartment blocks on Burrell's Wharf, you pass the yard where Brunel's *Great Eastern* was built **141**. The *Great Eastern*, 680 foot (207 metres) long, was vastly bigger than anything previously conceived and was built and launched sideways; had a conventional launching been attempted, the stern of the vessel would have hit the south bank of the river. The timber baulks you see today are the last reminders of the shipbuilding industry that thrived along Limehouse Reach for many years. Burrell's Wharf itself retains some original features: an octagonal chimney, gantry house and mast house, in an oddly Italianate square. Burrells were paint manufacturers who took over here in 1888 when shipbuilding was no longer viable. Keep on along a promenade **H** until it ends just beyond

water from a nearby pumphouse. Return to the riverside past the lock-keeper's office, then by a landing stage and over the lock gates of the smaller South Dock **151**. You are now walking towards Deptford Strand, passing, on the way, the boundary stone between Rotherhithe and Deptford parishes. On the Strand **152,** with its watergate, the buildings are reminders of the great naval dockyard established here in Henry VIII's time. These are rum storehouses, dating from around 1790. Most of the dockyard area is now high-rise housing, but a link remains, in that the name of Samuel Pepys, distinguished Secretary to the Admiralty, was chosen for the estate.

Where the walkway ends, turn right on a path through gates and ahead in a tiny grass area – part of Pepys Park. Go down some steps between housing blocks and across a drive **R** into a further area of park. Bear left to follow the red-surfaced cycle path round to an exit into Grove Street **S**. Turn left now until, just around a bend, you come to gates on the left leading into Sayes Court Park. This name, too, preserves a slice of Deptford history. Sayes Court, which stood near the dockyard here until 1729, was the house of John Evelyn, diarist and keen gardener. Walk forward in the little park, then go right and exit via a gate

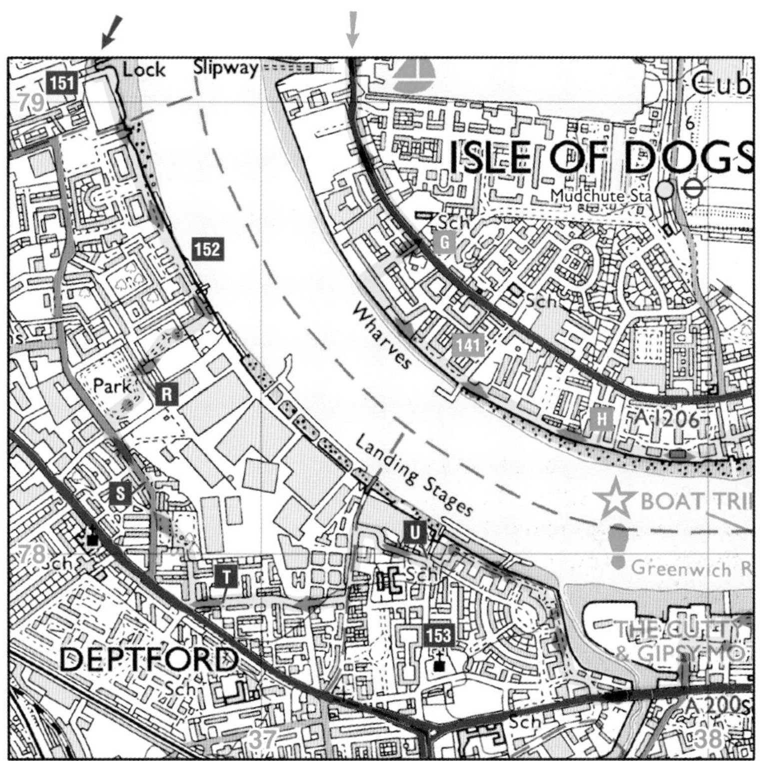

Contours are given in metres
The vertical interval is 5m

in the farthest right-hand corner, into a cobbled estate road. Coming up to a main road, turn left down Prince Street **T** and follow it past The Navy Arms and The Dog & Bell. Where Prince Street ends, turn left into Watergate Street, going right at the bottom into Borthwick Street. On the corner, the watergate is ahead, while to your right is a little park with a charming lily pond. Reaching the foot of Deptford Green **U**, your route goes left onto a riverside walkway, but a brief detour to the right leads to St Nicholas **153**, a church with a fine tower of Kentish ragstone and some morbid touches – a charnel house in the churchyard and weathered death's heads leering down at you from the gate pillars.

The walkway takes you along the riverside to Deptford Creek. On the bend you will meet Peter the Great, an elaborate statue presented by the people of Russia in recognition of the time the Emperor spent as a guest at nearby Sayes Court. Where the broad walkway ends, turn into a narrow road that bends up the Elephant Royale restaurant, where you bear up left beside a car park to the obvious exit beside The Ferry House pub, to the corner of Ferry Street **I**. This was the point where the waterman's ferry once plied across to Greenwich.

Keep ahead towards Island Gardens, with a tempting view of the river over Johnson's drawdock **J** on the way. Before the gardens themselves, a left-hand turn leads to Island Gardens DLR station. Ahead, the 'Thames Path Greenwich quarter mile' sign may suggest walking on water, but only points to a glass-topped tower with stairs leading down to Greenwich Foot Tunnel. A lift operates from 7am to 9pm, Monday to Saturday, and 9am to 9pm on Sunday. The tunnel was completed in 1902 to replace the ferry passed earlier, as an easier way for dockers to reach work in the West India Docks. But do not leave Island Gardens without crossing the garden itself **142** past the café to the river wall for the view across to the Royal Naval Hospital, the Queen's House and Greenwich Park beyond – probably the grandest architectural vista the Thames has to offer.

to join the main road, Creek Road **V**, beside The Hoy pub, and turn left over Deptford Creek. Take the first left turning after the Creek, go right at The Thames pub, then left in Horseferry Place **W** to the Greenwich riverside, bearing right to the pier, using the tall masts and spars of *Cutty Sark* **154** as your guide.

In close-up, the *Cutty Sark* is a revelation of how beauty can spring from the purest function. Last of the great clipper ships, she was built to harness the power of the wind for sheer speed – racing with tea from China, or later, wool from Australia, to get the best market prices. Inside, there is a museum of the sailing era and a unique collection of ships' figureheads. From the quayside, it is a short walk up to the tourist shops of Church Street with Cutty Sark station just off to the right. *For Greenwich station, walk on to the church and bear right along the High Road. To reach the north bank Thames Path, enter the circular, domed tower on the quayside. The steps or a lift take you to the foot tunnel leading to the other bank.*

The Thames Path continues from the quay as a narrow way beside the pier entrance, soon squeezing along the river frontage of the Royal Naval College **155**, now the Greenwich University campus. The whole breathtaking composition is best seen from across the river, but from a central point on our path, the main elements fall into place. You can see how the two wings of the college

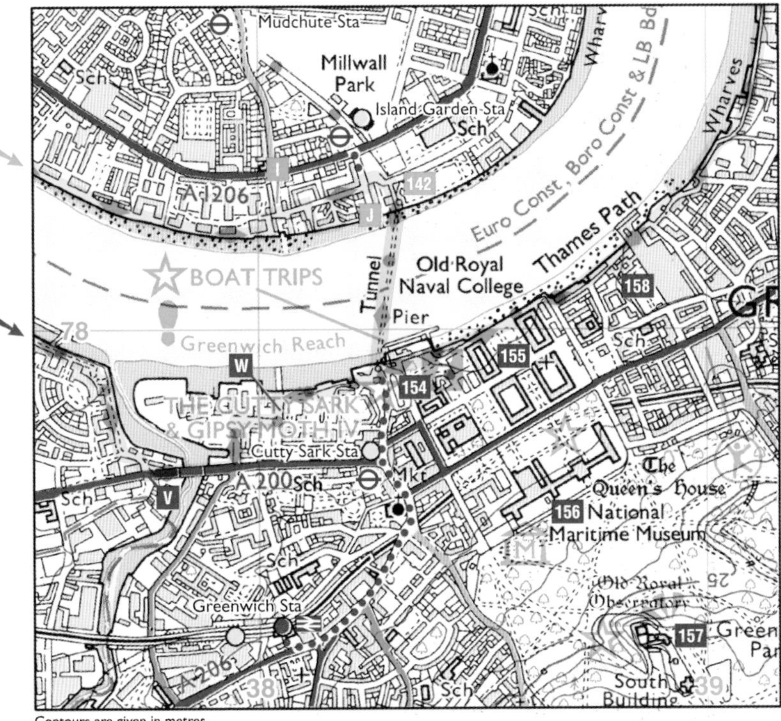

Contours are given in metres
The vertical interval is 5m

– built from 1696 on as a very grand hospital for disabled seamen – carefully preserve the river view from the Queen's House **156**, the little Palladian villa further back. This was designed by Inigo Jones for James I, and with wings and colonnades added later, it now forms part of the National Maritime Museum. As a backdrop to all this, you can see the rise of Greenwich Park, crowned by the Royal Observatory **157**, through which runs that prime meridian line dividing east from west.

The path turns up to the right in front of The Trafalgar Tavern, built in 1837. In passing, you will want to stop and admire its elegant Regency river frontage. Then, turn left between bollards on a paved way towards the flaky, white slab of a disused power station. Before this, however, you pass a delightful little creation on a different scale and from a different time. The almshouses of Trinity Hospital **158** were first established under the will of Henry Howard, Earl of Northampton, in 1613, although they seem to have been given

Beyond Greenwich, the Thames Path gives brief glimpses of working river wharves.

their battlements and rendering in an 1812 restoration. The effect, nevertheless, is very charming. The wardens have clearly had problems in keeping the Thames at bay, and the river wall they built here in 1817 has plates recording some 'extraordinary high tide' levels.

Beyond the power station you cross the riverside of Anchor Iron Quay, then take the cobbled road along Ballast Quay **X**. First, you pass The Cutty Sark pub, which claims to date from 1695; then a handsome terrace leads to the four-square Harbour Master's Office of 1854. Now, skirting Lovell's Wharf, you enter the only true industrial length of the Thames Path.

The red-tiled walkway angles around inlets, past barges and silos, with rumbling, drumming sounds, mysterious pipes belching steam, even some exotic smells to confirm that this is still a working river. After circling round the river frontage of two industrial sites, the Thames Path turns away from the river. Shortly after leaving the river, a fenced path on the left crosses a vacant site and returns to the riverside. It crosses two working wharves, crunchy with gravel underfoot, then Delta Wharf and a greener stretch that leads to a drawdock. *The road ahead leads to North Greenwich Underground station and buses.*

The Thames Path doubles back to follow the walkway and cycleway around the Millennium Dome. Look out for the steel channel across the path, with markers on a nearby jetty, that record your crossing of the Greenwich Meridian. There are artworks too – *Slice of Reality* by Richard Wilson is a sawn-off section of a ship, while beyond the piers, *Quantum Cloud* by Anthony Gormley must have been a welder's nightmare!

Coming to a broad new riverside walk, you have views ahead to the Thames Barrier **159**. The walkway turns up behind

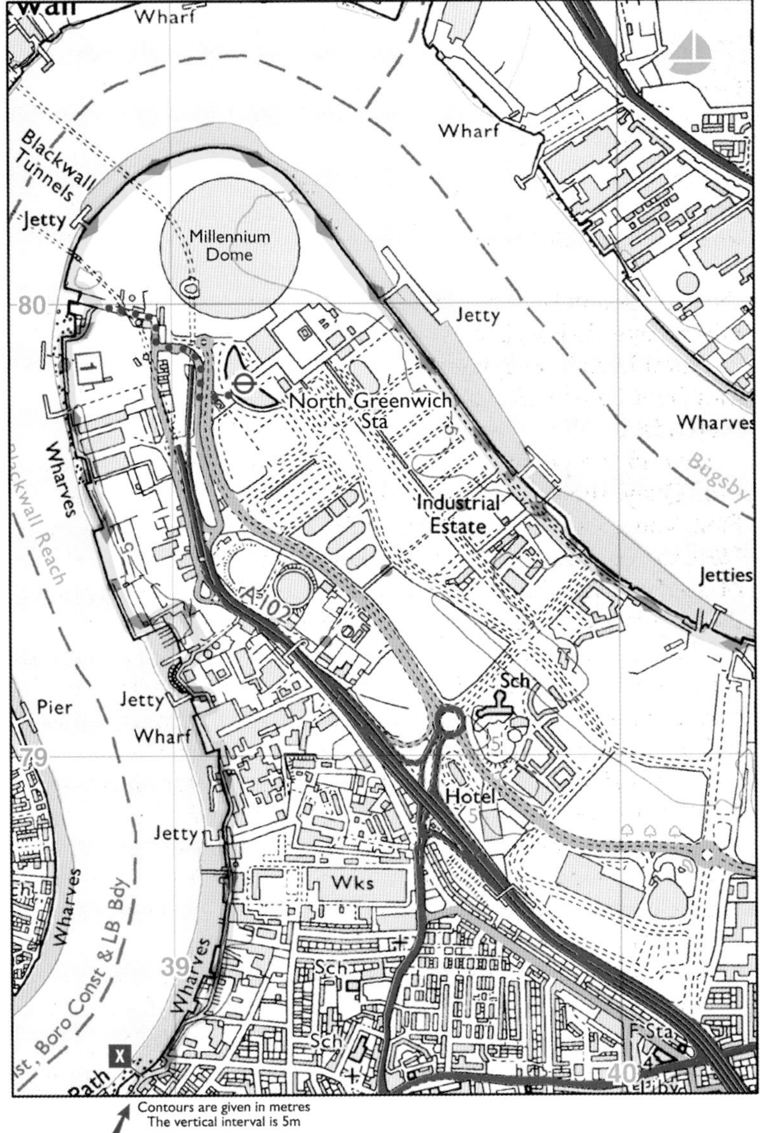

a yacht club, then joins the older Mudlarks Way. The river is broader now, and with barges and boats drawn up on the foreshore, its character has changed; Old Father Thames is smelling the sea.

The broad promenade offers brave attempts at seating and planting, but the visual drama comes from the great gravel conveyors overhead. For a while it seems there is sand everywhere, but the paved path continues by an industrial road to reach The Anchor & Hope pub, from where it becomes a riverside promenade again, continuing on to the Barrier. *For Charlton station, turn up Anchor & Hope Lane by the pub of that name; keep ahead when it joins a road from the right, and carry on straight up the rise beyond traffic lights.*

For some time now you have been looking at the stainless steel hoods of the Barrier – suggesting a procession of giant monks crossing the river – but close up you see more of the operating works underneath. You may also be wondering where the gates are. The answer is that the four vast 200-foot (61-metre) shipping gates and the six lesser gates are all of curved profile, lying face down on their riverbed sills ready to pivot up through 90 degrees to close off the river. As it approaches the control centre, the path goes up and down steps, then under the centre, where you will see the *Profile of the River Thames* by Simon Read, etched into the concrete wall. It charts your journey from the source to the Thames Barrier. A flight of steps finally leads up to the Barrier Buffet and – no doubt – to celebratory refreshments. Here, beyond the Barrier, you have a satisfying sense that the river you have followed from its first modest trickle is opening out to its estuary, ready to greet the sea.

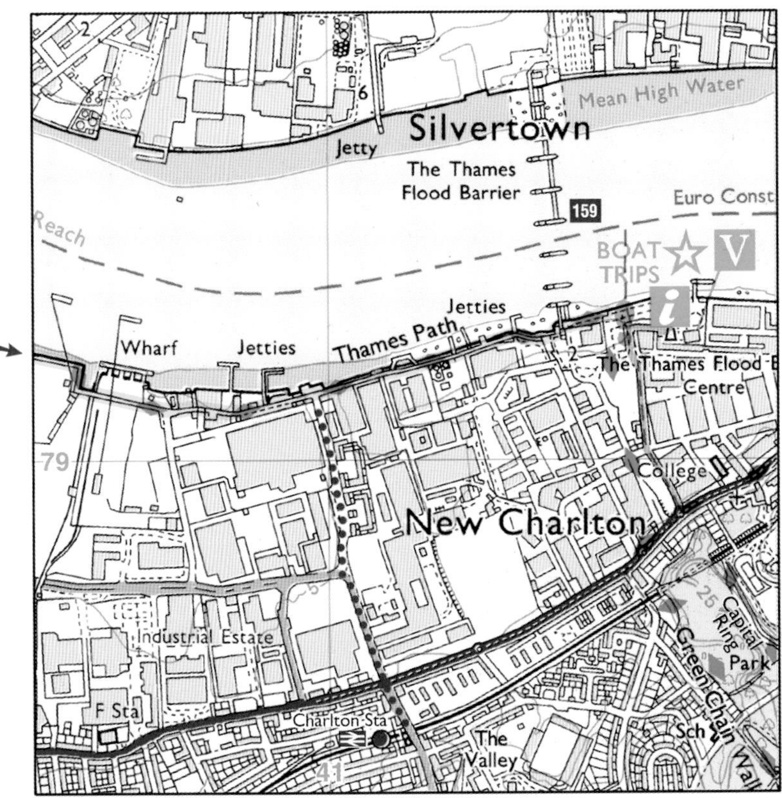

Contours are given in metres
The vertical interval is 5m

The final image of the Thames Path is provided by the great, gleaming, stainless steel hoods of the Thames Barrier, concealing the working machinery beneath.

USEFUL INFORMATION

Public transport

The Thames Path is unique amongst National Trails in that it is accessible by public transport along most of its length. From Oxford downstream the opportunities offered by train or bus links are excellent, and in London almost unlimited. In public transport terms, the Thames Path divides into three sections.

The source itself is within easy reach of Kemble station, with fast and reasonably frequent services from London Paddington to Cheltenham and Gloucester via Swindon. But after that you are dependent on bus services to Cricklade and Lechlade from Swindon, detailed in Wiltshire timetables. As with many other country services, there are around 10 buses a day and fewer on Sundays. From Lechlade downstream you are in remote Oxfordshire and buses are rare for a while. Useful services run to Oxford from Faringdon via Kingston Bagpuize, Appleton and other villages a mile or two from the path. North of the Thames, a bus service via Clanfield, Bampton, Aston and Standlake also runs into Oxford. At Newbridge a weekday service runs to Abingdon and Clifton Hampden, cutting off a vast loop of the Thames, while from Eynsham there are frequent buses every day over Swinford Bridge to Oxford.

From Oxford station there are services from Paddington to Banbury, Worcester and Hereford, plus Intercity services to Birmingham, and a stopping service which links conveniently to the Thames Path at Radley, Culham, Cholsey, Goring, Pangbourne, Tilehurst, Reading and Maidenhead. With the Twyford to Henley and Maidenhead to Marlow branches providing further links, on First Great Western you can take a return ticket to your further station and walk back to another station – still on the same ticket. Below Oxford it is worth noting that buses from Abingdon back to Oxford are frequent. Oxford has frequent 24-hour express bus services to central London, Heathrow and Gatwick. Another useful express bus service links Oxford with Dorchester and Wallingford.

Reading station has Intercity services to Paddington and to Bristol and the West Country, with an alternative South West Trains service to London Waterloo. Windsor has two stations, Windsor & Eton Riverside with a good South West Trains service to Waterloo and useful Thames Path links at Datchet and Staines, and Windsor & Eton Central with a shuttle service to Slough, connecting with services to Paddington, Reading etc. By Old Windsor you are entering Surrey, and after Staines there are further station links at Shepperton, Hampton Court and Hampton Wick, offering a range of services to Waterloo.

Then from Kingston on, the Thames Path begins to be served by bus and train services with a London frequency – so high that you need have little recourse to timetables. The major transport centres, Richmond, Hammersmith, Putney and Vauxhall, may offer a choice of national rail, Underground or bus connections in all directions, and in central London the walk passes near main line termini at Waterloo and Charing Cross, Blackfriars, Cannon Street and London Bridge. Through Docklands the most valuable rail links are provided by the Docklands Light Railway with its frequent services from Tower Gateway out to Limehouse, Canary Wharf, Island Gardens and Cutty Sark stations. On the south bank route there are station links at Greenwich and Charlton just half a mile from the Thames Barrier, with services back to London Bridge and Charing Cross. North Greenwich Station is now open on the Jubilee Line, too.

For train services, timetable information can be obtained via the central enquiry number.

For bus services you have two options: call the national enquiry service (see opposite), or alternatively get the free map folder from the National Trails Office (see 'useful addresses' overleaf). It shows you all the bus routes currently serving key points along the Thames Path, and lists the operators and their telephone numbers. With this folder you can see clearly where bus links are available, from Kemble right down to Richmond, then make enquiries or obtain timetables direct from the operator.

National Rail Enquiries: 08457 484950
Net: www.nationalrail.co.uk

London Transport Enquiries – for all London bus and Underground services, including the Docklands Light Railway:

Enquiries: 020 7222 1234
Net: www.tfl.gov.uk

National Public Transport Enquiry Service: 0870 608 2608

Boat Services
These are the major services that could be helpful to Thames Path walkers in summer, with the operators and their telephone numbers:

Oxford to Abingdon, also Reading, Henley, Marlow, Maidenhead, Windsor, Runnymede and Staines: Salter Brothers, tel. 01865 243421.

Hampton Court, Richmond and Kew to Westminster: Westminster Passenger Service, tel. 020 7930 4097.

Westminster to the Tower, Greenwich and Thames Barrier: City Cruises, tel. 020 7740 0400 (to Greenwich); Thames River Services, tel. 020 7930 4097 (to Greenwich and Thames Barrier).

Embankment to the Tower and Greenwich: Catamaran Cruisers, tel. 020 7987 1185.

River Trip Enquies: 0839 123432 or net: www.tfl.gov.uk/river

Accommodation

The Thames Path Companion, an up-to-date and comprehensive guide to the facilities and accommodation along the length of the Thames Path is available from the National Trails Office, Environment and Economy, Holton, Oxford OX33 1QQ.
Tel: 01865 810224. Or e-mail: mail@rway-tpath.demon.co.uk

Tourist Information Centres

These can provide guidance on local features, opening times etc., will hold local transport timetables and, with the exception of the City of London office, can usually advise on accommodation.

Cirencester: Corn Hall, Market Place, Cirencester GL7 2NW. Tel. 01285 654180. Fax. 01285 641182

Faringdon: 7A Market Place, Faringdon SN7 7HL. Tel./Fax. 01367 242191

Witney: 51A Market Square, Witney OX8 6AG. Tel. 01993 775802. Fax. 01993 709261

Oxford: 15–16 Broadstreet, Oxford OX1 3AS. Tel. 01865 726871, Fax: 01865 240261

Abingdon: 25 Bridge Street, Abingdon OX14 3HN. Tel. 01235 522771. Fax. 01235 535245

Wallingford: Town Hall, Market Place, Wallingford OX10 0EG. Tel. 01491 826972. Fax. 01491 832925

Reading: Town Hall, Blagrave Street, Reading RG1 1QH. Tel. 0118 956 6266. Fax. 0118 939 9885

Henley-on-Thames: King's Arms Barn, King's Road, Henley-on-Thames RG9 2DG. Tel. 01491 578034. Fax. 01491 411766

Marlow: 31 High Street, Marlow SL7 1AU. Tel. 01628 483597. Fax. 01628 471915

Maidenhead: The Library, St Ives Road, Maidenhead SL6 1QU. Tel: 01628 796502. Fax: 01628 781110.

Windsor: 24 High Street, Windsor SL4 1LH. Tel. 01753 743900. Fax. 01753 743904

Kingston: The Market House, Market Place, Kingston upon Thames KT1 1JS. Tel. 020 8547 5592. Fax. 020 8547 5594

Richmond: Old Town Hall, Whittaker Avenue, Richmond TW9 1TP. Tel. 020 8940 9125. Fax: 020 8940 6899

City of London Information Centre, St Paul's Churchyard, London EC4M 8BX. Tel. 020 7332 1456. Fax. 020 7332 1457

Southwark: 6 Tooley Street, London Bridge, Southwark SE1 2SE. Tel. 020 7403 8299. Fax. 020 7357 6321

Greenwich: Pepys House, 2 Cutty Sark Gardens, Greenwich, London SE10 9LW. Tel. 0870 608 2000. Fax. 020 8853 4607

Useful addresses

Countryside Agency *see* Natural England

English Tourism Council, Thames Tower, Black's Road, Hammersmith W6 9EL. Tel. 020 8563 3000. Fax. 020 8563 0302. Net: www.englishtourism.org.uk

Environment Agency (Thames Region), Kings Meadow House, Kings Meadow Road, Reading RG1 8DQ. Tel. 0118 953 5000. Fax. 0118 950 0388. *Official environmental regulator, including river management.* **Flood information line**: 0845 988 1188.

Long Distance Walkers Association, Tom Sinclair, Bank House, High Street, Wrotham TN15 7AE. Tel. 01732 883705. Net: secretary@ldwa.org.uk

National Trails Office, Cultural Services, Holton, Oxford OX33 1QQ. Tel. 01865 810224. Fax. 01865 810207. Net: www.nationaltrail.co.uk *Responsible for day-to-day management of the Thames Path.*

Natural England (South East & London Region), Dacre House, 19 Dacre Street, London SW1H 0DH. Tel. 020 7340 2900. Fax. 020 7340 2999. Net: www.naturalengland.gov.uk *Official government body on countryside matters.*

Open Spaces Society, 25A Bell Street, Henley on Thames RG9 2BA. Tel. 01491 573535. Net: www.oss.org.uk *Protects common land, greens and open spaces.*

Ordnance Survey, Romsey Road, Southampton SO16 4GU. Tel. 08456 050505. Fax. 023 8079 2615. Net: www.ordnancesurvey.co.uk/leisure *Mapping agency for Great Britain.*

Ramblers' Association, 2nd Floor, Camelford House, 87–90 Albert Embankment, London SE1 7TW. Tel. 020 7339 8500. Fax. 020 7339 8501. Net: www.ramblers.org.uk *Promotes walking and protects rights of way.*

River Thames Society, Side House, Middle Assendon, Henley on Thames, Oxon RG9 6AP. Tel. 01491 571476. *Represents the interests of all river users.*

Transport for London, Windsor House, 42–50 Victoria Street, London SW1H 0TL. Tel: 020 7941 7536. Net: www.tfl.gov.uk/walking *Information and leaflets on London walks.*

Youth Hostels Association, Trevelyan House, 8 St Stephens Hill, St Albans AL1 2DY. Tel. 01727 855215. Net: www.yha.org.uk *Low-cost hostel accommodation for all ages.*

Bibliography

There are numerous books about all aspects of the River Thames, but here is a brief selection of the more interesting titles. Some are now out of print, but should be available through public libraries.

Batey, Mavis, Buttery, Henrietta, Lambert, David and Wilkie, Kim, *Arcadian Thames* (Barn Elms Publishing, 1994).
Bolland, R.S., *Victorians on the Thames* (Midas Books, 1974).
Ebel, Suzanne and Impey, Doreen, *A Guide to London's Riverside* (Constable, 1985).
Jenkins, Alan, *The Book of the Thames* (Macmillan London, 1983).
Mackay, Duncan *The Secret Thames*, (Ebury Press/Countryside Commission, 1992).
Phillips, Geoffrey *Thames Crossings*, (David & Charles, 1981).
Pritchard, Mari and Carpenter, Humphrey *A Thames Companion*, (Oxford Illustrated Press, 1975).
Weightman, Gavin, *London River* (Collins & Brown, 1990).

Ordnance Survey Maps covering the Thames Path

Landranger Maps (scale 1:50 000): 163, 164, 174, 175, 176, 177.

Explorer Maps (scale 1:25 000): 168 Stroud, Tetbury and Malmesbury; 169 Cirencester and Swindon; 170 Abingdon, Wantage and Vale of White Horse; 180 Oxford; 171 Chiltern Hills West; 172 Chiltern Hills East; 160 Windsor, Weybridge and Bracknell; 161 London South; 173 London North; 162 Greenwich and Gravesend.

Motoring Maps: Reach the Thames Path by using Travelmaster Map 9 (scale 1:25 0000) South East England.

Responsibility for the Thames Path

The Thames Path was designated a National Trail by the Countryside Agency (now Natural England) and opened in 1996. A National Trails Officer and other staff are funded by the Agency and employed by Oxfordshire County Council to manage the trail in conjunction with the highway authorities along its route.

Natural England also funds most of the maintenance work. Much of the important practical work, such as monitoring the route, litter collecting, signposting and vegetation clearance, is carried out by enthusiastic members of the National Trails Volunteer Scheme, under the supervision of National Trails staff.